Built for More

The Role of Out-of-School Time in Preparing Youth for the Future of Work

A Volume in
Current Issues in Out-of-School Time

Series Editor

Helen Janc Malone
Institute for Educational Leadership

Current Issues in Out-of-School Time

Helen Janc Malone, Series Editor

Built for More:
The Role of Out-of-School Time in
Preparing Youth for the Future of Work (2024)
edited by Byron Sanders and Shannon Epner

The Heartbeat of the Youth Development Field:
Professional Journeys of Growth, Connection, and Transformation (2023)
edited by Georgia Hall, Jan Gallagher, and Elizabeth Starr

It Takes an Ecosystem: Understanding the People, Places, and Possibilities of
Learning and Development Across Settings (2022)
edited by Thomas Akiva and Kimberly H. Robinson

Measure, Use, Improve! Data Use in Out-of-School Time (2021)
edited by Christina A. Russell and Corey Newhouse

At Our Best:
Building Youth-Adult Partnerships in Out-of-School Time Settings (2020)
edited by Gretchen Brion-Meisels,
Jessica Tseming Fei, and Deepa Sriya Vasudevan

Changemakers! Practitioners Advance Equity and
Access in Out-of-School Time Programs (2019)
edited by Sara Hill and Femi Vance

Social and Emotional Learning in Out-Of-School Time:
Foundations and Futures (2018)
edited by Elizabeth Devaney and Deborah A. Moroney

The Growing Out-of-School Time Field: Past, Present, and Future (2017)
edited by Helen Janc Malone and Tara Donahue

Built for More

The Role of Out-of-School Time in Preparing Youth for the Future of Work

Editors

Byron Sanders and Shannon Epner
Big Thought

INFORMATION AGE PUBLISHING, INC.
Charlotte, NC • www.infoagepub.com

Praise for *Built for More: The Role of OST in Preparing Youth for the Future of Work*

We are witnessing the fifth industrial revolution to reshape human society. Unlike steam, mass production, electronics and even the internet, this revolution—powered by artificial intelligence, has the potential to unlock human potential and innovation like never before. The skills of creative problem solving will never be more applicable to as many people as right now. It is into this breach *Built for More: The Role of OST in Preparing Youth for the Future of Work*, ventures forward—with a bold vision of how out-of-school time nurtures creativity and prepares our students for the world of tomorrow, today. Drawing on decades of experience, and pulling together the most talented authors, Byron Sanders and Shannon Epner stare unblinking to the future of work, uplift the voice of youth, and elevate an integrated vision of learning for every young person, in every place. This is the moment, and this is a book to prepare us to meet it.

—David Adams, CEO,
Urban Assembly & Board of Directors, CASEL

As we all seek to prepare young people for successful futures where they can pursue their passions, care for their families, and build their futures, we must look to an entire ecosystem of support and robust learning opportunities that empower them to realize their full potential, especially as workforce needs evolve more rapidly than ever before. We in the out-of-school time (OST) field know that programs in this space are an essential part of that ecosystem we hope to sustain, and just as importantly we know that informal settings are some of the richest and most ideally suited to developing skills and mindsets for the workforce of tomorrow. The learnings in *Built for More: The Role of Out-of-School Time in Preparing Youth for the Future of Work* can inform and improve all of our practice and help us to build more thoughtful spaces, places, and systems in which our kids can thrive.

—Jenna Courtney, Chief Executive Officer, *TXPost*

Decades of research has shown time and time again that high-quality out-of-school time activities help develop essential skills to prepare youth for success in career and life. Skills like teamwork, perseverance, leadership, problem-solving and more can be further nurtured outside of the traditional school day and year. We're at a precipice in a society where the future of work is evolving rapidly. At this juncture, we need entire ecosystems to come together to ensure that our youth development systems are equitably working in concert to ensure all youth have opportunities to thrive. *Built for More, The Role of OST in Preparing Youth for the Future of Work*, edited by Byron Sanders and Shannon Epner of Big Thought, a leading OST organization in the country, provides a blueprint for practitioners, researchers, funders, and policymakers to design programs and policies that foster transformative opportunities for youth to thrive in the workforce of tomorrow.

—Jessica Donner, Executive Director,
Every Hour Counts

Every day children are asked by adults, "What do you want to be when you grow up?" We've often encouraged young people to respond, "What are all my options?" Summer youth employment and internships provide some of the highest level and most impactful forms of summer learning. They expose young people to an array of options and opportunities they might not be able to access or afford otherwise. *Built for More, The Role of OST in Preparing Youth for the Future of Work* highlights how and why the out-of-school time field is uniquely well positioned to help millions of America's young people discover their passions, explore careers, and develop skills they'll need to succeed in class, communities and life.

—Aaron Philip Dworkin, CEO,
National Summer Learning Association

Built for More: The Role of Out-of-School Time in Preparing Youth for the Future of Work is an important clarion call; the world is changing fast, and far too many conventional schools are still primarily teaching in the abstract through textbooks, online, and/or lecture. In our increasingly turbulent world, it is vital to get the content off the page or screen in a way that's relevant to young people's interests, otherwise it's not going to stick with them. Young people need to explore, play, experience trial and error, and learn from experiences and relationships with adult mentors/experts that enable a more "big picture" approach. The diverse author perspectives in this book insightfully engage with key facets of learning that elucidate that the adage "know and be able to do," would be better phrased "do and be able to know."

—Andrew Frishman, *Big Picture Learning*

The skills that enable workforce success in this century and beyond have changed so drastically from what our education system was created to produce that we are in an all-hands-on-deck moment to ready our young people for the new world of work. If you're not yet convinced of the magnitude of the shift, this book clearly lays it out. But more importantly, it offers a tangible set of opportunities for what we might do better—and the urgency of starting now—from experts and practitioners in the field. For young people to be prepared to contribute and thrive, we must take advantage of every opportunity to support their development. *Built for More* highlights the critical role that out-of-school time plays and offers valuable best practices for building these durable human skills—through formal and, more importantly, informal education spaces—in your community.

—Courtney Reilly, Founder, *Skillsline*

Built for More highlights vital issues as youth face a changing economy by elevating diverse, proximate voices across the education and workforce system. It illuminates how we must implement innovative, evidence-informed strategies, including whole-learner approaches, to strengthen equitable outcomes for young people. This volume will be a critical resource for policymakers, advocates, and practitioners.

—Chase Sackett, Policy Director, *America Forward*

Built for More: The Role of OST in Preparing Youth for the Future of Work is a vital and timely series that examines the crucial role of out-of-school time (OST) programs in preparing youth for the rapidly evolving future of work. With contributions from leading educators and innovators, this volume offers a diverse range of perspectives on how these programs can empower youth, foster creativity, and build essential skills for tomorrow's workforce. Its insightful analysis and practical case studies make it an indispensable resource for educators, policymakers, and anyone invested in the future of education and youth development.

—D'Andre Weaver, PhD,
—Chief Digital Equity Officer, *Digital Promise Global*

Built for More: The Role of Out-of-School Time in Preparing Youth for the Future of Work embodies the idea that we can't solve problems by using the same kind of thinking we used when we created them. In order to unlock the potential of out-of-school learning and development, innovative yet empirical thinking is needed. The diversity of ideas presented here will be useful to creative practitioners and researchers alike. Anyone who is invested in seeking new and equitable ways of thinking about collaboration and innovation in educational and workforce opportunities will benefit from this volume.

Dr. Annie Wright, Executive Director,
Southern Methodist University,
Center on Research and Evaluation

More praise on book's back cover

Current Issues in Out-of-School Time Book Series Board

Dr. Helen Janc Malone (Series Editor), *Senior Vice President for Strategy, Research, and Policy, Institute for Educational Leadership.* **Dr. Jaynemarie Angbah,** *Director, REDI Change Learning Journey, Charles and Lynn Schusterman Family Philanthropies.* **Brodrick Clarke,** *Vice President of Programs, National Summer Learning Association.* **Jessie Dickerson,** *Manager of Program Quality Systems, American Camp Association.* **Edward Franklin,** *President/ CEO, Voice of Hope Ministries.* **Dan Gilbert,** *Senior Program Manager, Afterschool Alliance.* **Dr. Georgia Hall,** *Director, National Institute on Out-of-School Time (NIOST), Wellesley Centers for Women at Wellesley College.* **Jessica Hay,** *Education and Healthcare Policy Advocate, California School Employees Association.* **Dr. Ryan Heath,** *Assistant Professor in the School of Social Work, Syracuse University.* **Dr. Elizabeth Hilvert,** *Manager of Research & Evaluation, Afterschool Matters.* **Dr. Car Mun Kok,** *Director of College Opportunity Programs, UC Davis School of Education.* **Angelica Portillo,** *Director of Advocacy and Workforce Initiatives, National AfterSchool Association.* **Michelle Rodriguez,** *Senior Manager, Organizational Learning & Development, YMCA OF THE USA.* **Christina Russell,** *Managing Director, Policy Studies Associates.* **Dr. Tanya Wiggins,** *Clinical Associate Professor, Foundations & Adolescent Education, Pace University.* **Dr. Steven Worker,** *4-H Youth Development Advisor, University of California, Agriculture and Natural Resources, Cooperative Education.* **Dr. Jill Young,** *Senior Researcher, Youth, Family, and Community Development, American Institutes for Research.*

DEDICATION

We dedicate this book to Rage Almighty aka Adam Tench. A poet. A person. A pillar who changed lives by changing the air of the rooms he filled. Come soon, a world that values the value of his humanity as divinely it deserves.

We also dedicate this book to Mary Hernandez. Because of all things to dedicate to her, a book is most fitting. The wearer of the warrior helm for literacy, her belief that youths' "who" mattered as much as their "what" or "how" in the books they read. Thank you for your clarity of purpose and always the best words.

Library of Congress Cataloging-in-Publication Data

CIP record for this book is available from the Library of Congress
http://www.loc.gov

ISBNs: 979-8-88730-631-5 (Paperback)

979-8-88730-632-2 (Hardcover)

979-8-88730-633-9 (ebook)

Copyright © 2024 Information Age Publishing Inc.

All rights reserved. No part of this publication may be reproduced, stored in a retrieval system, or transmitted, in any form or by any means, electronic, mechanical, photocopying, microfilming, recording or otherwise, without written permission from the publisher.

Printed in the United States of America

CONTENTS

Foreword
Chike Aguh .... *xiii*

Acknowledgments .... *xxi*

Introduction
Byron Sanders .... *xxiii*

SECTION I: THE FUTURE OF WORK

1. Transforming Education Through Learner-Centered
   Ecosystems: Empowering All Children for a Thriving Future
   Bobbi R. Macdonald *3*

2. The Impact of AI Technology on Future Generations in the
   Workforce and the Role of Out-of-School Time Providers
   Shannon Epner and ChatGPT-4 .... *23*

3. Tomorrow's Workforce in Afterschool Programs Today:
   STEM-Focused Afterschool Programs and Systems
   Terri Ferinde, Teresa Drew, Nicole Evans, and Sheronda Witter *41*

SECTION II: IMPORTANCE OF YOUTH WORKERS IN PREPARING YOUTH FOR THE FUTURE OF WORK

4. Importance of Youth Workers in Preparing Youth for the
   Future of Work
   Carlos Santini *59*

xi

xii CONTENTS

5. Post-Traumatic Growth in OST: Creating Nurturing Conditions for Growth and Transformation in the Youth Development Workforce
Melea Meyer 79

6. Higher Education and Youth Work: Opportunities for Expanding the Field
Nancy L. Deutsch and Melissa K. Levy 95

7. Supporting the Youth Fields Workforce: Lessons Learned From the Power of Us Workforce Survey and the Field
Jill Young and Rebecca Goldberg 121

SECTION III: ROLE OF OST IN SPARKING CAREER PATHWAYS

8. Creating Authentic Spaces for Youth: A Conversation About the Role of Youth Agency & Its Future
Monique Miles, Angelica Portillo, and Byron Sanders 141

9. Non-Artificial Authentic Intelligence: Creating Ecosystems of Development for Young People Outside of School and in the World of Work
Gabrielle Kurlander and Christopher Street. 153

10. Leveraging the Community as a Civic Classroom
Fernande Raine and Emily Wegner 173

11. Pathways to College and Career Readiness in South Los Angeles: A Case Study of the Al Wooten Jr. Youth Center
Naomi McSwain 191

12. Creating Creators: How an Out-of-School Time Ecosystem is Redefining Creativity and Building Learning Pathways to Future Success
Greg MacPherson, Evan Cleveland, and Armando Banchs 211

13. A Conversation With Ania Hodges: A Youth Changemaker's Story and Call to Action
Ania Hodges and Byron Sanders 237

Conclusion 245

Author Biographies 251

FOREWORD

Chike Aguh

Over nearly the last two decades, I have spent my career focused equally on how we, as Americans, can lift up the educationally and economically the most disadvantaged in our society, and at the same time, how we can have the most competitive and innovative economy in the world. Until recently, these two conversations have not been joined. We are beginning to realize, as I have felt in my bones for a long time, that these two conversations are actually one and the same. In the pages of this visionary volume, these conversations come together.

One might argue that this is a grand proposition for a tome on out-of-school time (OST) and its intersection with the future of work. The grandness of the proposition makes it no less true. From my time as a teacher in America's largest school system, my time as a member of the Council on Foreign Relations' task force on the future of work, to my time as the Chief Innovation Officer at the U.S. Department of Labor, I am more convinced than ever that OST will be a critical lever for this nation to create the workforce that can secure America's future. If we do this right, this century will be defined by both the American innovation and dominance, and by shared prosperity and less division.

How does OST get us there? Let's first define the dilemma and challenges posed by the future of work. First, we have the challenge of jobs that may be obviated entirely by technology. There are many examples, but one of the most visible is autonomous vehicles. According to industry estimates, we will likely have autonomous vehicles on American roads en masse between 2030–2040, with the first disruptions likely happening in commercial trucking and public transportation. This new technology will

---

Built for More: The Role of Out-of-School Time in Preparing Youth for the Future of Work,
pp. xiii–xix
Copyright © 2024 by Information Age Publishing
www.infoagepub.com
All rights of reproduction in any form reserved.

potentially add \$800B–\$1T of economic output to our economy. It will also obviate the most commonly held profession by Americans, driving a vehicle. There are almost as many Americans driving a vehicle for a living as there are teachers in the American public schools.

The second half of the challenge are jobs that will still exist but will be radically changed by technology; therefore, the people who do that job now may not have the capacity to do it in the future. The job that most encapsulates this is that of the loan officer. Forty years ago, a loan officer's job was to evaluate each borrower on a number of objective (and implicitly subjective) criteria like loan need, previous financial history, and so on. Upon reviewing those criteria, that individual would make the decision about whether to approve that loan. Today, that job is very different. The decision about whether a loan is approved or not is not made by a human being, but more likely by a machine. Today, the job of the loan officer is much more about bringing potential borrowers in the door and keeping them happy so that they will make additional loans with the same institution in the future. The question in this instance is: who is preparing those who were able to do the loan officer's job before to being able to perform the job now? Too often, there is not an answer. The pillars of that answer are fivefold.

Pillar #1: Creating the Work of the Future

While many academics and economists are optimistic that this new economy will create as many jobs as it destroys and will produce enough decent work for everyone, there is no guarantee. Like in past economic transitions, new technologies have created jobs that never existed before, but they also make it possible for firms to replace humans with machines in ways they never could. What is different today is the speed of the transition. In the past, they took decades; now they are measured in short years or even months. The government must and can take action to create the conditions to make sure that we have an economy that creates fulfilling jobs for everyone.

Pillar #2: Investing in the Workers of the Future

To prepare the workers of the future, we must ensure that workers have the skills that are just-in-time (skills that are directly tied to current needs of the market) and timeless (those skills that have made humans successful throughout history like leadership, communication, and targeted curiosity). Along with those skills, we need to make sure that they have the social capital and connections to get the jobs they need. According to Matt

Youngquist of Career Horizons, over 70% of job postings are filled without a job posting (Kaufman, 2011). This means that it is likely that there are candidates for certain jobs who have the requisite skills who cannot apply for the appropriate job because they do not even know it exists.

Pillar #3: Matching Americans Who Need Work With Work That Needs Doing

In February 2019, there were 7.3 million open jobs, according to the U.S. Labor Department. While there is always some degree of open jobs in the economy, this is a historic number. While there is much attention paid to the skills gap (workers not having the skills required), there is also not a smooth system for matching the work that needs to be done with the people who need work. Once workers have the skills necessary to do the job, there is no guarantee that they will know it exists, find it, and be able to compete for it.

Pillar #4: Moving From a Social Safety Net to an Economic Trampoline

In the 20th century, we created a social safety net of benefit to blunt the hardest edges of capitalism when Americans fell on hard times. These benefits consist of Medicare, Social Security, Medicaid, unemployment benefits, and so. These benefits are critical and have kept many Americans over the decades from falling off an economic cliff. However, this safety net must be transformed into an economic trampoline: more than simply catching people when they fall out of the job market, it must be strong enough to bounce them back into that market at a similar or better position than they were in before.

Pillar #5: Ensuring That Every Worker Is Respected, Protected, and Dignified on Job

In a labor market that is tighter than ever before, workers have choices about to whom they give their labor. In July 2023, there were 8.8 million open jobs. Workers deserve and are now demanding not just a job but a quality job. As defined by joint principles released by the U.S. Departments of Commerce and Labor in the summer of 2022 (U.S. Department of Commerce and U.S. Department of Labor, 2022), those jobs are defined by the right to organize, freedom from discrimination, family sustaining wages and benefits, and access to training and advancement.

Cross-cutting these pillars are additional considerations, namely the change in work modality (remote and hybrid work) and the rise of emerging technologies (generative AI, quantum, XR) that will be woven into everyday work. These two considerations have a feedback effect on each other, where the rise of remote/hybrid work necessitates the use of these new technologies. These new technologies make these new work arrangements easier, which increases their prevalence.

Winning this future of work matters because it fuels the economic inequality and lack of social mobility that defines this age. The economic inequality of the U.S. currently rivals countries like China and Russia, and that is because the economic gains of our new economy have flowed to an increasingly smaller group of Americans who live in the right places, have the right education and, at times, have had the power to institute policies that protect those gains. This trend will only accelerate unless a response equal to the size of this challenge is taken. According to McKinsey and Company, over one-third of jobs overall could be automated by 2030 (Manyika et al., 2017). The cost of not stepping up here will be grievous and will be visited most heavily upon communities that have already disproportionately suffered: communities of color and residents of our industrial heartland.

Winning the future of work is critical because that aforementioned inequality and lack of social mobility is also what helps fuel our political divisions. While we must confront the racism and xenophobia that characterize much of our current political debate, we must also see the historical pattern of economic anxiety, making it easier to divide people along lines of difference. Real wages for Americans in the middle of the income distribution are up a mere 3% since 1979, and those at the bottom have lost ground (Mishel, 2015). Additionally, the U.S. lost some 6 million manufacturing jobs in the 2000s before recovering slightly in recent years: the remaining 12 million manufacturing jobs today account for less than 10% of nonagricultural employment (Charles, 2019). As Richard Haass of the Council on Foreign Relations has argued, unless we solve this challenge, we will succumb to political sclerosis and civic division that will destroy our ability to be a world power (Haass, 2023).

Lastly, winning the future of work is a necessity if we are going to truly have intergenerational justice. If we do not solve this challenge, we will see massive economic harm visited upon Americans who have borne the brunt of this transition for the last 40 years. However, if our people and our government can step up in the way we have historically, then these new technologies and their equitably shared gains can fuel a new

American century greater than the last. To do right for our children and grandchildren, we must step up.

The last time America faced an economic transition akin to what we are facing today was at the turn of the 20th century. During that time, we were moving from a country in which most Americans relied on agriculture to make a living, to one in which families supported themselves with jobs in manufacturing, in industries such as textile and steel. During that time of economic and demographic change (as new immigrants were arriving on our shores), the American government didn't step back, but rather it stepped up. And it did so with actions that matched the magnitude of the problems. Our government outlawed child labor, instituted the 40-hour workweek, and safeguarded the right to organize (FLSA, 1938). Furthermore, it also made two of the most massive investments in workers in human history up to that point: universal American public education and the GI Bill (Greenberg, 2004). These actions by our government, supported by the American citizenry in ways large and small, helped us conquer that change and lay the economic foundation of the American century.

As we proceeded into the postwar era, another shift began to take place: one defined by globalization, service delivery, and technology. A new transition had to face trading regimes that did not always prioritize American workers and new technologies that moved at speeds heretofore unseen. At the same time, Americans were moving from the factory floor to service and content delivery enterprises. Importantly, that content and those services were not just delivered to people in America, but around the world. This trend was accelerated exponentially with the advent of the internet and is now being further augmented with the advent of artificial intelligence, machine learning, and autonomous vehicles. However, unlike the past, our government has not stepped up during this transition, but rather has stepped back. Since the dawn of the Reagan era, we have been told that government cannot and should not step in to help us meet this challenge. It is the average Americans, from Black communities in our biggest cities to former industrial centers of our heartland, who have paid the price for this inaction. We must step up to win the future of work.

To win this future of work, we must come back to two fundamental questions that undergird education, knowledge, and how we seek to train up the next generation: What should our students know? How will effectively ensure that they learn it? The future and present of work that has been previously described points the way. The aforementioned trends and technologies will create a world where workers' prime value will not be the strength of their backs, the ability to follow orders or routines, or to simply repeat what has already been done. Workers' prime value to the economy and our society will be their ability to do and excel at the things that only humans can do. These are things that we have taught since the days of xviii C. AGUH

Songhai and Greece, Egypt and Rome, Britannia, and the Ming Dynasty: communication, problem identification, leading others, pinpointing not just what people do but why, and so many other "intangible" skills that we all know make the difference between success and failure on the job and in life. This "human work" as the Lumina Foundation's CEO Jamie Merisotis calls it, and each worker's ability to master these new technologies to further it, is what will define the future (Merisotis, 2020). There are many who say that these skills cannot be totally taught in a classroom setting. I agree and would go a step further; to teach these skills, we have to redefine the world and each person's lived experience as the classroom for this future of work. This is where a reimagined paradigm for OST can point the way.

In this paradigm, OST is not simply a place to shore academic weaknesses, but it is a place where students from a young age are flexing the mental and emotional muscles to shoulder this human work that will define their career. This training will take place under a caring adult who serves as a caring mentor, demanding coaching, and wise guide for these students. These adults will not only help them learn, but teach them how to learn. In this paradigm, OST will give students the space to lead their peers towards identifying and solving problems meaningful to them and important to the world. In this paradigm, as Dr. Tony Wagner put it, the worlds of work and school will be far closer together and students will travel between them seamlessly (Wagner, 2010). This paradigm is possible, this future is possible and the brilliance within the following pages will show us how.

Chike Aguh
Senior Advisor, Project on Workforce at Harvard University
Former Chief Innovation Officer, U.S. Department of Labor

REFERENCES

Charles, K. K., Hurst, E., & Schwartz, M. (2019). The transformation of manufacturing and the decline in US employment. *NBER Macroeconomics Annual*, *33*, 307–372. https://doi.org/10.1086/700896

Greenberg, M. (2004, June 18). *How the GI bill changed higher education—The chronicle of higher education.* https://www.chronicle.com/article/how-the-gi-bill-changed-higher-education/

Haass, R. (2023, January 22). *Why we need civics.* The Atlantic. https://www.theatlantic.com/ideas/archive/2023/01/american-identity-democracy-civics-education-requirement/672789/

Kaufman, W. (2011, February 3). *A successful job search: It's all about networking.* NPR. https://www.npr.org/2011/02/08/133474431/a-successful-job-search-its-all-about-networking#:~:text=Most%20Jobs%20Are%20Not%20Published,not%20published%2C%22%20he%20says.

Manyika, J., Lund, S., Chui, M., Bughin, J., Woetzel, J., Batra, P., Ko, R., & Sanghvi, S. (2017, November 28). *Jobs Lost, jobs gained: What the future of work will mean for jobs, skills, and wages*. McKinsey & Company. https://www.mckinsey.com/featured-insights/future-of-work/jobs-lost-jobs-gained-what-the-future-of-work-will-mean-for-jobs-skills-and-wages

Merisotis, J. (2020). *Human work in the age of smart machines*. RosettaBooks.

Mishel, R., & B. L. (2015, January 6). *Wage stagnation in nine charts*. Economic Policy Institute. https://www.epi.org/publication/charting-wage-stagnation/

The Fair Labor Standards Act (FLSA) of 1938, as amended (1938).

Wagner, T. (2010). *The global achievement gap*. Basic Books.

U.S. Department of Commerce and U.S. Department of Labor. Joint Communication on Guidance to States on Addressing the Workforce Needs. (2022, December 6). https://www.dol.gov/sites/dolgov/files/ETA/advisories/TEN/2022/TEN%2010-22/TEN%2010-22%20%28Complete%20PDF%29.pdf.and https://www.dol.gov/sites/dolgov/files/ETA/advisories/TEN/2022/TEN%2010-22/TEN%2010-22%20(Complete%20PDF).pdf

ACKNOWLEDGMENTS

This publication could not have come to fruition without collaboration and commitment from Big Thought's team, the Current Issues in Out-of-School Time Editorial Review Committee, and the Contributors. Grateful to our families and friends for their continued support —you all have made this possible. Thank you to our youth for playing the largest role: being the inspiration for furthering this work and making it better for your world.

Built for More: The Role of Out-of-School Time in Preparing Youth for the Future of Work,
pp. xxi–xxi
Copyright © 2024 by Information Age Publishing
www.infoagepub.com
All rights of reproduction in any form reserved.

INTRODUCTION

Byron Sanders

In a world teetering on the cusp of unimaginable change, our young people stand at the nexus of unprecedented challenges and unparalleled opportunities. And while the public school system serves as the traditional cornerstone of education, it's the Out-of-School Time (OST) programs as their vital partner that often provide the crucible where innovation, creativity, and adaptability thrive. This book, *Built for More: The Role of Out-of-School Time in Preparing Youth for the Future of Work*, is a declaration of the invaluable role that OST plays in preparing our youth for the constantly evolving landscape of the future workforce.

We find ourselves navigating through the Fourth Industrial Revolution, a seismic shift in how work is structured and accomplished. Automation, machine learning, and other technological marvels are rewriting the script on what constitutes essential skills. McKinsey, LinkedIn, Institute for the Future, Boston Consulting Group, and even the U.S. Department of Education agree on this: 21st-century skills like creativity, critical thinking, collaboration, and adaptability are not just beneficial but crucial for succeeding in tomorrow's workforce.

Out-of-school time helps knit the space-between in a child's life. Afterschool programs on campuses and in community settings during the year, summer learning to include both academic and enrichment experiences, career-related on-site learning experiences with employers, the OST ecosystem produces the opportunities for youth across the age spectrum to continue their personal and academic development beyond the 8 A.M.–3 P.M. paradigm most typically think of as *education*. Soccer club, theater camps, robotics competition, service-learning movements,

---

Built for More: The Role of Out-of-School Time in Preparing Youth for the Future of Work,
pp. xxiii–xxvi
Copyright © 2024 by Information Age Publishing
www.infoagepub.com
All rights of reproduction in any form reserved.

the forms are as varied as the young lives they serve. But what we are learning is that the sector itself has even more utility than traditionally attributed. This book lays out that claim in pristine account across three units described below.

Section I: The Future of Work

In this section, as we peel back the layers to uncover the underpinnings of the future of work, we realize that this is not solely a discussion about technological advancement. The issue is far more nuanced. Even our concept of the future must recalibrate—the future of work is not a distant abstraction; it is unfolding before our very eyes. The scale and immediacy of the shift is striking: As put forth by the World Economic Forum, by 2025, an estimated 85 million jobs could be displaced by automation, yet 97 million new roles may emerge, roles more adapted to the new collaboration between humans and machines (Zahidi et al., 2020, p. 29). Demographic shifts, such as an increasingly diverse population and an aging workforce, are adding layers of complexity and urgency to our evolving human development ecosystems. We must grapple with how these shifts compound the exigence for curricula and experiences that transcend traditional academic boundaries. These tectonic shifts require us to reimagine education and youth development not merely as a conduit for information but as a laboratory for skill development and character formation. Our contributors deftly lay out the need for change and the urgency with which our systems must evolve to meet it.

Section II: The Importance of Youth Workers in Preparing Youth for the Future of Work

Here, we contend with the notion that just as youth stand on the cusp of a radically changing world, so too do the professionals dedicated to guiding them through it. Gone are the days when a youth worker's role was limited to supervision and administrative tasks. According to a report by the Afterschool Alliance, these professionals have a direct impact on shaping positive learning experiences, particularly in marginalized communities (Afterschool Alliance, 2014, p. 18). Today, these individuals are mentors, coaches, and collaborators. They require a different set of skills that are attuned to the needs of a 21st-century young person and are eminently important to the new kind of skills-building structures that will be required. The training of youth workers must now include a focus on emotional intelligence, trauma-informed care, and systemic equity. This book will delve into innovative ways that youth worker training is shifting to become more responsive, adaptable, and relevant to the changing demands of a future that is perpetually in flux.

Section III: The Role of OST in Sparking Career Pathways

In this final unit, you will notice a common theme of OST programs and systems that make them the ideal medium for spurring youths' career discovery and economic activation: their flexibility and adaptability. The advantages of more programmatic flexibility, the leveraged power of location-specific learning, and the freedom to enlist workers with a broader range of professional backgrounds make OST an essential partner in youth career preparedness. OST, through its multi-faceted and often pioneering approaches, offers experiences and environments where young people can explore, learn, and innovate beyond the scope of standardized curriculum. They serve as incubators for the creative problem-solving skills and resilience that will become increasingly critical in the future work landscape. Data and studies continually show that formal education, though vital, is often insufficient alone in preparing youth fully for real-world challenges. LinkedIn's Most In-Demand Skills List indicates a growing demand for those skills that we used to call "soft" but are increasingly being relabeled as "critical," "durable," and "power" (Pate, 2020, p. 2). The chapters you'll read in this section lay bare powerful stories of practice and approaches that are pushing the possibilities and expectations of OST's contribution to this calling.

It is essential to note that as we explore the transformative role of OST, we also aim to amplify voices often relegated to the margins—those from BIPOC, rural, and other marginalized communities. Disparities in access to OST programs are, unfortunately, reflective of larger systemic issues. By showcasing research and practices that are inclusive and equitable for a diaspora of thoughtful contributors, this book seeks to remedy that omission, recognizing the inherent worth and potential in every young person and youth work professional, irrespective of their background. And in these sharings, you will see voices of a diverse mosaic of experts in the work reflected. Their stories matter and can illuminate the humanity behind the practice.

As the COVID-19 pandemic has illustrated with just how suddenly the world can shift, the future is now; it is here, demanding that we adapt, innovate, and thrive. This book serves as a testament to the incredible work already being done in the OST space, as well as a call to action for educators, policymakers, and thought leaders. It is a comprehensive exploration of the multi-faceted roles that OST plays in shaping our future workforce and, by extension, the fabric of our society.

Whether you are an educator, a researcher, or someone invested in the holistic development of our youth, we invite you to engage deeply with the insights and discussions that follow. Policymakers can shift the goalposts to focus on skills rather than grades alone. Researchers can delve deeper into the work to make visible the connections between OST learning and skills-building that lead to youths' economic empowerment. Practitioners can reimagine their programs to ensure youth know the full value of the learning encounters incite. Let us move forward collectively, with resolve and creativity, to ensure that our youth are not just participants in the future but the architects of a more just, inclusive, and innovative world.

Byron Sanders
President & CEO, Big Thought

REFERENCES

Afterschool Alliance. (2014). *Taking a deeper dive into afterschool: Positive outcomes and promising practices.* https://afterschoolalliance.org/documents/deeper_dive_into_afterschool.pdf

Pate, D. (2020). *The top skills companies need most in 2020—And how to learn them.* LinkedIn. https://www.linkedin.com/business/learning/blog/top-skills-and-courses/the-skills-companies-need-most-in-2020and-how-to-learn-them

Zahidi, S., Ratcheva, V., Hingel, G., & Brown, S. (2020). *Future Jobs Report of 2020.* World Economic Forum. https://www.weforum.org/publications/the-future-of-jobs-report-2020/

SECTION I

THE FUTURE OF WORK

CHAPTER 1

TRANSFORMING EDUCATION THROUGH LEARNER-CENTERED ECOSYSTEMS

Empowering All Children for a Thriving Future

Bobbi R. Macdonald
Education Reimagined

INTRODUCTION

Imagine a future where children and families are supported in caring communities to navigate vibrant ecosystems of learning experiences. In this public education system, the community and world serve as the playground for learning, promoting equity as well as the worth and dignity of every child is fostered. Silos between youth development, employment, K–12, higher education, and the community are broken down in the service of creating cohesive, enlivening, and community-embedded experiences for children. In this future, the purpose of education is to support young people—regardless of who they are, or where they are from—to discover and explore their identity, their unique gifts, and how to contribute those gifts meaningfully to the world.

A burgeoning movement is underway, aimed at redefining public education by harnessing the power of community involvement through the development of learner-centered ecosystems. Practitioners involved in out-

---

Built for More: The Role of Out-of-School Time in Preparing Youth for the Future of Work,
pp. 3–21
Copyright © 2024 by Information Age Publishing
www.infoagepub.com
All rights of reproduction in any form reserved.

3

of-school time (OST) learning have long recognized the value of engaging learners through activities that resonate with their interests. This approach not only fosters vital, equitable learning experiences, but also ignites a child's sense of purpose and identity and provides valuable exposure to a myriad of life and career possibilities. Remarkably, however, it remains outside the realm of accredited education.

At Education Reimagined, we envision a transformative system that fully embraces community-centered learning as integral to public education. In this vision, education is purposefully designed to seamlessly integrate all facets of learning and becomes the backbone infrastructure to something that supports much more than academic learning or even career goals. It aims to provide a focus for the community. This shared focus creates unwavering support to learners, attuned to their unique needs and preferences. Above all, it endeavors to contextualize all accredited learning within the framework of what truly matters to our youth and our communities.

Neuroscientist, Dr. Pamela Cantor, has been a pioneer and field-builder in understanding the dynamic systems that support whole-child development. Her most recent work, along with the Science of Learning and Development (SoLD) Alliance, states, "We should not expect children to adapt their learning to our flawed system; we must re-design our systems to understand and adapt to each learner, with the goal of helping them to discover and realize their potential" (Cantor et al., 2020, p. 15).

To achieve this vision and consistently prepare our young people to excel in the global economy while actively participating in civic life, we must embark on a new era of profound cross-sector collaboration. This endeavor calls for a passionate, shared commitment to reinventing education, ensuring that every child receives a holistic, community-driven education that empowers them to thrive.

I. Learner-Centered Ecosystems: A Bold Paradigm Shift in Education

> Living systems are dynamic living webs of interdependent relationships—inherently whole, abundant, creative and self-organizing. Their organizing principles, creative processes, and dynamic interdependence must guide our design of generative human systems, especially those that nurture the growing minds of our children. (Marshall, 2021)

Imagine a future where the journey of education is not confined within the walls of a classroom but rather extends across vibrant landscapes of intentional, learner-centered experiences. This is a world where the growth of children and their families is nurtured within supportive communities, and learning seamlessly intertwines into the fabric of everyday life.

Within this learner-centered ecosystem, every child's inherent potential is recognized and cherished, while the artificial barriers that segregate fields like youth development, academia, and employment dissolve, giving rise to a unified and enriching experience for every learner. At the heart of this transformation lies a commitment to honoring the innate worth of every individual and the recognition that our learning is socially embedded. The burgeoning idea of learner-centered ecosystems introduces a transformative approach that places the importance of fostering learner agency within nurturing communities. In this paradigm, each and every young person is not just a learner, but a whole human being, a valued member of an active community, deserving of recognition, acceptance, and unwavering support. This vision underscores the significance of building caring communities where learners can flourish both in the present and as they step into the future.

There are numerous examples of learner-centered sites that focus on learner agency embedded in communities, such as the schools of the Big Picture Learning (BPL) network. In the BPL model, learners are organized in small advisories where peers stay together for years with a caring advisor. There is a high value placed on becoming your authentic self. Advisory serves as a space where you are known, you are supported in finding and developing your interests, and navigating your learning journey. In a longitudinal study of students and alumni of schools within the BPL network, early findings showed that 97% of BPL students were admitted into 2-year or 4-year colleges and 96% of BPL alumni reported maintaining contact with their high school advisors more than 2 years after graduation (Arnold & Mihut, 2020).

Many initiatives that prioritize learner-centered approaches within conventional K–12 models often find themselves operating within systems designed for an entirely different purpose. These systems are rooted in the industrial model, inspired by mass production and mass consumption, and driven by standardization for the sake of efficiency, catering to the "average" child. This approach no longer aligns with the current needs of our economy, communities, and, most importantly, the learners themselves. It is clear that none of us can bring about this transformation in isolation. It is time to build an ecosystem that can support the broader societal goals and the outcomes we truly desire for every child. Reaching every child with a transformative model that is unique to each community will take bringing a transformative, systems-level approach to scale. The approach is founded on principles of belonging, agency, and building strong communities.

Achieving scalability requires us to develop a new kind of system—one that has dynamic relationships and flexible networks while also providing

6   B. R. MACDONALD

a reliable structure families can count on. Ecosystems in each community will be unique and a reflection of the shared vision of many partners who come together to bring the ecosystem to life. Scaling will be a different concept than the one we have come to know through the industrial age of mass production. In our work with communities, we have identified some essential components of the ecosystem that have the potential to shake up the current blueprints of education, which are guided by the principles of belonging, agency, and community building. We offer three distinct yet interconnected learning environments: home bases, learning hubs, and field sites. These components work harmoniously to craft and sustain a transformative educational experience.

1. Home Bases

Imagine a nurturing and secure space, facilitated by an advisor, where a young learner's educational journey is carefully planned and cultivated over time. In these home bases, learners not only receive personalized guidance but also find a profound sense of belonging within a consistent group of peers and dedicated adult advisors. Here, relationships are fostered, trust is built, and learners embark on their educational quests, knowing they have a steadfast support system. A home base could be located in a variety of places—similar to the micro-schools we see organically emerging across the country—or they could be grouped together in existing school buildings. The home base can serve as the main connection for families and as the anchoring structure dedicated to the academic growth of learners. It would also be designed to foster a deep sense of camaraderie. In contrast to big box school filled to maximum capacity based on square footage and budgetary needs, home bases are right-sized, responsive to the developmental needs of the learners served, and purposefully designed so that the advisor can know and be engaged with each learner and family.

2. Learning Hubs

Picture dedicated spaces designed to foster intellectual growth, cultivate academic skills, and nurture competencies in subjects such as reading, mathematics, science, and art. These places of learning cater to learners' developmental needs and aspirations and offer a diversity of experiences and learning environments that reflect the local ecosystem that developed it. Given that ecosystems are developed by the community through a highly participatory process, each learning hub will be unique. Learning hubs can include spaces in the community and existing organizations that provide learning environments such as recreation centers, YMCAs, gyms, libraries, museums, community colleges, and universities. These hubs allow learners to explore subjects they're passionate about, experiment with new ideas, and strengthen their sense of agency. For example, a well-equipped maker space—a creative environment that inspires learners to actively participate in the processes of design, experimentation, construction, and innovation. Within such a setting, young people immerse themselves in the worlds of science, engineering, and math, fostering a deep and enthusiastic engagement with these subjects.

3. Field Sites

Consider commercial, public, or nonprofit organizations that have formed approved partnerships with the ecosystem to host young learners for defined periods. Within these field sites, learners serve as interns who actively contribute to the host organization's objectives while simultaneously addressing their own learning goals. This is real-world experience. Field sites are another way the ecosystem makes deeper connections, bringing together businesses, education, the civic structure, and because there is such a strong local element to this idea, the land itself becomes an acknowledged partner. This symbiotic relationship enables learners to gain authentic, real-world experience and see the direct impact of their education on the world around them. For instance, a local environmental nonprofit might host learners who work on projects related to conservation, aligning with the organization's mission and the learners' interests in environmental science. For the community, the work and engagement of learners becomes a new force for the achievement of shared goals and objectives.

This design inherently necessitates the seamless coordination of OST learning and real-world resources. By bringing together these autonomous yet interdependent learning environments, we envision a system that not only builds a profound sense of belonging and identity but also actively engages learners within their communities. It creates clear and navigable learning pathways, ultimately leading to meaningful careers and greater job satisfaction.

Numerous examples of OST intermediaries exist. These organizations have developed a strong network of opportunities for youth, connecting them to learning experiences, internships, and mentors intentionally designed for career exploration and personal development. For example, Big Thought operates the Dallas City of Learning designed to actively foster a network of opportunities focused on equipping young people with essential skills for the 21st century through its innovative Creator

Archetype framework. Inspired by research and educational models like the Business-Higher Education Forum and Battelle for Kids' Portrait of a Graduate, this framework identifies five crucial domains: (1) Social and Emotional Foundation, emphasizing strong SEL skills; (2) Academics and Artistry, promoting lifelong learning in STEAM and the arts; (3) Digital Fluency, emphasizing digital asset use for self-expression; (4) Design Thinking, highlighting solution-oriented innovation; and (5) Civics and Service, encouraging active community participation. These domains are the foundation for Big Thought's programs, including the Learning Pathways Fellowship, connecting youth's out-of-school experiences to higher education, career development, and livable wages.

At the core of learner-centered education lies a powerful concept: Education is not designed solely for the future of work. Instead, education is designed for the future of our communities, economy, and planet—the future of us. It is a collaborative endeavor that engages the young learners, their peers, and the adults surrounding them in a system designed for thriving. This approach acknowledges that education isn't a one-sided process of knowledge transfer, but rather a shared journey, where the experiences and insights of each participant contribute to collective growth. Central to this approach is the empowerment of each learner's agency—the inherent ability to act independently and make impactful decisions about their learning and the role they play within their families, communities, and the broader world. This emphasis on agency is not just about gaining knowledge; it is about cultivating the capacity to navigate one's own path, make informed choices, and contribute meaningfully to various aspects of life.

This sentiment resonates deeply with the aspiration of empowering all children to thrive in an unpredictable future. The education landscape must evolve from its conventional role of imparting static knowledge to equipping young minds with the tools to navigate a dynamic world. The context for that learning must be dynamic, giving learners the opportunity to grow and learn immersed in a sustainable and reliable ecosystem designed for thriving. It seems that now more than ever we are able to bring to life the idea that John Dewey (1916) aptly noted, "Education is not preparation for life; education is life itself" (p. 239). Dewey's words underscore the concept that education is a lived experience, and not a "preparation" for a future state of being, but rather an integral part of our way of life and collective existence.

Empowering learners' agency is not merely a lofty ideal; it is a pragmatic and well-founded approach that stands at the forefront of the changing landscape in the future of work. This strategy is underpinned by a wealth of research and trends that shed light on its pivotal role. The World Economic Forum's (2020) "Future of Jobs Report" underscores the growing

Transforming Education Through Learner-Centered Ecosystems

imperative of lifelong learning in the contemporary job market. This report demonstrates that the skills demanded by many occupations are in a state of constant flux, demanding individuals who possess the capacity to adapt and learn continuously. Consequently, it becomes apparent that those who can take the reins of their own learning and education will be better equipped to navigate the dynamic job market. This brings lifelong learning into a new focus, and we have the opportunity to nurture inter-generational relationships and the sharing of wisdom and perspectives that come with every developmental age while also strengthening the fabric of each community.

Empowering learners' agency emerges as a well-informed and strategic response to the evolving demands of the future workforce. Grounded in a robust foundation of research and data, this approach equips individuals with desirable and essential skills for personal and professional success in a dynamic job market. The Association of American Colleges and Universities underscores the resounding value employers place on critical thinking and decision-making skills (Flateby & Rose, 2021). These competencies are not merely advantageous; they are imperative for tackling the intricacies of modern job roles, which often involve addressing complex challenges. Consequently, individuals who foster these skills through self-directed learning are primed for success in the evolving world of work. By fostering the ability to independently shape one's learning journey and roles within communities and workplaces, learners are not just preparing for the future—they are actively shaping it. In an era where self-starters thrive, those who can seize control of their own learning and proactively shape their opportunities stand on solid ground for professional success.

When we contemplate the creation of a learner-centered environment, as Education Reimagined distinguishes it, this environment is designed to promote learner agency that is socially embedded, competency-based, open-walled, personalized, relevant, and contextualized. The transformative concept of learner-centered ecosystems offers a fitting metaphor where learning intertwines with life, and where both local and global communities serve as fertile grounds for exploration and growth. The problems we face on a global level will take a collaborative approach if we are to solve them. Our capacity to face this complex work together can be nurtured through ecosystems where learners experience growing up together as respected members of the community—engaged participants, supported, and known as unique individuals.

An ecosystem acknowledges that learning is not a linear assembly line but rather an intricate interplay of diverse elements, much like the natural world. The conventional notion of education fixated on rote memoriza-tion and standardized assessments falls short in preparing learners for the complexities of modern existence. It is essential to challenge the outdated purpose of education that seeks to transmit information and instead embrace an approach that cultivates critical thinking, adaptability, and collaboration—the very skills that define success in the 21st century. Learner-centered practices shift the focus from a teacher-centric model to one that honors each learner's unique interests, strengths, and aspirations. These practices invite exploration, experimentation, and deep engagement, fostering a love for learning that extends beyond formal institutions. In addition, everyone is seen as a learner. Educators are seen as expert navigators and facilitators of learning. The ecosystem organizes time, people, and spaces for long-term relationships, inspiration, iteration, and shared decision-making.

As we embark on this exploration of transforming education through learner-centered ecosystems, it becomes evident that this work will take new ways of talking about education. The journey ahead demands a departure from convention, a willingness to challenge established norms, and a commitment to crafting an educational experience that aligns with the values of today's society. The subsequent sections of this chapter will delve deeper into the nuances of this transformation, outlining the redefinition of learning, the creation of sustainable frameworks, and the embodiment of shared aspirations.

II. Embracing Adaptability: Integrating OST With Future Skills

The World Economic Forum (WEF) *Future of Jobs Report* consistently underscores the growing demand for skills such as complex problem-solving, critical thinking, creativity, and cognitive flexibility—attributes that are closely linked to adaptability. The report explores how technological advancements and automation are reshaping the workforce, necessitating skills that enable individuals to pivot and excel in dynamic environments (WEF, 2020). In a world which is rapidly changing, the importance of adaptability cannot be overstated. As highlighted in research by McKinsey & Company on workforce skills for the future, resilience and adaptability are quintessential in a world of work characterized by rapid change (Lund et al., 2021). Individuals who can bounce back from setbacks and swiftly adjust to new circumstances are not only sought after by employers but are also more likely to flourish amidst the evolving employment landscape. Adaptable life skills encompass qualities such as critical thinking, problem-solving, creativity, and emotional intelligence. These skills form the bedrock of a resilient individual, someone who can navigate unforeseen challenges with confidence, embrace change as an opportunity, and continue to learn and grow in the face of uncertainty. Research conducted by

Carol Dweck, a renowned psychologist at Stanford University, highlights the significance of developing life skills and fostering resilience and a growth mindset. Dweck found that individuals with a belief in the malleability of their abilities are better equipped to face challenges and adapt to change. This growth mindset encourages the development of critical thinking and problem-solving skills, enabling individuals to view setbacks as opportunities for learning and growth (Dweck, 2006).

The traditional view of education, rooted in static knowledge and rote learning, falls short of preparing learners for the uncertainties that lie ahead. The call for adaptable life skills goes beyond workforce demands; it's a necessity for thriving in a future characterized by the rapid acceleration of artificial intelligence (AI), technological advancements, and economic shifts.

Within the terrain of educational ecosystems, we must glean wisdom from OST experiences that have often thrived outside the confines of traditional classroom structures and the constraints of standardized teaching and learning paradigms. OST programs, free from many of these limitations, present a reservoir of insights for cultivating adaptability in learners. Operating beyond conventional hours, OST experiences provide unique avenues for learners to immerse themselves in diverse, hands-on encounters. These experiences are intentionally designed to nurture the very skills essential for adaptability—skills that transcend the confines of the traditional curriculum and empower learners to thrive in dynamic contexts. Recent educational research echoes the importance of experiential learning in shaping meaningful educational experiences. The "Deeper Learning for All" report by the William and Flora Hewlett Foundation (2021) underscores that hands-on experiences foster critical thinking, problem-solving, and collaboration. Experiential learning transcends the textbook, extending into communities, workplaces, and real-world contexts. In this vein, community engagement becomes pivotal. The "Civic Learning and Democratic Engagement" study from the American Association of State Colleges and Universities (AASCU) highlights the role of community engagement in cultivating active citizenship (AASCU, 2012). These ecosystems blur the lines between education and reality, offering learners authentic encounters with the world around them.

The power of OST programs within educational ecosystems is evident in various reports. The "Expanded Learning and Time" report by the Wallace Foundation delves into the impact of OST programs on students' academic and social-emotional development (Wallace Foundation, 2021). These programs transcend traditional classroom hours, offering learners opportunities to explore their passions, build skills, and connect with mentors. The "Promising Afterschool Programs" study by the RAND Corporation emphasizes that OST programs enhance learning in diverse domains,

12   B. R. MACDONALD

from STEM to the arts (RAND Corporation, 2020). These programs inject authenticity into education, bridging the gap between theoretical knowledge and real-world application.

In our journey beyond classroom boundaries, we heed the lessons from these studies and recognized reports. We are crafting dynamic ecosystems that cultivate learner agency, foster experiential learning, and harness the potential of OST programs. It is a visionary departure from traditional constraints, aligning education with the evolving needs of learners and society.

Educational ecosystems recognize that adaptability is not solely about acquiring theoretical knowledge; it's about applying that knowledge in real-world contexts. When learners engage in experiential learning that encourages them to grapple with complex challenges, explore innovative solutions, and collaborate with peers of various backgrounds, these experiences mirror the demands of an ever-evolving landscape, where adaptability is not just a trait but a requirement for success. Our challenge is to design a system that values and nurtures these kinds of experiences.

The acceleration of AI and economic change reshapes the professional landscape, rendering the traditional career path a relic of the past. The economy of the past benefited those who stayed with a company over many years, and the career path and advancement was mapped by a series of promotions and pay raises. Technical specialists relied on union contracts and credentials as a career pathway. However, as we move from mass production to a new era the landscape has changed significantly. In this era, businesses are seeking individuals with more than specialized knowledge—they seek individuals with the ability to pivot, learn new skills, and adapt to unforeseen circumstances. The demand for adaptability extends to every sector, from tech-driven industries to creative fields, underscoring its universal importance. Recent studies, such as the report by the National Academies of Sciences, Engineering, and Medicine (2018) titled "How People Learn II," emphasize that traditional classroom structures often stifle active learning and engagement. Learner agency—the ability to drive one's learning—emerges as a pivotal focus. As learners actively shape their educational journey, they develop autonomy, curiosity, and a sense of ownership over their growth. A study from the Organization for Economic Co-operation and Development (OECD) underscores that learner agency is essential for lifelong learning and adaptability (OECD, 2018). Thus, dynamic ecosystems become the canvas where agency flourishes, empowering learners to navigate an unpredictable future.

Adapting to an AI-accelerated world and economic transformation requires more than technical know-how—it demands adaptable life skills that empower individuals to confidently navigate uncertainty. Through the strategic integration of OST experiences, learner-centered ecosystems become a launchpad for cultivating this adaptability. As learners participate

Transforming Education Through Learner-Centered Ecosystems 13

in hands-on projects, engage in real-world problem-solving, and collaborate across disciplines, they hone the very skills that will empower them to thrive amidst AI-driven disruption and economic transformations. By emphasizing adaptable life skills, these ecosystems empower learners to remain agile, regardless of economic and workforce shifts.

III. Inclusivity and Equity: Empowering All Learners in Ecosystems

The conventional design of the public education system has, over time, contributed to cultural erasure, community displacement, and the enforcement of compliance and conformity to authoritarian models. This structure has perpetuated long-standing inequalities, resulting in the marginalization of entire communities. The focus of learner-centered ecosystems lies in creating something new together and providing access to opportunities for every child. The traditional silos that have long perpetuated disparities can be replaced by learning journeys that honor the diverse experiences and strengths each learner brings. As we reimagine the possibilities, we are called to design ecosystems that inherently value and celebrate the varied backgrounds, cultures, and perspectives of each and every learner. From the start, this work is grounded in each learner's uniqueness. That shift has the potential to make diversity our greatest strength and enrich our society. At the core of this journey is the elevation of learner agency—a force that has the potential to dismantle barriers and rewrite narratives. By granting learners the agency to shape their educational journeys, we create a seismic shift. No longer passive recipients, our youth become architects of their destinies. This empowerment is a formidable tool against marginalization, allowing even the most silenced voices to be heard, valued, and catalyzed into action.

However, fostering inclusivity and equity is not just solely about providing equitable opportunities and promoting learner agency; it is about creating a profound sense of belonging and an unwavering belief that every child is inherently valuable. It involves cultivating ecosystems that not only recognize diversity but also always actively work to dismantle racist practices, to humbly develop our shared capacity for compassion and to intentionally view the work through the lens of equity and community as a natural function of the ecosystem. It is about nurturing environments where learners, regardless of their race, socioeconomic status, gender, and identity, can truly thrive without the fear of exclusion.

For example, consider Norris Academy in Mukwonago, Wisconsin, where innovative approaches to education are making a remarkable impact. Norris Academy serves approximately 100 learners, the majority of whom

14 B. R. MACDONALD

come from economically disadvantaged backgrounds and represent a rich tapestry of racial and cultural diversity, making up about 69% of the student body. A significant portion of these students, over 75%, are identified with disabilities. Norris also serves adjudicated youth. This adds another layer of focus and intention on the trauma of incoming learners, some of whom are placed with Norris for short amounts of time.

Norris begins with every learner by focusing on developing a unique learner profile. They dedicate 10 days with each learner during "orientation" period to build connections and relationships. They actively seek to find their interests, cares, likes, and dislikes. They start with the story of each unique individual, and as the learner begins to build their profile, trust and connection develop. Learners are then supported in creating and navigating their learning journey, including being connected to various businesses for exploration, mentorship, and career guidance. They are also deeply engaged in service-learning initiatives that support community missions and are focused on developing achievement centers in the community for learners post-graduation to continue the relationship and provide further support and connection to careers and services.

In the past, Norris was often characterized by a perception as a "school for troubled kids." However, today, it is a different story. Families and the local community are now witnessing individual success stories among the youth. Norris continuously evaluates and iterates on their practices and intentionally develops a shared vision for approaching each learner as unique, powerful, and capable. As one learner named Sean commented, after being at Norris for only three weeks, "They just keep telling me I'm good at something. Every day. Day after day. I'm starting to believe it myself."

As we navigate the path of inclusivity and equity within learner-centered ecosystems, we're not just shaping a future for individuals; we are shaping a future for society at large. The echoes of inclusion ripple outward, influencing communities, industries, and the world. Our commitment to providing equal opportunities, empowering learner agency, and championing belonging and equity is not just about education—it is about crafting a legacy of social transformation. It's about the belief that every child's journey matters and that, together, we can create ecosystems where every young learner can truly thrive.

IV. Nurturing Empowerment and Collaboration in Ecosystems

The core components that drive learner empowerment and agency in learner-centered ecosystems are the environment, the people, and the strength of the connections. In the realm of these ecosystems, a profound transformation takes place with two foundational pillars: learner agency and a culture of collaboration among a diverse array of stakeholders. To fully appreciate this transformative landscape, it is imperative to dissect the fundamental components that fuel these dynamics and explore how they reshape the terrain of education and community engagement.

At the heart of these learner-centered ecosystems lies the pivotal concept of empowerment and agency. In this context, learners are not passive recipients but active architects of their educational journeys. As previously mentioned, ecosystems begin with individual interests, strengths, and aspirations. Placing learners squarely at the center ensures that education harmonizes with their distinctive needs, nurturing a profound sense of ownership over their personal growth.

However, this transformation extends far beyond individual empowerment alone. In these ecosystems, community serves as the guiding principle. The ecosystem weaves together a rich tapestry, incorporating the contributions of youth development organizations, civic structures, local businesses, and the entire community. Together, these stakeholders jointly craft a shared vision, collaborating to provide an immersive and comprehensive educational experience. The shared process of imagining, implementing, learning, reflecting, and revising is the work of the ecosystem.

Learner-centered ecosystems are a collective endeavor involving educators, parents, community leaders, and learners themselves, all coming together to foster a culture of lifelong learning and growth. Within these ecosystems, the community emerges as a treasure trove of resources. OST programs, local businesses, museums, libraries, and credentialing institutions all contribute to an array of learning opportunities. The community takes center stage, offering a wealth of knowledge and experiences. It is about embracing and championing these resources and recognizing their indispensable role in the educational journey. At the local level, the ecosystem develops highly participatory practices to form the bedrock of operations. Active engagement from all stakeholders ensures the vibrancy of the ecosystem, making it responsive to the ever-evolving needs of the community. It is a collective commitment to continuous improvement and growth.

In addition, the institutions that are directly influenced and connected to K–12 education are influenced through this new way of functioning. Higher education alignment with a variety of transcripts has already begun to emerge across the country. For instance, many universities have moved away from standardized test scores and have instead embraced the idea that an incoming learner with various work or leadership experiences carries the merit to join the institution.

16 B. R. MACDONALD

Parent involvement undergoes a profound transformation in learner-centered ecosystems. Parents evolve from passive observers to active partners, deeply engaged in shaping their children's educational pathways. For example, Rock Tree Sky is a learning environment in Ojai, California supported by a cooperative of homeschool families. The parents are in a community supporting the growth and development of their learners and use Rock Tree Sky as a home base and learning hub. Learners are also placed at field sites for experiences with other organizations based on their interests. In this community, many of the courses of study have developed over time based on the interests of learners and educators. Parents also participate in community conversations aimed at learning, governance, and social connections.

Equitable, community-based ecosystems require transformational infrastructure. This includes developing transportation services, learning management systems, transcripts and portfolios, portable credentials and badges, funding models, and policies. It is about reimagining infrastructure, not as a utility, but as an enabler of education, community, and connection. Our challenge in designing the future of work is to recognize we are also designing the future of our society.

V. From Vision to Reality: Strategies for Building Learner-Centered Ecosystems

The transition from vision to reality will take a movement of people working together to grow demonstrations of this transformational approach. At the same time, we must think like systems engineers—learning from models what infrastructure, policy, and conditions are needed to allow the widespread adoption of ecosystems.

We find ourselves at a critical crossroads where the future of work is advancing rapidly, and the education system is not aligned with the needs that have been identified. In response, we observe districts attempting to forge partnerships and school models attempting to add or pivot programming to serve these evolving needs, striving to provide future-forward opportunities to their learners. However, these efforts exist within the confines of a system not originally designed for these purposes. For this reason, system-level change is imperative.

To advance this movement, we must bring fully realized, equitable, community-based, learner-centered ecosystem demonstrations to life. These living examples will be powerful showcases of what becomes achievable when learners, parents, educators, and communities immerse themselves in the complete vision of learner-centered education. They will demonstrate the profound impact and potential of education when it genuinely revolves around the learner.

The journey of iteration and piloting is indispensable. Systems invention requires continuous research and development. The field needs proofs of concepts by conducting iterative cycles with a wide range of communities to collectively accumulate the insights necessary to construct an equitable learner-centered system capable of serving all children. We can only comprehend the intricate requirements of this transformation by actively engaging in the process.

While we bring these examples to life, we must concurrently construct the essential infrastructure that not only empowers these demonstrations but also facilitates future leaders' ability to establish learner-centered ecosystems in their own communities with ease. This comprehensive infrastructure includes some of the most daunting challenges, including programmatic, technological, and policy barriers.

In essence, the transition from vision to reality is a multifaceted endeavor that involves not only the creation of ecosystem demonstration but also the creation of infrastructure, research initiatives, policy frameworks, funding mechanisms, and knowledge dissemination required to propel this transformative movement forward. It is a collective journey of learning by doing, building, and refining—a movement that can reshape education, align it with the future of work, and empower learners and communities alike.

VI. Cultivating a Ripple Effect: Ecosystems and Societal Transformation

Learner-centered ecosystems hold the potential for a far-reaching and transformative impact that extends well beyond the individual learner. These complex networks of interconnected educational experiences have the capacity to set in motion a ripple effect that not only shapes individuals but also reverberates through communities and plays a pivotal role in the landscape of community and workforce development. As we delve into the broader influence of these ecosystems, we begin to understand their profound implications for societal transformation.

At the heart of learner-centered ecosystems, there exists a foundational principle of interconnectedness. These ecosystems go beyond merely imparting knowledge and skills; they also cultivate a deep sense of community and belonging. When learners engage in a diverse array of learning experiences deeply embedded within their communities, they not only acquire valuable competencies but also actively contribute to shaping the social fabric of their communities.

In their research on collective learning processes and journeys, the authors emphasize that this approach has the potential to "generate and sustain meaningful collective purposes, identities, and actions that promote co-creation, collaboration, and collective learning" (Spencer-Keyse et al., 2020, p. 21). By enabling individuals to collectively explore, co-create, and evolve across various disciplines in engaging and thought-provoking ways, this approach allows them to experience a profound sense of belonging to something greater.

Learner-centered ecosystems, when strategically implemented in urban and rural environments, can serve as powerful catalysts for reinvention and community-building. By seamlessly integrating diverse learning opportunities into the urban landscape, ecosystems can contribute to the revitalization of regions and neighborhoods. Consequently, communities experience not only economic growth but also a rekindling of hope and aspiration. Research by the Urban Institute (2020) highlights the profound impact of well-designed educational ecosystems, as they attract investments, improve local infrastructure, stimulate entrepreneurship, and ultimately foster a thriving urban environment.

Organizations continue to develop infrastructure that can support ecosystems and build community. These digital platforms serve as a one-stop "human library" to quickly match community members with PK–12 educators. For instance, the Big Picture Learning platform, B-Unbound, initially established to connect youth with supportive adults who share their interests and foster peer learning, has now evolved to create multigenerational networks of support for both youth and adults. Using proprietary technology, B-Unbound manages these community relationships and partners with trusted community-based organizations to train co-navigators who guide youth navigators in connecting with supportive adults on their platform. This expansion also includes the introduction of adult navigators, further broadening the program's reach and impact through collaborations with local organizations.

Unlocking the full potential of learner-centered ecosystems necessitates a concerted effort from a diverse array of stakeholders, including educational institutions, local governments, businesses, and community members. This collaborative endeavor transcends traditional boundaries and fosters a shared vision of education as a unifying force. As we unite to harness the capabilities of learner-centered ecosystems, we collectively pave the way for a more inclusive, compassionate, and equitable future. In the words of Nelson Mandela, "Education is the most powerful weapon which you can use to change the world" (Mandela, 1990). Embracing the holistic approach of learner-centered ecosystems empowers us to generate a collective force to drive societal transformation.

CONCLUSION

Just as every child is seen for their unique gifts, stories, and aspirations, each community has a unique story to tell. Rather than approaching public education as a mass-produced industry, we must find a way to understand that each community will have a unique story. If we want to create learner-centered ecosystems and have them be available through public education—where most of the learners are—we must ask ourselves: What should be scaled? What shouldn't be scaled?

The positive impact of growing learner-centered ecosystems extends beyond the realm of education, nurturing a society characterized by inclusivity, empathy, and adaptability. The potential ripple effect of this transformation stands to shape resilient communities and future generations, equipping them with the skills, values, and resilience needed to navigate a rapidly evolving world. As this collective journey unfolds, it invites us to aspire to ambitious goals while grounding our efforts in practical strategies. The transition to learner-centered ecosystems calls for a departure from established norms and an embrace of innovative approaches that prioritize the holistic development of learners.

In the spirit of nurturing these ecosystems, stakeholders are encouraged to be both trailblazers and partners in redefining education. By doing so, we acknowledge the potential for profound change while acknowledging the challenges that lie ahead. As we embrace this transformative shift, we realize that education is not just about preparing for the future; it is about equipping learners with the tools and experiences to shape the future themselves. It is about creating strong connected communities where we can raise our children together in a loving environment, create spaces designed for thriving, and tell a new story. A story of us.

REFERENCES

American Association of State Colleges and Universities (AASCU). (2012). *Civic learning and democratic engagement: A review of the literature.* https://www.aascu.org/civic/

Arnold, K., & Mihut, G. (2020). Post-secondary outcomes of innovative high schools: The big picture longitudinal study. *Teachers College Record, 122*(8), 1–42.

Cantor, P., L. Darling-Hammond, B. Little, S. Palmer, D. Osher, K. Pittman, & T. Rose. (2020). *How the science of learning and development can transform education.* Science of Learning & Development Alliance. https://soldalliance.org/wp-content/uploads/2021/12/SoLD-Science-Translation_May-2020_FNL.pdf

Dewey, J. (1916). *Democracy and education: An introduction to the philosophy of education.* Macmillan.

Dweck, C. S. (2006). *Mindset: The new psychology of success.* Random House.

20   B. R. MACDONALD

Flateby, T., & Rose, T. (2021, July 16). *From college to career success*. AAC&U. https://www.aacu.org/liberaleducation/articles/from-college-to-career-success-how-educators-and-employers-talk-about-skills

Lund, S., Madgavkar, A., Manyika, J., Smit, S., Ellingrud, K., & Robinson, O. (2021). *The future of work after COVID-19*. McKinsey and Company. https://www.mckinsey.com/featured-insights/future-of-work/the-future-of-work-after-covid-19

Mandela, N. (1990, June 23). *Nelson Mandela visits Madison Park High School in Roxbury in 1990* [Video]. YouTube. https://www.youtube.com/watch?v=b66c6OkMZGw

Marshall, S. P. (1997). Creating sustainable learning communities for the twenty-first century. *The Organization of the Future*, 177–188.

Marshall, S. (2021). *Living systems*. Stephanie Pace Marshall. https://stephaniepacemarshall.com/livingsystems

National Academies of Sciences, Engineering, and Medicine. (2018). *How people learn II: Learners, contexts, and cultures*. The National Academies Press.

Organization for Economic Co-operation and Development (OECD). (2018). *Education 2030: The future of education and skills*. OECD Publishing.

RAND Corporation. (2020). *Promising afterschool programs*. https://www.rand.org/pubs/research_reports/RR2491.html

Spencer-Keyse, J., Luksha, P., & Cubista, J. (2020). *Learning ecosystems: An emerging praxis for the future of education*. Moscow School of Management SKOLKOVO & Global Education Futures. https://www.rand.org/pubs/research_reports/RR2491.html

Urban Institute. (2020). *The economic and community development benefits of education ecosystems*. https://www.urban.org/sites/default/files/publication/102413/making-education-and-employment-work-for-high-school-students_1.pdf

Wallace Foundation. (2021). *Expanded learning and time: A guide to successful out-of-school time (OST) programs*. https://www.wallacefoundation.org/knowledge-center/pages/expanded-learning-and-time-a-guide-to-successful-out-of-school-time-ost-programs.aspx

William and Flora Hewlett Foundation. (2021). *Deeper learning for all: Five powerful strategies*. https://hewlett.org/deeper-learning-for-all-five-powerful-strategies/

World Economic Forum. (2020). *Future of Jobs Report*. https://www.weforum.org/reports/the-future-of-jobs-report-2020

ADDITIONAL READINGS

Coates, T. N. (2015). *Between the world and me*. Spiegel & Grau.

Hannon, V. (2018). *Thrive: Schools reinvented for the real challenges we face*. New Frontiers in Education.

Hooks, B. (1994). *Teaching to transgress: Education as the practice of freedom*. Routledge.

Lonechild, L. (2003). Indigenous ways of knowing and learning. *Education Canada*, *43*(1), 16–19.

Senge, P. M. (2020). *The necessary revolution: How individuals and organizations are working together to create a sustainable world*. Crown Currency.

Tyson, N. D. (2000). *The sky is not the limit: Adventures of an urban astrophysicist*. Prometheus.

Wahl, D. C. (2016). *Designing regenerative cultures.* Triarchy Press.

Wallis, J. (2009). *The divine matrix: Bridging time, space, miracles, and belief.* Hay House.

The Wellbeing Economy Alliance (WEAll). (2020). *WEAll primer: An economy based on well-being.* https://wellbeingeconomy.org/wp-content/uploads/2020/10/WEAll-Primer.pdf

The Wellbeing Economy Alliance (WEAll). (2020). *WEAll policy design guide: Wellbeing economy policies for national governments.* https://wellbeingeconomy.org/wp-content/uploads/Wellbeing-Economy-Policy-Design-Guide_Mar17_FINAL.pdf

CHAPTER 2

THE IMPACT OF AI TECHNOLOGY ON FUTURE GENERATIONS IN THE WORKFORCE AND THE ROLE OF OUT-OF-SCHOOL TIME PROVIDERS

Shannon Epner and ChatGPT-4

INTRODUCTION BY AUTHOR

The out-of-school time (OST) community has a long history of embracing innovative practices and staying abreast of evolving trends throughout their years of dedicated work. Hence, the introduction of artificial intelligence (AI) tools and resources should come as no surprise. However, we are now witnessing the substantial impact that this new tool and its capabilities can have on the field. Youth are coming into programs with new technology, wanting to work on new projects, and professionals are racing to keep up.

As we delved into the development of this publication, the emergence of AI technology and tools started to make waves in news headlines and global discussions. In an incredibly short span of time, the discourse shifted from casual inquiries like, "Have you explored AI for creating meal plans? It's fascinating to experiment with!" to a scenario where every virtual meeting starts with AI-assisted reading software and collaborative sharing of notes with action items when the meeting ends. This transformation prompted

Built for More: The Role of Out-of-School Time in Preparing Youth for the Future of Work,
pp. 23–39
Copyright © 2024 by Information Age Publishing
www.infoagepub.com
All rights of reproduction in any form reserved.

us to explore the notion of, "Let's request ChatGPT to compose a chapter and see what insights it can offer to the OST community."

Below, you'll find a chapter authored by Chat GPT-4 in response to the directive: "Write an essay about the impact of AI technology on future generations in the workforce and the role that out of school time providers can have on that impact. Essay needs to be between 6,000–7,000 words and cited using APA format." This was compiled on August 9, 2023.

Information Age Publishing (IAP) has approved the following for publication.

THE IMPACT OF AI ON THE FUTURE WORKFORCE BY CHATGPT-4

The rapid advancement of artificial intelligence (AI) technology has ignited profound discussions about its transformative influence across various sectors of modern society, notably the workforce. As AI continues to progress at an astonishing pace, its implications for future generations entering the job market have gained unprecedented significance. This essay endeavors to comprehensively explore the potential impact of AI technology on employment trends, skills development, and socioeconomic inequality among future generations. Additionally, it highlights the pivotal role that out-of-school time providers can play in preparing young individuals to not only navigate but also flourish within an AI-driven job landscape.

Employment Trends in the Age of AI

The assimilation of AI technology into workplaces has initiated a transformative shift in the dynamics of employment. A critical point of contention revolves around the divergent viewpoints concerning the impact of AI on jobs. On one end of the spectrum, proponents assert that AI's automation capabilities may lead to substantial job displacement. This viewpoint finds validation in instances where routine, repetitive tasks are progressively being automated by AI-powered systems. For example, industries like manufacturing and logistics have begun witnessing the integration of AI-powered robots to replace human workers in tasks involving precision and repetition (Bessen, 2019).

On the opposite end of the spectrum, a contrasting perspective contends that AI will give rise to novel job opportunities and roles. Particularly evident in areas such as AI research, programming, data analysis, and the management of AI systems (Brynjolfsson & McAfee, 2014), this viewpoint underscores AI's potential to amplify productivity, efficiency, and market niches. For instance, the emergence of industries centered around voice assistants, chatbots, and autonomous vehicles reflects AI's capacity to generate entirely new job categories, thereby countering job displacement concerns (Acemoglu & Restrepo, 2018).

The amalgamation of these perspectives underscores the nuanced nature of AI's influence on the future workforce. As AI evolves, its impact on job markets is likely to encompass a complex interplay of job displacement in routine tasks and the emergence of fresh positions demanding specialized AI-related skills. Preparing upcoming generations for this dynamic landscape necessitates a comprehensive understanding of the multifaceted employment trends under the influence of AI.

Skills Development and AI

The increasing infusion of AI technology across diverse industries necessitates a recalibration of the skill sets demanded by the job market. While AI excels in executing routine tasks, it struggles when confronted with tasks demanding human qualities such as creativity, complex problem-solving, emotional intelligence, and ethical decision-making (Davenport & Kirby, 2016). This dynamic underscores the growing significance of skills traditionally viewed as quintessentially human, like critical thinking and creativity, in an AI-driven society.

As a result, a growing demand is emerging for individuals possessing a well-rounded skill set that complements the capabilities of AI. Instead of perceiving AI as a threat, a more constructive approach is to regard it as a tool augmenting human abilities. This perspective accentuates the importance of nurturing skills that augment AI's strengths, including cognitive flexibility, emotional intelligence, and creativity. Out-of-school time providers occupy a crucial position in this landscape, as they can offer tailored educational experiences designed to foster these essential skills.

Out-of-school programs provide a conducive environment where students can engage in problem-based learning, collaboration, and critical thinking exercises. For instance, hackathons, robotics competitions, and design thinking workshops encourage students to tackle real-world challenges, fostering creativity and innovation. Through these activities, young individuals not only cultivate technical skills but also learn how to approach intricate problems from diverse interdisciplinary perspectives (Hirsh-Pasek et al., 2019).

Socioeconomic Inequality and the Digital Divide

While the integration of AI technology holds the promise of transforming industries and catalyzing economic growth, concerns linger regarding its potential to exacerbate existing socioeconomic inequalities. Notably, one avenue through which inequality could be perpetuated is the digital divide. This phenomenon encompasses the disparities in access to AI education, resources, and opportunities, with marginalized communities often bearing the brunt of limited access to technology infrastructure and quality education. Consequently, these communities are at heightened risk of being left behind in an AI-driven world.

The intricate relationship between AI and socioeconomic inequality underscores the necessity for proactive measures. Despite AI's capacity to amplify productivity and stimulate economic advancement, its benefits may not be evenly distributed across society. The absence of equitable access to AI education and training could result in the widening of the digital divide, deepening existing disparities. Herein lies the potential of out-of-school time providers to mitigate this divide through the provision of inclusive AI education programs targeting underserved communities. By democratizing access to AI education, these providers can contribute to a more equitable distribution of AI-related opportunities and benefits.

The formation of collaborations among out-of-school time providers, community organizations, and local educational institutions holds the potential to extend the reach of AI education to marginalized communities. Initiatives such as coding camps, AI workshops, and mentorship programs can be tailored to address the specific needs of these communities, ensuring that the benefits of AI education are accessible to all (Bevan et al., 2017). Furthermore, these collaborations can engender a sense of belonging and empowerment among individuals historically underrepresented in the STEM fields.

IMPACT OF AI CONCLUSION

The amalgamation of AI into the workforce ushers in both challenges and opportunities for future generations. The evolution of the employment landscape, the shifting demands for skills, and the potential for socioeconomic inequality underscore the imperative of proactive measures in preparing young individuals for a workforce dominated by AI. In this transformative era, out-of-school time providers, through their innovative educational initiatives, assume a pivotal role in equipping students with the skills and knowledge requisite for thriving in an evolving landscape shaped by AI.

THE ROLE OF OUT-OF-SCHOOL TIME PROVIDERS IN PREPARING FOR THE AI-DOMINATED JOB MARKET

The relentless progression of AI technology into various sectors casts a compelling spotlight on the urgency to recalibrate education to match the demands of an AI-centric workforce. Out-of-school time providers, encompassing afterschool programs, summer camps, and community organizations, emerge as instrumental agents in nurturing the preparedness of future generations to confront the myriad opportunities and challenges spawned by a job landscape dominated by AI. This section underscores the profound significance of out-of-school time providers in readying students for the dynamic workforce evolution, accentuating the criticality of cultivating essential skills, fostering creativity and innovation, and nurturing adaptability and lifelong learning.

Equipping Students With Essential Skills

The assimilation of AI into the professional realm precipitates a perceptible shift in the skills that hold prime currency in the contemporary job market. Beyond the realm of mere technical prowess, a burgeoning emphasis is placed on skills that resonate with uniquely human attributes. Out-of-school time providers, armed with their dexterity and adaptability, occupy an enviable vantage point in fostering these indispensable skills. Instead of limiting their purview to the mere transfer of knowledge, these providers wield the power to engender the development of competencies that remain resilient in the face of automation. Skills such as critical thinking, problem-solving, effective communication, and collaboration have unequivocally risen to prominence as prerequisites for individuals to seamlessly mesh with AI systems (World Economic Forum, 2020).

Crafting experiential learning that is tailored to the cultivation of these essential skills is the forte of out-of-school programs. Envision collaborative projects that compel students to grapple with intricate challenges, engage in interdisciplinary problem-solving, and communicate cogently—these initiatives possess the potential to nurture skills that are immensely coveted in an AI-tinged workforce (Sawyer, 2006). By fostering an environment wherein students enthusiastically collaborate and immerse themselves in real-world scenarios, out-of-school time providers spearhead a pivotal role in preparing individuals for roles that entail not only technical mastery but also the acumen of human-centered skills.

Within these programs, scenarios mirroring the complexities of real-world challenges can be meticulously designed to train participants in dissecting intricate problems, evaluating multiple perspectives, and

Fostering Creativity and Innovation

Among the gamut of faculties that define human cognition, creativity, and innovation reign supreme. These qualities embody an inherent value that existing AI capabilities find arduous to replicate. As AI's ascent progresses, the nurturing of creativity and innovation ascends to even greater significance. In this context, out-of-school time providers emerge as trailblazers in fostering these attributes by creating environments that nurture experimentation, ideation, and unconventional thinking.

By infusing activities like design challenges, art projects, and open-ended problem-solving tasks, these providers can effectively galvanize and hone creative thinking (Hidi & Renninger, 2006). By urging students to traverse the boundaries of convention, embrace ambiguity, and experiment with offbeat concepts, these providers cultivate a mindset that is indispensable not only for navigating the dynamic terrain forged by AI but also for propelling progress across multifarious fields.

Through the integration of interdisciplinary activities, out-of-school programs have the capacity to facilitate the recognition of synergies between seemingly disparate domains of knowledge. This perspective augments cognitive flexibility, propelling students to transcend traditional confines and fostering innovative thinking—an imperative for spearheading AI's development and seamless integration into diverse sectors.

Promoting Adaptability and Lifelong Learning

The relentless cadence of technological evolution underscores the heightened need for adaptability and lifelong learning. As AI remains an ever-present force reshaping industry, the skills coveted by the job market remain in a perpetual state of flux. It is within this flux that out-of-school time providers are uniquely poised to cultivate adaptability by infusing a growth mindset and kindling an enduring passion for lifelong learning.

Central to this pedagogical approach is project-based learning, a cornerstone of numerous out-of-school programs. Beyond endowing participants with domain-specific knowledge, this methodology nurtures the dexterity required to navigate a professional realm characterized by rapid transformations (Dweck, 2006). Furthermore, these providers can facilitate direct exposure to emerging technologies and industries, fostering an authentic ardor for learning that transcends the limits of conventional classroom settings.

Incorporating students into AI applications spanning diverse sectors—ranging from healthcare and finance to entertainment and agriculture—kindles curiosity and sparks a fervor for exploration. Additionally, these experiences illuminate the ethical dimensions intrinsic to AI's use, fostering conscientious AI practices and nurturing awareness regarding potential challenges embedded within AI technologies.

THE ROLE OF OUT-OF-SCHOOL TIME PROVIDERS IN PREPARING FOR THE AI-DOMINATED JOB MARKET CONCLUSION

The convergence of AI and the workforce ushers forth a multifaceted tapestry of challenges and opportunities for the emerging generations. As AI's capabilities burgeon, the unique human attributes—critical thinking, creativity, adaptability, and effective communication—achieve an even loftier zenith of significance. Out-of-school time providers, occupying the pivotal juncture of education and personal development, constitute the bedrock of preparing students for this transformative landscape. Through the nurturing of essential skills, incubation of creative capacities, and promotion of adaptability and lifelong learning, these providers empower students to harness AI as a vessel for innovation and growth, thereby transforming it from a mere force to be grappled with into a potent catalyst for human progress.

Best Practices and Strategies for Out-of-School Time Providers

In the midst of the AI revolution that is redefining the global job landscape, the role of out-of-school time providers stands as a critical conduit in equipping future generations with the skills, knowledge, and ethical sensibilities requisite for success in an AI-driven world. While the preceding sections underscored the integral role of these providers in cultivating essential skills, fostering creativity and innovation, and promoting adaptability and lifelong learning, this section delves into a more nuanced exploration of the best practices and strategies that can empower out-of-school time providers to effectively prepare students for the burgeoning AI-centric workforce. The following subsections elucidate the paramount importance of collaboration with educational institutions and industry partners, the seamless integration of AI education into program curricula, and the cultivation of ethical and responsible AI application.

COLLABORATION WITH
EDUCATIONAL INSTITUTIONS AND INDUSTRY

Realizing the full potential of their impact necessitates that out-of-school time providers engage in robust collaborations with both educational institutions and industries. This triadic partnership generates a dynamic synergy that enables a comprehensive approach to sculpting students for the multifaceted challenges posed by an AI-saturated job milieu. Through these partnerships, a cohesive and holistic learning journey can be forged, spanning from conventional classrooms to out-of-school programs and ultimately integrating seamlessly into real-world industries.

Educational institutions, acting as bastions of foundational knowledge, offer the quintessential bedrock upon which out-of-school time providers can build. To ensure an uninterrupted continuum of learning, these providers can strategically align their offerings with the curricular frameworks of these institutions. By harmonizing their programs with classroom teachings, providers can deliver an educational experience that reinforces, amplifies, and extends the tenets of formal learning. Collaborative initiatives, such as supplementary AI education that delves deeper into AI principles and applications, enhance students' mastery of the subject beyond the classroom's confines.

Furthermore, a symbiotic relationship with industries is instrumental in keeping pace with the ever-evolving trends, technologies, and skill requirements of the AI landscape. By collaborating with experts from various industries, out-of-school time providers can glean insights into the specific skills, knowledge, and competencies that are paramount for excelling in AI-related careers. These industry connections serve as invaluable guides in tailoring program offerings to ensure students' readiness for the demands of the AI-dominated professional world.

Incorporating insights from both educational institutions and industries, out-of-school time providers can co-create holistic learning experiences that encompass the entire spectrum of skills needed to thrive in the AI era.

Integrating AI Education Into Programs

Central to the mission of out-of-school time providers is the seamless integration of AI education into their program offerings. By infusing AI-related content across a diverse range of disciplines and activities, these providers can not only demystify AI but also inspire a generation of students to embrace its intricacies and potentials.

Workshops, seminars, and hands-on projects constitute an effective means of introducing students to the foundational concepts of AI, machine learning, and data analytics. Engaging in these activities imparts not only theoretical understanding but also practical experience in applying AI principles. For instance, coding challenges involving the creation of AI algorithms or the design of chatbots can foster both technical expertise and creative problem-solving abilities.

Furthermore, out-of-school time providers can proactively develop specialized AI-focused tracks within their programs. These specialized tracks cater to varying interests and aptitudes, allowing students to explore AI-related fields of study in greater depth. By tailoring offerings to specific subjects such as robotics, AI ethics, or data analysis, providers empower students to delve into the intricacies of AI disciplines that resonate with their passion and potential.

Cultivating Ethical and Responsible AI Use

The rapid advancement of AI technologies accentuates the criticality of instilling ethical awareness and responsible AI use among students. Ethical AI practices encompass a wide spectrum of considerations, including fairness, transparency, accountability, and the societal impact of AI technologies. Out-of-school time providers are uniquely positioned to foster ethical AI practitioners who consider not only technical prowess, but also the broader implications of their actions.

Incorporating discussions on AI ethics into program curricula encourages students to critically analyze the ethical dimensions of AI technologies. Case studies, debates, and group dialogues enable students to explore complex issues, such as algorithmic bias and the potential societal consequences of AI-driven decision-making. By engaging in these activities, students develop the ethical reasoning and critical thinking skills necessary to navigate the moral complexities of AI.

Moreover, providers can emphasize the ethical imperative of leveraging AI for the greater good and societal advancement. Encouraging students to brainstorm and develop AI solutions that tackle real-world challenges—such as disparities in healthcare or environmental concerns—instills a sense of responsibility and purpose. By showcasing the positive impact AI can have on society, out-of-school time providers contribute to the cultivation of AI practitioners who are committed to ethical and responsible innovation.

COLLABORATION WITH EDUCATIONAL INSTITUTIONS AND INDUSTRY CONCLUSION

Out-of-school time providers shoulder a profound responsibility in molding the workforce of the future within an AI-imbued world. By embracing best practices and strategies that encompass collaboration with educational institutions and industries, the integration of AI education into programs, and the cultivation of ethical and responsible AI application, these providers wield the power to nurture students who are not merely adept in technical skills, but are also equipped with the holistic insights, ethical values, and innovation mindset necessary to excel in the AI-dominated professional realm. As AI's footprint continues to expand, the role of out-of-school time providers will prove indispensable in shaping a workforce that is not only technologically proficient but also ethically conscious, resilient, and poised to seize the opportunities and surmount the challenges presented by the accelerating AI revolution.

CHALLENGES AND ETHICAL CONSIDERATIONS

The exponential growth of AI technology and its pervasive influence across industries beckon a landscape fraught with intricate challenges and ethical conundrums. As AI's omnipresence continues to redefine the contours of the future workforce, a profound exploration of the multifaceted challenges and ethical considerations becomes paramount. This section delves into the intricacies woven within this narrative, shedding light on the imperative of addressing issues related to access and equity in AI education, the ethical dimensions encompassing AI use and data privacy, and the transformative impact on employment opportunities.

Access and Equity in AI Education

In the grand tapestry of AI's rise, one of the most pressing challenges emerges in the form of access and equity in AI education. As AI technologies weave their influence into a plethora of industries, they usher in unprecedented opportunities for innovation, progress, and transformation. However, the darker underbelly of this revolution lies in the growing divide between those who can access AI education and its resultant benefits and those who find themselves marginalized and left on the fringes of this technological advancement.

Education has historically been a realm where inequities have been vividly mirrored, and the foray of AI education is no exception. This challenge is

The Impact of AI Technology on Future Generations in the Workforce   33

multifaceted—often stemming from the uneven distribution of educational resources across socioeconomic lines. Schools and educational institutions that serve marginalized communities frequently lack the resources to offer comprehensive AI education, perpetuating a cycle of exclusion and disparity.

The intersection of AI with issues of gender and race further compounds the access conundrum. The dearth of female and minority representation in AI fields reflects broader social imbalances and biases. This not only results in missed opportunities for underrepresented groups, but also stifles innovation by limiting the diversity of perspectives that can contribute to AI's evolution.

Out-of-school time providers wield a formidable mantle in tackling this challenge head-on. Through strategic alliances with schools, community organizations, and local governments, these providers can help bridge the gap by offering inclusive AI education programs. By creating learning environments that embrace diversity and inclusivity, these programs can empower students from all walks of life to develop AI-related skills. By actively seeking out opportunities to engage marginalized communities and underrepresented groups, out-of-school time providers can foster a generation of AI practitioners that reflects the kaleidoscope of humanity's diversity.

Ethical Use of AI and Data Privacy

As AI technologies burgeon and their tendrils delve into every facet of human existence, the ethical considerations surrounding their use and the preservation of individual data privacy emerge as pressing concerns. The crux of AI's efficacy often hinges on the accumulation, analysis, and utilization of vast amounts of data. However, this voracious appetite for data has ignited a veritable minefield of ethical dilemmas, including consent, transparency, and the specter of unchecked surveillance.

The ethical pitfalls associated with AI are multidimensional and extend across sectors. Industries such as healthcare, finance, criminal justice, and marketing now grapple with the implications of algorithmic decision-making that can significantly impact lives. Biased algorithms, often a reflection of historical prejudices embedded within training data, can perpetuate societal injustices, exacerbating disparities along lines of race, gender, and socio-economic status.

The challenge becomes twofold: not only must AI systems be developed with robust ethical considerations embedded, but mechanisms of accountability, transparency, and recourse must be established to hold AI technologies and their creators to ethical standards. This calls for regulatory

34 S. EPNER and CHATGPT-4

frameworks that ensure responsible AI deployment while safeguarding individual rights and societal values.

Out-of-school time providers hold a pivotal role in shaping the ethical consciousness of future AI practitioners. By integrating discussions on bias, transparency, and the responsible use of AI in their educational programs, these providers can instill a profound understanding of the ethical dimensions inherent to AI technologies. Equipping students with the ability to critically dissect the ethical implications of AI applications empowers them to navigate the intricate terrain of AI with a heightened sense of responsibility. This combination of technical acumen and ethical consciousness contributes to the cultivation of AI practitioners who are attuned not only to the potential of AI but also to its broader social impact.

Impact on Employment Opportunities

The advent of AI heralds an era of unparalleled transformation in employment opportunities. Yet, this promise of disruption also encapsulates the specter of upheaval. AI's integration into various industries has led to concerns about potential job displacement and the need for a workforce replete with adaptable skills.

The transformative impact of AI on employment opportunities is a dual-edged sword. On one hand, AI has the potential to automate routine and repetitive tasks, freeing human workers to focus on creative and strategic endeavors. On the other hand, there exists a genuine fear that the very technology designed to augment human capabilities could render certain jobs obsolete.

The challenge lies not just in the potential job losses, but in the transition and reskilling of the workforce. The rapid pace of technological change necessitates a workforce that is agile, flexible, and able to continuously learn and adapt. However, this transition is fraught with obstacles, including access to retraining opportunities, cultural resistance to change, and the need to equip workers with a new skill set that aligns with the evolving demands of the job market.

Out-of-school time providers can serve as vanguards of this transition by embracing an ethos of continuous learning. By instilling in students, the value of adaptability and lifelong learning, these providers cultivate a mindset that is poised to navigate the evolving professional landscape. Furthermore, by exposing students to emerging industries and technologies, out-of-school time providers foster an environment where AI is not seen as a threat but as a catalyst for innovation. This paradigm shift from disruption to opportunity is pivotal in ensuring that the AI era is marked by the empowerment of the workforce rather than its displacement.

The formidable ascent of AI into the workforce arena is fraught with challenges and ethical considerations that transcend mere technical prowess. The issues of access and equity in AI education, the ethical dimensions surrounding AI use and data privacy, and the transformative impact on employment opportunities all loom large in the narrative of the AI era. Out-of-school time providers, by taking a proactive stance, embracing diversity, and fostering a culture of ethical consciousness and continuous learning, emerge as architects of a workforce that is not only equipped with technical skills but is also ethically aware, adaptable, and ready to harness the potential of AI to chart new frontiers of innovation and progress.

CHALLENGES AND ETHICAL CONSIDERATIONS CONCLUSION

The relentless surge of AI technology promises to reshape the very foundations of the future workforce. This essay embarked on a comprehensive journey to unravel the multifaceted impacts of AI on future generations in the workforce and the instrumental role that out-of-school time providers can play in shaping this landscape. By delving into the integration of AI technology in employment trends, the evolving skill sets demanded by the job market, the potential for socioeconomic inequality, and the paramount importance of preparing the next generation, this essay illuminated the intricate interplay between AI and the future workforce. It explored how out-of-school time providers are poised to emerge as catalytic forces in equipping students with essential skills, fostering creativity and innovation, promoting adaptability and lifelong learning, and crafting ethical and responsible AI practitioners. Moreover, the essay probed the complexities surrounding access and equity in AI education, ethical AI use and data privacy, and the transformation of employment opportunities, elucidating the pressing challenges and ethical considerations that will define the AI era. Finally, the essay culminated in a nuanced reflection on the findings and the presentation of actionable recommendations for a future marked by AI's indelible influence.

Summary of Findings

Throughout this essay, a tapestry of findings has been woven, showcasing the profound impact that AI is set to exert on the future workforce. The employment landscape is set to undergo a seismic shift, marked by both the creation of novel opportunities and the displacement of traditional roles. The skills requisite for success in this AI-forged terrain transcend mere technical expertise and extend into the realms of critical thinking, problem-solving, creativity, and adaptability. However, the evolution of AI also poses challenges, notably those concerning equitable access to AI education, the ethical dimensions of AI use, and the ramifications for employment opportunities.

The pivotal role of out-of-school time providers in shaping this trajectory cannot be overstated. By fostering essential skills, promoting creativity, nurturing adaptability, and infusing ethical considerations into AI education, these providers emerge as architects of a workforce that is both technically adept and ethically conscious. Their strategic collaborations with educational institutions and industries, seamless integration of AI education, and focus on ethical AI use are poised to equip future generations with the tools needed to navigate the AI landscape with integrity and innovation. Additionally, the role of these providers in cultivating a culture of continuous learning and facilitating exposure to emerging industries ensures that the Smart Technology Era becomes one marked by empowerment rather than displacement.

Recommendations for Future Action

As the canvas of the future workforce is painted with the strokes of AI's influence, a series of recommendations emerge as signposts for the path forward:

Policy Formulation and Collaboration: Governments, educational institutions, and industries should collaborate to establish comprehensive AI education policies that promote inclusivity, diversity, and ethical considerations. Out-of-school time providers can actively contribute to these discussions by bringing their experiential insights to the table.

Ethical AI Curriculum: Out-of-school time providers should weave ethical considerations into their AI curricula, fostering students' understanding of bias, transparency, and responsible AI use. This prepares them to navigate the ethical dimensions of AI technologies with acumen and integrity.

Lifelong Learning Emphasis: Providers should underscore the importance of continuous learning, equipping students with the adaptability and resilience to navigate evolving employment landscapes. A culture of lifelong learning ensures that AI's disruptions are harnessed as opportunities for growth.

Partnerships for Equity: Collaboration between out-of-school time providers, educational institutions, and communities can bridge the access gap in AI education. By extending AI education to marginalized communities, these partnerships can ensure a diverse and inclusive AI workforce.

Impact on Employment Ecosystem: Out-of-school time providers should collaborate with industries to create avenues for students to gain exposure to emerging AI-driven industries. By connecting education with real-world applications, providers can facilitate seamless transitions into AI-centric careers.

Promoting Responsible AI Use: Providers can engage in dialogue and awareness campaigns to raise awareness about the ethical implications of AI technologies. By encouraging students to contemplate the societal impact of AI, providers nurture a generation of responsible AI practitioners.

CONCLUSION

The age of AI dawns upon us with the promise of unprecedented innovation and progress, accompanied by the challenges and ethical considerations that are emblematic of profound technological revolutions. The future workforce stands at the crossroads of this transformation, poised to navigate a landscape that is both invigorating and uncertain. Out-of-school time providers are positioned as beacons, illuminating the path ahead. Their commitment to equipping students with essential skills, fostering creativity and innovation, promoting adaptability and lifelong learning, and nurturing ethical and responsible AI use stands as a testament to their role as architects of the AI era. As we stand on the threshold of this new era, the collaborative efforts of educational institutions, industries, policymakers, and out-of-school time providers will define the trajectory of AI's influence on future generations in the workforce.

CONCLUSION BY AUTHOR

With just a quick prompt explaining the desired content, ChatGPT generated the section above within minutes. While it may not be flawless and still requires a human touch for adjustments, what's abundantly clear is the transformative potential of this tool and its imminent impact within the out-of-school time (OST) community.

Within the OST community, a significant facet of our mission is to foster the development of vital skills among our youth. We are well-positioned to leverage the evolving landscape of AI tools and technologies to further enhance our support for youth development. AI, with its capacity for data analysis, personalization, and real-time feedback, can become an invaluable ally in the educational journey of young individuals. It can help tailor learning experiences to suit the unique needs and interests of each student, ensuring that no one is left behind in their quest for knowledge and skill attainment.

Moreover, AI can empower us to track and measure the progress of the youth we serve more comprehensively, providing data-driven insights to fine-tune our programs and strategies. As we integrate AI into our OST initiatives, we have the opportunity to extend our reach and impact, making high-quality education and skill-building accessible to a broader and more diverse demographic. This, in turn, can contribute to bridging educational gaps, fostering inclusivity, and equipping our youth with the competencies they need to thrive in a rapidly changing world. It's a remarkable synergy between human dedication and technological innovation that has the potential to redefine the landscape of youth development and education for generations to come.

As demonstrated by ChatGPT's capabilities, the OST community finds itself in a novel and rapidly evolving environment. Adapting to this paradigm shift is imperative, but it cannot be accomplished in isolation. Collaboration with key stakeholders, including funders, policymakers, families, and, most importantly, the youth themselves, is paramount to ensure a synchronized and effective response to the challenges presented by this new landscape. While there will undoubtedly be experiments and innovations, some successful and others less so, the OST community's commitment to navigating this terrain alongside AI remains steadfast.

AI is here for the long run, and so is the OST community. These two forces, when harnessed collectively, possess the potential to usher in a new era of youth development and empowerment. By embracing the opportunities AI offers while upholding our commitment to human guidance and support, we can work together to unlock the full potential of this technological revolution for the benefit of the youth we serve.

REFERENCES

Acemoglu, D., & Restrepo, P. (2018). The race between man and machine: Implications of technology for growth, factor shares, and employment. *American Economic Review, 108*(6), 1488–1542. https://doi.org/10.1257/aer.20160696

Bessen, J. E. (2019). AI and jobs: The role of demand. *Artificial Intelligence, 170*, 103–116.

Bevan, B., Ghosh, R., & Penuel, W. R. (2017). Connecting in-school and out-of-school learning: New directions for research and practice. *American Journal of Education, 123*(2), 225–227.

Brynjolfsson, E., & McAfee, A. (2014). *The second machine age: Work, progress, and prosperity in a time of brilliant technologies.* W. W. Norton & Company.

Davenport, T. H., & Kirby, J. (2016). *Only humans need apply: Winners and losers in the age of smart machines.* HarperBusiness.

Dweck, C. S. (2006). *Mindset: The new psychology of success.* Random House.

Hidi, S., & Renninger, K. A. (2006). The four-phase model of interest development. *Educational Psychologist, 41*(2), 111–127. https://doi.org/10.1207/s15326985ep4102_4

Hirsh-Pasek, K., Zosh, J. M., Golinkoff, R. M., Gray, J. H., Robb, M. B., & Kaufman, J. (2019). Putting education in "educational" apps: Lessons from the science of learning. *Psychological Science in the Public Interest, 20*(1), 3–34. https://doi.org/10.1177/1529100615569721

Sawyer, R. K. (2006). Educating for innovation. *Thinking Skills and Creativity, 1*(1), 41–48.

World Economic Forum. (2020). *The Future of Jobs Report 2020.* https://www.weforum.org/reports/the-future-of-jobs/

CHAPTER 3

TOMORROW'S WORKFORCE IN AFTERSCHOOL PROGRAMS TODAY

STEM-Focused Afterschool Programs and Systems

**Terri Ferinde, Teresa Drew,
Nicole Evans, and Sheronda Witter**

INTRODUCTION

"STEM means so many things. It has changed my life so drastically. I would say that STEM means community. It means this family of people that all want to see you succeed. We all work in so many different fields. My friends, our friends in engineering, biology, computer science, chemistry, all of these different fields. And we all come together for the common goal of improving society through science and STEM in general. It's a community of people working for the greater good. That's the greatest part about STEM, the impact potential is really vast."

—Mackenzie H, 2022, Million Girls Moonshot Flight Crew
(STEM Next Opportunity Fund, 2023)

How can afterschool and summer programs inspire the leaders, thinkers, and innovators of tomorrow?

A recent high school graduate from Hazel Green, Alabama, Mackenzie got hooked on computer science in an afterschool STEM (science, technology,

Built for More: The Role of Out-of-School Time in Preparing Youth for the Future of Work,
pp. 41–56
Copyright © 2024 by Information Age Publishing
www.infoagepub.com
All rights of reproduction in any form reserved.

engineering, and math) program called Kode with Klossy. She joined Girls Who Code and served as an instructor in both programs. She called these programs a "catalyst" exposing her to STEM broadly. Mackenzie was selected to the inaugural Million Girls Moonshot Flight Crew in 2022 where she could become an ambassador for afterschool STEM programs. She is now a computer science major at Cornell University pursuing her passions in biomedical engineering, computer science, and astrophysics.

Like Mackenzie's experience, afterschool and summer learning opportunities have been found to be powerful forces in girls' lives that can provide experiences leading to a lifelong engagement with STEM fields (Kekelis, 2018). For example, over 160,000 Girl Scouts participate in STEM programs annually, and more than 77% of these girls are considering a career in technology because of their Girl Scout experiences. Similarly, Techbridge Girls, another afterschool program, has served more than 15,000 girls, with 95% of participating girls thinking engineering is a good career for women, 94% are more confident trying new things, and 80 percent plan to study computer science in college (Kekelis, 2018). These programs have been successful in increasing female students' interest in science careers (Allen et al., 2019).

The youth in today's afterschool programs are clearly the workforce for tomorrow. The opportunity is abundant for afterschool programs to catalyze interest, expose youth to career options, develop early workforce skills, and support young people's dreams and aspirations. STEM-focused afterschool programs have unique opportunities and responsibility to support young people to pursue STEM careers (Allen et al., 2020), addressing some of the nation's most pressing career gaps. To take on this responsibility, systems–known as intermediaries, networks, and ecosystems–are stepping up to help afterschool programs succeed. This chapter explores the demand, offers the example of STEM Next Opportunity Fund as a backbone organization, and details how today's afterschool programs are supporting and developing tomorrow's workforce.

Developing Workforce Interests and Skills in STEM-focused Afterschool Programs

Nationally, 62% of K–12 students are interested in STEM careers—but 33% say school is doing a bad job of preparing them (Walton Family Foundation, 2023). And while afterschool programs can expose youth to a range of possible careers, STEM-focused afterschool programs are also particularly well-positioned to address pressing workforce needs in the nation (Abeel, 2023). The ability of all students to build skills and capacities to help them successfully participate in the workplace depends on their exposure to high-quality STEM opportunities.

With STEM jobs growing two times faster and paying two times more than non-STEM jobs, our economy needs 821,300 more workers by 2031 (U.S. Bureau of Labor Statistics, 2023). This is why improving and enhancing STEM education is a national priority. "Perhaps we ought to shift from asking 'how many STEM workers do we need?' to 'what knowledge and skills do all of our workers need to be successful now and in the future?'" said Kelvin Droegemeier, vice chairman at the National Science Board and meteorology professor and vice president for research at the University of Oklahoma, in a statement accompanying the 2016 National Science Board report (National Science Board, 2015).

The demand to support women in STEM careers is even greater. Women make up half of the total U.S. college-educated workforce, but less than one-third of the science and engineering workforce. Latinx and African American women make up less than 3% of the STEM workforce (Fry et al., 2021). There is a strong need to retain women in STEM occupations after college graduation. Among women with engineering degrees, only 24% are employed in engineering professions (compared to 30% for men.) Among women with computer science degrees, only 38% are employed in the field (compared to 53% for men) (Fry et al., 2021).

Afterschool programs are particularly well-positioned to develop workforce skills. Notably, high-quality programs with adequate resources and staff development can:

- Enhance 21st-century skills: Afterschool programs, particularly those focused on STEM, have been shown to positively impact students' 21st-century skills, including perseverance, critical thinking, and quality of relationships with adults and peers (Allen et al., 2017)
- Integrate science learning and 21st-century skills: The integration of science learning opportunities into afterschool programs has shown a positive correlation with the development of critical thinking skills and positive relationships. These skills are not only essential for succeeding in science but also in the 21st-century workforce (Krishnamurthi & Bevan, 2018).
- Increase STEM career knowledge and positive STEM identity: Afterschool programs have been found to increase students' knowledge of STEM careers and foster a more positive STEM identity (Allen et al., 2016).
- Be a solution for filling STEM jobs: With the number of STEM-related jobs increasing at a faster rate than overall employment, afterschool programs have been identified as an effective part of

the solution to engage youth early and help build the skills they will need for the future (Allen et al., 2016).

- Integrate youth development and informal science learning: Afterschool programs can simultaneously address the social-emotional/21st-century needs of students while also sparking their curiosity and skills in science. This integration of youth development and informal science learning can enhance every child's potential to learn and thrive in science. (Krishnamurthi & Bevan, 2018)

According to the U.S. Department of Labor, more than 65% of today's students will grow up having careers that do not exist yet (Krutsch & Roderick, 2022). Our world is changing rapidly—from AI to driverless cars, to 3D-printed rockets. To keep pace and ensure that our workforce is future-ready for the next wave of innovations in nanotechnology, advanced manufacturing, exploration to Mars, or whatever comes next, we must prepare the kids today with STEM skills to problem solve, build, and create. By exposing youth to hands-on, inquiry-based STEM learning early and often, we not only support them in mastering the fundamental STEM disciplines. We can also foster an Engineering Mindset in young people, preparing them to think critically, problem-solve in a real-world context, collaborate, apply math and science skills, and innovate. Afterschool and summer programs provide a ripe opportunity to leverage existing national infrastructure to reach more youth with STEM experiences that build skills, change narratives, and nurture interest (Allen et al., 2019).

Growing a System Supporting STEM-Focused Afterschool Programs

While there is solid evidence that STEM in afterschool and summer is highly effective at engaging youth (Allen et al., 2019), and there are many examples of effective programs, to effect large-scale adoption of quality STEM programming requires a systems-level approach. Enter the STEM Next Opportunity Fund and the commitment to provide STEM-learning opportunities in afterschool and summer programs.

To catalyze funders and develop a conceptual framework for the broad-scale spread of STEM-focused afterschool programs, STEM Next launched the Million Girls Moonshot, a national, collective impact initiative engaging millions more girls, youth of color, and youth from low-income households in STEM by 2025. Grounded in a research-based theory of change (Figure 3.1), the Moonshot builds the capacity of the STEM learning system now and into the future by raising awareness and demand for high-quality

STEM in informal learning across the country, helping informal educators shift to the best practices that, in turn, engage more youth, and produce better STEM outcomes for them.

Figure 3.1

Moonshot Theory of Change

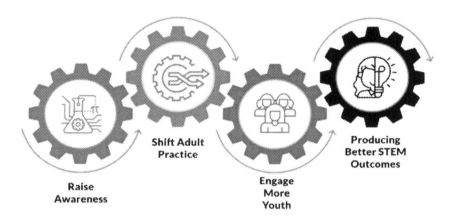

As of summer 2023, the Moonshot has reached 1.7 million girls, 3 million total youth, and more than 200,000 educators across the U.S. Among youth served, two-thirds are from low-income households, half are from minority groups underrepresented in the STEM workforce, and over a third live in rural or frontier areas. Program evaluation sampling demonstrates that youth are improving important STEM outcomes, including increased engagement in STEM, and improved 21st-century skills (like critical thinking and perseverance) when compared to national data.

The Moonshot is a systemic approach to eliminating barriers for youth in STEM and creating a more equitable, diverse STEM workforce. Through the Moonshot, STEM Next ensures informal educators in afterschool and summer programs have the resources, support, mentorship, and expert guidance they need to deliver high-quality, hands-on STEM learning experiences built on the following Moonshot transformative, evidenced-based principles:

- Culturally responsive program design matters. To promote equity and increase gender and racial diversity in STEM, Moonshot includes an Access STEM Framework that is youth-centric and culturally responsive (Sammet & Kekelis, 2016). The framework illustrates the particular concepts and variables that are connected to equity and inclusion and provides a map for identifying strategies and actions to eliminate barriers.

- Socially-relevant projects are a huge draw for girls. With increased training and access to engaging STEM activities and curriculum, the Moonshot increases opportunities for girls to solve problems that matter to them and their communities (Billington et al., 2019).
- Build STEM identity by creating a continuum of experiences that draw on interests, knowledge, skills, culture, and lived experiences. This is critical to increasing a sense of belonging (Billington et al., 2019). The Moonshot works with programs to create effective transitions and handoffs between programs that provide youth with a seamless continuum of experiences from elementary to middle to high school.
- Create opportunities for hands-on STEM early and often. Attracting students into STEM fields is best started in elementary and middle school, prioritizing Grades 4–8.
- Engage role models and mentors to inspire career awareness and increase youth interest in positive attitudes toward and identification with STEM (Maltese & Tai, 2010). The Moonshot partners with private industry and industry associations to engage employees as role models and mentors and other national initiatives aimed at increasing visibility and awareness, such as the Lyda Hill Philanthropies IF/THEN Initiative and Women@NASA.
- Empower families by supporting programs to scale family engagement (Kekelis & Sammet, 2019). Encouragement matters, especially for girls. The Moonshot includes families as critical stakeholders, scaling and evaluating family engagement communities of practice through the 50 State Afterschool Networks, using the Institute for the Study of Resilience in Youth at McLean Hospital Harvard STEM Family Engagement Tool. The tool is a culturally responsive, research-informed program planning tool to better evaluate and inform the implementation of quality programming for families to engage their young children in STEM across broad contexts and diverse communities.

To scale and spread STEM-focused afterschool and summer programs, STEM Next worked in collaboration with the 50 state afterschool networks. STEM Next serves as a hub for the networks, providing funding, new partners, content packages in the form of "Booster Packs," professional development, and communications tools. The networks, in turn, provide access and support to hundreds of thousands of afterschool programs nationwide, reaching millions of youth.

Diffusion of Innovation: Intermediaries, Ecosystems, and Statewide Afterschool Networks

An intermediary aligns partners, resources, money, expertise, and more with the needs of a community. They act as connectors, the glue between people and organizations working on a common mission, but often in siloes (Moritz & Ottinger, 2023). In the STEM learning field, there are many varied organizations at local, state, and national levels working to link resources to front-line programs and create a collective movement to support youth people to engage in STEM learning.

At the local level, STEM Learning Ecosystems are cross-sector collaborations including schools, afterschool and summer programs, science centers, libraries, and any place in a community that supports STEM learning. There are 100+ communities affiliated with the STEM learning ecosystems working to spark young people's engagement, develop their knowledge, strengthen their persistence, and nurture their sense of identity and belonging in STEM disciplines.

In each of the 50 states, there is a statewide intermediary known as an afterschool network. With funding in part from the Charles Stewart Mott Foundation—these networks are cross-sector statewide coalitions of partners from education, business, state government, philanthropy, law enforcement, health, and nonprofits working with a common vision and coordinated strategy to advance quality afterschool and summer learning programs. For more than 20 years in some states, these networks have been building momentum and support for afterschool programs. With data, research, stories, and champions, the networks make the case for the need and potential for afterschool and summer learning programs (Ferinde, 2021).

All 50 statewide afterschool networks are partners with the STEM Next Opportunity Fund to advance STEM learning. As part of the Million Girls Moonshot effort, the networks are engaged in four transformative practices that shape their approaches and programs in helping youth develop STEM workforce skills and mindsets. As developed by STEM Next, the practices are: Access to STEM Framework, Engineering Mindsets, Role Models and Mentors and STEM Transitions and Pathways.

Access to STEM Framework

The Access to STEM Framework presents research- and practice-based strategies to help out-of-school programs provide equitable STEM opportunities for historically disadvantaged youth. Partnering with the National Girls Collaborative Project (NGCP) and national experts, STEM Next supported the networks to consider innovative strategies in three categories: Increasing Access, Youth-Centric, and Skill Development. Part of increasing access is exposure; many of the networks work with partners to create STEM-related activities and events.

For example, in Tucson, Arizona, the Arizona Center for Afterschool Excellence hosted "The Festival of Books: Science City," with more than 350 young curious female-identifying students engaged in a hands-on engineering design challenge to create an animal crossing for Tucson's living creatures. In a statewide high school STEM competition, the network supported female high school students to utilize their Engineering Mindset and skills to create apps to stabilize diabetic individuals, cultivate native plants to replace harsh chemicals in makeup, and bioengineered masks to protect citizens in their community.

The Kansas Enrichment Network supports programs statewide with STEM-specific trainings, technical assistance, quality assessments and access to STEM experts. According to the Year 2 Evaluation report on the Million Girls Moonshot, they reported that nearly 90% of afterschool programs are incorporating STEM learning experiences including robotics competitions, 3D printing, LEGO and KEVA blocks for structural engineering challenges, drones, coding, music production, hydroponic gardens, and roller coaster design (Public Profit, 2022).

Engineering Mindset

An Engineering Mindset refers to the attitudes and thinking skills associated with engineering—using a systematic engineering design process, considering real-world problems, applying math and science, and working in teams. Using these skills and many more, engineers design objects, systems, or processes that address the needs and desires of people, animals, and society (Cunningham, 2018; Cunningham & Kelly, 2017). The statewide afterschool networks embraced the ten principles of the Engineering Mindset (Figure 3.2) in designing programs and experiences to engage youth.

Figure 3.2

Ten Principles of Engineering Mindset

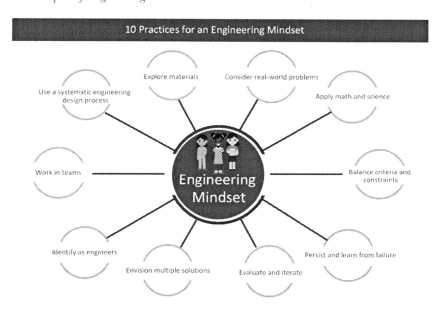

STEM Next Opportunity Fund

To introduce Engineering Mindset concepts, the Hawaii Afterschool Alliance partners with STEMworks Hawaii to host "Girl's Day! Introduce A Girl to Engineering" at the University of Hawaii, Manoa. In 2023, 150 girls from seven middle schools engaged with wahine (female) engineers. The youth had the opportunity to listen to wahines' talk-story of their career and experiences in the field. Additionally, the youth explored and created an engineering-specific kit.

To expose young people to engineering practices, a fleet of Think Make Create (TMC) Labs has rolled out across rural communities in the Western U.S. Developed by the Nebraska network, Beyond School Bells, the TMC Labs is a mobile maker platform housed in a 6 x 12 foot trailer that can easily be transported for use at afterschool and summer learning programs to inspire tinkering, hands-on learning, and inquiry. The trailer is carefully packed with tools and materials; when the trailer arrives at a program, TMC tables and pop-up canopies roll out, and learning facilitators help youth play and build using engineering concepts. In 2022–23, TMC Labs educators facilitated approximately 500 sessions with 10,000 K–8 youth using engineering-inspired inquiry-based hands-on learning experiences. The TMC Labs project staff are now working to thoroughly study and evaluate youth impacts regarding STEM identity, skills, understanding, and appreciation of science, technology, engineering, and mathematics.

The TMC Labs are spreading. In Idaho, more than 27 TMC Labs are roaming the state. The Idaho Out-Of-School Network and University of Idaho Extension 4-H Youth Development are deploying the pop-up maker space trailers in rural and underserved communities with help from the Idaho STEM Action Center, Idaho State Department of Education, Idaho Division of Career & Technical Education, GizmoCDA, and private partners. More than 5,000 youth are served annually, largely in rural communities, with the goal of leading them into STEM jobs. Organizers note that 19 of Idaho's 20 hot jobs through 2026 require STEM skills, and STEM jobs pay about twice as much as non-STEM jobs (Idaho EcosySTEM, 2021). The TMC Labs are also hosted by the South Dakota Afterschool Network, Utah Afterschool Network, and the Wyoming Afterschool Alliance.

Deepening understanding and adoption of the Engineering Mindset, Vermont Afterschool Inc., has created a course to be used in afterschool programs, Linking Engineering to Life, aimed specifically at middle school girls and non-binary youth who have historically been underrepresented in STEM fields. This two-part program includes a BASICS engineering course and a BIOMEDICAL engineering course. The engineering activities in LEL have real-life connections and relate to community issues the youth see in their lives. The BASICS course has activities that connect to communities, like designing and building a wind-powered water pump and creating safer vehicles. The BIOMEDICAL course has many real-life applications related to everyday life, like designing a grasping device for older adults and creating prosthetic limbs. The programs are intended to help program providers understand the importance of connecting to an Engineering Mindset and allowing youth to see applications in real life to what they are learning.

Role Models and Mentors

Role models, mentors, and family engagement in a young person's STEM education leads to increased interest, greater self-confidence, and ultimately a stronger STEM identity (Kekelis & Drew, 2023) Developing a science-related identity increases the likelihood that students will work toward developing science literacy, or even pursue a career in a science or STEM-related field. Conversely, when a young person lacks a STEM identity, this increases the chance for disengagement and makes it less likely for them to pursue STEM-related activities in the future (Techbridge Girls, 2014).

For example, in 2022, the Rhode Island Afterschool Network enhanced its STEM pathways initiative to include high school-aged students through a partnership with the Cranston, RI YMCA. The YMCA offered a STEM enrichment program for high school students, engaging 35 youth in day-long STEM learning activities, paired with field trips to local STEM-related workplaces. Participants visited other summer programs for younger students, as well, acting as near-peer mentors. The network hosted a Peer Mentor Leadership Academy in spring 2022, engaging 50 peer mentors to explore the mentorship role, practice leadership skills, and learn how to support STEM learning when working with younger students. Working across 16 programs, the participating peers mentored 450 youth.

The South Carolina Afterschool Alliance partners with Claflin University faculty to mentor students of color in grades 10 through 12 in a innovated summer internship program. The Biomedical/Biomaterials Internship incorporates entrepreneurial education, guest lectures by industry leaders and group discussions about social justice. The program works to build knowledge about STEM fields, connect youth to college and scholarships and provide hands-on experience with real lab equipment (Mott Foundation, 2022).

STEM Transitions and Pathways

The out-of-school time space provides a unique environment for fostering interest, especially in STEM. Continuous engagement and exposure, rather than limited one-time opportunities are needed to nurture the interest and motivation necessary for children to pursue STEM pathways long-term (Peppler, 2022). With STEM Next, afterschool networks are working to understand and support transitions and handoffs that remove barriers for youth by connecting STEM learning across ages and settings, ensuring youth interest and motivation persists, especially for underrepresented groups like girls, youth of color, and youth from low-income families.

Vermont Afterschool Inc. runs a program called STEM Pathways, where high school students work in an elementary afterschool program to lead younger kids through engineering activities using an Engineering is Elementary (EiE) kit, a set of hands-on learning activities developed by the Museum of Science in Boston. Teen staff members are mentored by an adult, who offers support and guidance on teens' future college and career path and the skills they need to develop to effectively lead EiE activities. These adult staff mentors use lessons from the Jobs for the Future: Possible Futures curriculum, a Moonshot Booster Pack. This nested approach to mentoring enables aspiring afterschool professionals to get real-world experience as an educator and to explore potential career paths while adult mentors hone their own skills in supervising and mentoring others (Public Profit, 2022).

Nebraska's network, Beyond School Hours, partners with the Peter Kiewit Foundation (PKF) to increase engineering skills, identity, and interest in rural Nebraska and raise awareness about a major scholarship program to encourage more women to pursue engineering degrees at the University of Nebraska. There are four rural sites building engineering pathways in their communities. The pathways are structured as a series of interconnected elementary and middle grades clubs led by trained high school students who then receive development and mentorship themselves with the aim that some of them will apply for the PKF engineering scholarship program and/or continue other engineering-relative career paths.

CONCLUSION

Developing workforce skills and mindsets in afterschool programs has positive impacts for individuals, communities, companies, and society. Together with the STEM Next Opportunity Fund, the statewide afterschool networks have built a foundation of partnerships and practices poised for extensive dividends.

For the young people in today's afterschool and summer programs, exposure to workforce ideas and skills can be highly engaging and relevant to their everyday lives. STEM concepts capture the imagination and spark curiosity. When afterschool programs allow exploration, young people have agency to pursue what most intrigues them. As youth mature, afterschool programs provide opportunities to delve deeper into STEM experiences, understand the pathways needed for STEM careers, and act as near-peer mentors for younger students.

For communities, STEM-focused afterschool programs meet critical needs. When programs are intentionally designed with context and culture in mind, programs can focus on the challenges of specific communities, like environmental issues. And, as many have documented, engaging, strong afterschool programs keep young people safe and occupied during potentially dangerous times for unsupervised youth (Afterschool Alliance, 2014).

For companies, tapping into afterschool and summer programs helps to build a more diverse, prepared talent pool earlier. In addition to a growing talent gap, industry is navigating low gender and racial representation among employee bases, limiting the diversity needed to fuel continued innovation. Without inspiring a larger, more diverse pool of youth earlier, this challenge threatens to persist: nationally, high schoolers interested in

STEM overwhelmingly look like the current workforce—predominantly White males (DiscoverE, 2023). More work is needed targeted to younger youth, especially the 4th-8th grade developmental window, to blunt this workforce shortage, position the U.S. ahead of global competition, and ensure these important careers are within reach for every American.

Perhaps most importantly, STEM careers can serve as a driver for economic and social mobility. From AI to climate or advanced manufacturing, STEM careers hold the potential to positively impact every aspect of human life. And high-paying STEM jobs can also serve as a critical pathway to economic prosperity for individuals and families. These lucrative careers pay, on average, twice as much as non-STEM jobs (U.S. Bureau of Labor Statistics, 2023). When we ensure that every young person has the access and STEM learning opportunities they deserve, we ensure that they have the chance to play a leading role in shaping our future world.

Actionable Recommendations

Beyond the successful implementation of STEM Next's innovative Million Girls Moonshot model, the following best practices are ripe for implementation in other youth workforce readiness programs:

- Build robust support networks for teens. Engage both adult and near-peer mentors in order to build supportive networks for young people. Research demonstrates that family engagement is particularly critical to supporting whole-child development and bridging the gap between school, home, and community for young people.
- Tap into the power of near-peer mentoring. Research shows that near-peer mentors can be particularly effective because they pair mentors and mentees who are roughly equal in age and power for the task and social-emotional support (Angelique et al., 2002). Peer mentoring approaches also provide advantages in the form of cost, volume of potential mentors, and increased likelihood of mentees following advice due to sharing a common perspective with their mentors (Collier, 2017).
- Leverage technology and media. Include social and digital training in addition to more traditional media coaching. This may enable youth to make effective use of new social media platforms that can authentically engage peers.
- Incorporate youth voice and choice. Youth have important opinions, perspectives, and experiences that adults need to hear. And research is clear that when students have higher levels of

self-efficacy, they will be more engaged, particularly in blended learning environments that take advantage of both virtual and in-person engagement (Vasile et al., 2011).

- Include STEM career exposure. Research demonstrates that career role models are particularly effective in engaging youth from underserved groups. Engage real-life STEM professionals as role models and mentors to youth and encourage them to share their own STEM stories and experiences (Bell et al., 2017)
- Invest in program capacity. Beyond intentional, structured experiences that grow the potential of STEM leaders, more work must be done to engage youth from diverse backgrounds in STEM. Research suggests that the majority of informal educators in out-of-school time programs lack strong STEM backgrounds (Freeman et al., 2009), leading to repeated calls for professional learning opportunities (National Research Council, 2015). STEM program leaders need more research-backed training and tools in order to create rich STEM learning environments that intentionally lift up girls and their participation and ideas.

We conclude with the experience of another member of the Million Girls Moonshot Flight Crew: Henrietta was drawn to Flight Crew's emphasis on supporting youth as ambassadors in STEM, and reports being especially grateful for the foundational skills the experience offered. The highlight of the Flight Crew experience, for Henrietta, was the connections she made to powerful women in STEM, including the other Flight Crew members. She offers, *"Meeting such powerful women who made such a huge difference in STEM and in my life was so, so special to me. I hold the Girls Build Solutions event so close to my heart because it opened my eyes to a world of possibilities for who I will become"* (STEM Next Opportunity Fund, 2023).

REFERENCES

Abeel, M., Altstadt, D., & Green, C. (2023). *Investing in out-of-school time STEM is an investment in a robust, diverse STEM workforce.* Jobs for the Future. https://www.jff.org/wp-content/uploads/2023/10/231023-STEMNextOSTReport-FD-V3.pdf

Afterschool Alliance. (2014). *Keeping kids safe and supported in the hours after school.* https://afterschoolalliance.org//documents/issue_briefs/issue_Keeping-KidsSafe_65.pdf

Allen, P. J., Chang, R., Gorrall, B. K., Waggenspack, L., Fukuda, E., Little, T. D., & Noam, G. G. (2019). From quality to outcomes: a national study of afterschool STEM programming. *International Journal of STEM Education, 6*(1), 1–21. https://doi.org/10.1186/s40594-019-0191

Allen, P. J., Lewis-Warner, K., & Noam, G. G. (2020). Partnerships to transform STEM learning: A case study of a STEM learning ecosystem. *Afterschool Matters, 31*, 12.

Allen, P. J., Noam, G. G., Little, T. D., Fukuda, E., Gorrall, B. K., & Waggenspack, L. (2016). *Afterschool & STEM system building evaluation.* The PEAR Institute: Partnerships in Education and Resilience.

Angelique, H., Kyle, K., & Taylor, E. (2002). Mentors and muses: New strategies for academic success. *Innovative Higher Education, 26*(3), 195–209. https://doi.org/10.1023/A:1017968906264

Bell, C., Jaravel, P., & Reenan A. (2017). *Who becomes an inventor in America? The importance of exposure to innovation.* National Bureau of Economic Research Working Paper. http://www.nber.org/papers/w24062

Billington, B., Britsch, B., Santiago, A., Schellinger, J., Carter, S., & Becker, N. (2019). *SciGirls strategies: How to engage girls in STEM.* https://www.scigirlsconnect.org/wp-content/uploads/2019/06/SciGirls-Strategies-Guide.pdf

Collier, P. (2017). Why peer mentoring is an effective approach for promoting college student success. *Metropolitan Universities, 28*(3). https://doi.org/10.18060/21539

Cunningham, C. M. (2018). *Engineering in elementary STEM education: Curriculum design, instruction, learning, and assessment.* Teachers College Press.

Cunningham, C. M., & Kelly, G. K. (2017). Epistemic practices of engineering in education. *Science Education, 101*, 486–505.

DiscoverE. (2023). *Messages matter full research findings.* https://discovere.org/resources/messages-matter-full-report/

Ferinde, T. (2022). Creating opportunities for young people: Statewide after-school networks. *Journal of Youth Development, 17*(1), 1–8.

Freeman, J., Dorph, R., & Chi, B. (2009), *Strengthening after-school STEM staff development.* Coalition for Science After School. https://www.informalscience.org/sites/default/files/Strengthening_After-School_STEM_Staff_Development.pdf

Fry, R., Kennedy, B., & Funk, C. (2021). *STEM jobs see uneven progress in increasing gender, racial and ethnic diversity.* Pew Research Center. https://www.pewresearch.org/science/2021/04/01/stem-jobs-see-uneven-progress-in-increasing-gender-racial-andethnic-diversity.

Idaho EcosySTEM. (2021). *Think Make Create mobile makerspaces deploying statewide.* Media Release. https://stem.idaho.gov/wp-content/uploads/Press-Releases/2021/tmcLabs_NewsRelease_FINAL.pdf

Keklis, L. (2018) *Engaging girls in STEM: At the crossroads. STEM Ready America: Inspiring and preparing students for success with afterschool and summer learning.* Collaborative Communications. http://stemreadyamerica.org/

Kekelis, L., & Drew, T. (2023). *Mentoring 2023: Access your superpower and make the Million Girls Moonshot a reality.* STEM Next Opportunity Fund Blog.

Kekelis, L. & Sammet, K. (2019). *Expanding access and inclusion in STEM through culturally responsive family engagement.* STEM Next Opportunity Fund.

Krishnamurthi, A., & Bevan, B. (2018). *From evidence to policy: The case forSTEM in afterschool inspiring and preparing students for success with afterschool and summer learning. STEM Ready America: Inspiring and preparing students for success with afterschool and summer learning.* Collaborative Communications. http://stemreadyamerica.org/

Krutsch, E., & Roderick, V. (2022). *STEM Day: Explore growing careers.* U.S. Department of Labor. https://blog.dol.gov/2022/11/04/stem-day-explore-growing-careers

Maltese, A., & Tai, R. (2010). Eyeballs in the Fridge: Sources of Early Interest in Science. *International Journal of Science Education, 32*(5), 669–685. https://doi.org/10.1080/09500690902792385

Moritz, M., & Ottinger, R. (2023). *The critical role of intermediaries in the STEM ecosystem.* STEM Next Opportunity Fund. https://stemnext.org/the-critical-role-of-intermediaries-in-the-stem-ecosystem

Mott Foundation. (2022). *South Carolina afterschool network forges bright futures for young people.* https://www.mott.org/news/articles/south-carolina-afterschool-network-forges-bright-futures-for-young-people/

National Research Council. (2015). *Identifying and supporting productive STEM programs in out-of-school settings/Committee on Successful Out-of-School STEM Learning, Board on Science Education, Division of Behavioral and Social Sciences and Education.* The National Academies Press.

National Science Board. (2015). *Revisiting the STEM workforce, A companion to science and engineering indicators.* National Science Foundation (NSB-2015-10)

Public Profit. (2022). *The Million Girls Moonshot Evaluation Report 2021–22, Year 2.*

Peppler, K., Ito, M., & Dahn, M. (2022). *Making connections to support STEM transitions for middle school girls.* Conference Presentation, Girls Build Solutions. Atlanta, GA.

Sammet, K., & Kekelis, L. (2016). *Changing the game for girls in STEM: Findings on high-impact programs and system-building strategies.* Techbridge Girls. https://www.chevron.com/-/media/chevron/stories/documents/changing-the-game-for-girls-in-stem-white-paper.pdf

STEM Next Opportunity Fund. (n.d.). *Meet Mackenzie H., Million Girls Moonshot.* https://www.milliongirlsmoonshot.org/meet-mackenzie-h

STEM Next Opportunity Fund. (n.d.). *Meet Henrietta, Million Girls Moonshot.* https://www.milliongirlsmoonshot.org/meet-henrietta

Techbridge Girls and National Girls Collaborative Project. (2014). *Creating connections with role models: The power of collaboration.* https://static1.squarespace.com/static/63ddd4d3686ac83bfa8c608d/t/643d3d8fda25427c4392bfce/1681735055851/NGCP-Role-Model-Guide-Web-Version-1.pdf

U.S. Bureau of Labor Statistics. (2023). *Employment projections.* https://www.bls.gov/emp/tables/stem-employment.htm

Vasile, C., Marhan, A.-M., Singer, F. M., & Stoicescu, D. (2011). Academic self-efficacy and cognitive load in students. *International conference on education and educational psychology 2010, 12,* 478–482. https://doi.org/10.1016/j.sbspro.2011.02.059

Walton Family Foundation. (2023). *Americans see need to better prepare students for national security careers of the future.* Private Correspondence.

SECTION II

IMPORTANCE OF YOUTH WORKERS IN PREPARING YOUTH FOR THE FUTURE OF WORK

CHAPTER 4

IMPORTANCE OF YOUTH WORKERS IN PREPARING YOUTH FOR THE FUTURE OF WORK

Carlos Santini

INTRODUCTION

It was the start of summer 2023 for my now eighth grade daughter, and we had some critical errands to run. One of these was the all-important bathing suit purchase. My wife was out of town, so I had the honor of filling in to choose the right colors, and more importantly, the right fit! On our way there, I happened to mention that she was lucky it was pay day, to which she responded, "Yeah dad, and they pay you good, too!"

As far as kids go, anything you make as an adult is a lot of money for them. I followed up her "oh yeah" outburst by reflecting aloud saying that it had taken her father 20+ years of hard work to get to a place where the family felt taken care of. You see, the growth trajectory of my family and career have been parallel. I began my work in out-of-school-time (OST) programs just over a year into marriage, and to a darn good educator, at that. I had my first child in 2006, soon after the implementation of Proposition 49, a statewide ballot initiative that has funded afterschool programs across the state of California for the past 20 years. My second daughter was just five years old when I transitioned from leading work at the local level in Los Angeles, to national level leadership with the After-School All-Stars,

---

Built for More: The Role of Out-of-School Time in Preparing Youth for the Future of Work,
pp. 59–78
Copyright © 2024 by Information Age Publishing
www.infoagepub.com
All rights of reproduction in any form reserved.

a nationwide organization currently providing programs for 118,000 youth in 78 cities across the country. My family has been there every step of the way. I must admit that I have seized many moments when it came to the Santini crew volunteering in several events and experiences over the span of my career. One such experience was my youngest daughter joining me for a week-long career pathway retreat in 2019 with 40 high school youth from the After-School All-Stars, Los Angeles. I remember her drawing emoji stickers and blowing up balloons. She knew I was "leveraging" our relationship to have an extra pair of hands and a more capable artist to prepare workshop materials.

I share this context to make a key point: youth *can* and *will be* influenced and hopefully inspired by not only WHAT adults in their lives do for a living, but HOW they do it. As far as I was concerned and what my children have seen through listening to what they saw and hearing what they have commented on, I have learned that the various relationships and connections I have made with people over the years stood out to them. So much so that they ask how my current and past colleagues are doing. I am proud and grateful that my professional journey has been about family and relationships!

Just as quickly as my children have grown up right before my eyes, so has the outlook and perspective on what youth need to succeed in life, school, and career. This is especially true as the prospects of a faster, more digital, and increasingly automated world have come into sharper view. *The Economist* published report that looked at the automation probability of various tasks within several industries, ranging from food preparation, construction, sales, science and engineering to healthcare and teaching (The Data Team, 2018). It indicated that 210 million jobs across 32 countries were vulnerable to automation. This data is not meant to make progress and automation out to be the villain as we look at the importance of youth workers in preparing youth for the future of work. I cite this research to consider how fundamental principles of identity development, relationships, and connection should merge with a changing skills landscape in the workplace to create a thriving and fulfilled workforce of the future.

Looking at how today's field of youth development professionals influences, inspires, and equips youth for a radically different future work landscape, we will explore how identity development, personal storytelling, relationship-building, the emergence of self-care in the workplace, and the growing world of virtual learning communities all come together to redefine who a youth worker is and the skills needed to continue guiding their pursuit of success. One of the first and most important skills that youth developers can model and transfer to youth as a career pathway competency is relationship building.

RELATIONSHIP BUILDING

There was something about turning 50 that had me doing some reflecting in 2023, especially as I came across family pictures shared by my siblings that I had not seen before. Some of these pictures included high school graduation, my cross-country races, and even myself as a kid in Honduras before I immigrated to the United States. I found myself connecting more dots between my early adolescence and the adults in my life. It was a personal therapy of sorts to look back at my youth through the lens of theories, practices, and research that I have engaged with in my years as a youth development professional.

At a recent keynote I gave for Texas's annual state conference, OSTI-CON, I shared findings from a 2019 study published by the Frameworks Institute and sponsored by the Search Institute that examined the impact of Developmental Relationships on young people. As part of the Search Institute's work on examining the state of young people's relationships and how these relationships affect who they are, the study entitled, *Reframing Youth Development Relationships,* produced some emerging insights that many youth development professionals have become familiar with (O'Neil et al., 2019). Adult relationships featured included:

- Family Relationships
- Student-Teacher Relationships
- Relationships in Youth Programs
- Relationships with Peers

Insights from this work showed the following:

- The positive elements of family relationships tend to decline through adolescence.
- Too few students experience strong relationships with their teachers.
- Young people do not consistently experience elements of developmental relationships with staff/volunteers when participating in youth-based programs.
- Peer relationships are critical in identity formation but are often overlooked.

In reflecting on the adults in my life, specifically those involved in my K–12 education, it is safe to say the majority did not intentionally leverage and lean into relationship-building as a teaching and learning strategy. The ones that did so did it because they had a predisposition towards connection. I can recall my college counselor and my track and field coach as individuals who knew me because they understood me and were aware of what I was going through in my young life. This level of connection required two key ingredients: they wanted to get to know me, and I let them in. The latter was a result of trust being built over time through their actions. These actions looked like my track and field coach, Mr. Richardson, coming to my house to check on me after I walked out of an important competition distraught over my father's passing. He advocated for me! The other featured my college counselor, Mrs. Debrah Collins, monitoring my college application process to ensure I was giving myself every opportunity to attend the best university possible (I ended up being accepted into UCLA). Part of her commitment to my success came from her knowing my story and believing in me.

These interactions align with findings from the Framework Institute's research, emphasizing the importance of students forming strong relationships with core day teachers and youth developers. The roles of adults in my academic journey have made a significant difference in my life's trajectory. They modeled essential elements of their professions as educators and, by extension, as youth developers.

As a known practice, youth development professionals have demonstrated an ability to connect with students in learning environments outside of the regular school day. Even so, findings from the Search Institute's work on adult relationships indicate that youth are not exposed enough to these important adults in their lives:

> Youth programs provide important contexts where young people can develop trustworthy, lasting relationships with adults and peers. However, participating youth do not consistently experience all elements of developmental relationships with program leaders when they participate. ("What We're Learning" 2016)

The Developmental Relationships Framework, an accompanying matrix to the Search Institute's work on adult relationships, lists five key components in relationship building between youth and adults. Among these, one component involves adults helping Expand Possibilities for young people. This is an intentional process by which an adult serves as a guide, inspiration, mentor and/or coach as youth begin to engage with career interests and possibilities. This was a dynamic that was absent in my experience with my regular school day teachers. While Coach Richardson and Mrs. Collins contributed greatly, there were few deliberate or guiding conversations about my interests, aspirations, or the initial steps towards crafting my career path. Today's youth development professionals have an incredible opportunity to leverage the concept of Expanding Possibilities in young people, making it a useful tool and competency in their toolkit.

Mentoring Practices and Relationship Building

I previously mentioned my engagement with high school youth and career exploration programming in California's Eastern Sierras in 2019. One constant interaction over that four-day period was a real desire from youth to share their lives with staff. In starting with identity work on the first night (we will unpack this further in the next section of the chapter) the staff had set up a safe and familial environment. This activated an authenticity in what and how youth shared when it came to their future aspirations. Although this might seem informal and spontaneous, it aligns with the Mentor organization's *developmental style* approach, which places a primary focus on nurturing relational interactions first, with the ultimate goal of engaging in competency or skill-building activities. Based in Boston, MA, with programs nationwide, Mentor has built a youth mentoring field and movement over the past three decades serving as the expert and go-to resource on quality mentoring. Developmental interactions as cited in Mentor's *Elements of Effective Mentoring Practice for Mentoring* have been associated with a range of positive outcomes, including more positive quality mentoring relationships and longer relationship durations (Garringer et al., 2015).

In response, youth development organizations such as out-of-school-time, summer learning, and non-formal learning programs should prioritize intentional relationship-building initiatives outlined by the likes of the Search Institute and Mentor. As workplace skills and competencies shift and evolve over time, the ability to connect and create spaces of belonging will continue to be an essential skill needed across sectors and industries. In conjunction with youth honing their relationship-building proficiencies, it is equally crucial for young individuals to cultivate self-awareness and forge a robust sense of identity.

IDENTIFY FORMING

The Science Behind Identity

Right before transitioning from my Los-Angeles based work with the After-School All-Stars to a role with the national office of the same organization, I designed and hosted an event inspired by South by Southwest (SXSW) that looked to blend arts and entertainment with innovation. The trick was to make STEM cool, so do not ask me how I came to land on psychology as one of the themes for the day! Nevertheless, I reached out to a well-regarded professor of psychology and neuroscientist at UCLA specializing in adolescent brain development named Dr. Adriana Galván. It was

64 C. SANTINI

a long shot, but my pitch to her was simple. First, we would come to her and bring 200 middle school youth to the Northwest Auditorium near her offices. Second, the goal was to provide young minds with a deeper insight into the roots of their behavior and engage them in exploring their own motivations. Seeing her presenting to youth via several YouTube videos only confirmed that she was the perfect fit. Secretly, I was also hoping she would accept the invitation because she was just a cool scientist! Her engaging TEDx Talk videos had convinced me that our primarily Latino student body would be drawn to a Latina scientist with such charisma.

Dr. Galván's work unveiled the fascinating science behind the adolescent brain. In her 2022 TEDx UCLA Talk, Dr. Galván described the adolescent brain, ranging from the age of 11 or 12 through the early 20s. This phase is marked by heightened levels of uncertainty as young individuals navigate many novel experiences for the first time. In her 2013 TEDxYouth Talk at Caltech, where she addressed a group of middle and high school students, Dr. Galván expounded on the role of adolescence in establishing independence from caregivers, with the adolescent brain exhibiting an aptitude for this task (Galván, 2022).

During my experience with Dr. Galván at this After-School All-Stars event, I was surprised by how interested young people were in knowing more about their own brains. More importantly, this experience acquainted youth to the scientific underpinnings of their desire for independence and autonomy during this period in their lives. A significant insight I gained was understanding how the adolescent brain was wired to respond to affirmation, validation, and approval. In essence, as young individuals make choices and navigate the complexities of growing up, they yearn for validation and attention to their evolving thought processes. This is especially true when young people are looking for spaces to belong and to connect with something or someone to identify with. This period of adolescence becomes a crucible for the development of identity.

My Personal Identity Formation Journey

The experience of identity formation is near and dear to me, especially as an immigrant. I recently wrote a piece for my organization's blog on the definition of heritage and my journey in finding and owning my identity:

> Heritage is defined as something transmitted by or acquired from a predecessor. Being an immigrant from Honduras, it was a struggle to fully understand what I acquired or brought with me from my country during my adolescent years. I was only seven when I came to California, with my early years focused on assimilating, learning the language, and in many ways, giving greater value and meaning to cultures and traditions that were not mine.

Importance of Youth Workers in Preparing Youth for the Future of Work   65

Coming to the U.S. was not just about adjusting to a new world and a new family, but it was a critical time of identity development as I tried to look back at my history, including the origins of my name. The circumstances surrounding my unconventional family situation, where I met my biological mother and stepfather upon my arrival in California, led me on a years-long exploration to find out my real name. The first step was discovering that I had a biological father I never met. Second, was understanding why I had an Italian last name. I often found myself having to explain how I had a stepfather who was Peruvian-Italian who met and married my mother while I was in Honduras. He passed away when I was 16, so I was never able to fully engage with him about my last name and how I came to receive it. My biological father is alive to this day and living in Honduras. Though we have spoken a few times over the years, I have never actively sought a connection with him.

The story behind my name is an important one. Dr. Galván's research into the well-being of the adolescent brain and my own experiences during that formative period vividly intersect in the pursuit of my personal truth. Who was I? Where did my name come from? Who gave it to me, and does it have a meaning? I had all these questions in the search for belonging and connection. Added to all this, I was an immigrant to the U.S.—I was a classic case study for Dr. Galván's work.

Identity Formation and Program Experiences

Let's go back to the four-day career pathway workshop experience mentioned earlier. As I contemplated the approach, I leaned into community-building and connection as an engagement strategy. This created a series of enlightening moments for students as they discovered the relationship between identity development and the awareness of character traits essential for achieving success and fulfillment across life, education, and career. A pivotal moment took place on the first evening with a young lady engaging in a "Name Exploration" activity. This exercise prompted participants to reflect on their names, including the origin and significance of their first names, and how they felt about them. She responded to the activity by defining her name as "nowhere," encapsulating her feelings of ambiguity regarding its origins and historical significance. She continued by sharing that she had never discovered who named her and what her name represented.

As OST programs continue to prioritize the social and emotional well-being of young people, it is both strategic and timely for youth-serving organizations to continue codifying practices that equip youth development professionals to design and facilitate identity development experiences for young people. This includes activities that build self-awareness, engage youth in identifying personal character traits and related strengths-based work like Gallup's CliftonStrengths initiative (Galván, 2013).

The non-formal education landscape, including OST, summer learning, mentoring programs, and related organizations, have a unique opportunity to continue building an ecosystem where youth development professionals model and transfer what I consider next-generation workforce skills such as identity development. As themes such as self-care, social and emotional learning, community, connection, and mental health emerged within the youth development space during the COVID-19 pandemic, I participated in and observed various efforts in which organizations partnered and leveraged their strengths and experiences to design and implement a human-centered approach to teaching and learning. This looked like the reimagining and redesigning of professional development initiatives, new staff onboarding experiences, focusing on community-building and connection as the foundation of student learning, and other holistic practices that promoted overall well-being and connection as part of the learning outcomes for youth and educators.

Identity Development and the Ever Forward Club

One organization has stood out in this important identity development work. The Ever Forward Club is an Oakland-based non-profit whose mission is to build character and transform lives by providing underserved middle and high school youth with safe, brave, and bold communities that provide them with opportunities for academic, personal, family, and community development. One of their signature program experiences and workshops, *Taking off the Mask*, helps youth, communities, and organizations unlock their potential and transform the way they interact and relate to each other and their communities. Founded by Ashanti Branch in 2004 as a first-year teacher in Alameda-Contra Costa County Unified School District, the Ever Forward Club started as an effort to provide a support group for African American and Latino males who were not achieving to the level of their potential.

I met Ashanti while starting out-of-school-time programs in the city of Oakland in 2016. Our work revolved around providing youth of color a safe and authentic space after school to engage with their true emotions, their history, and identity. This was one of the first times that I had come across a program that engaged in deep and intentional identity work rooted on youth engaging with their true self hiding behind a social and emotional mask to find authentic motivation and inspiration to succeed in school and

Importance of Youth Workers in Preparing Youth for the Future of Work   67

in life. Ashanti and the Ever Forward Club have since launched a global effort called the #MillionMaskMovement as part of their Taking off the Mask initiative:

> To help our young people, adults, and community gain a deeper understanding of how much we have in common. We invite people from around the world to participate in an activity of self-reflection and deep connection. (Branch, 2022)

Since the #MillionMaskMovement began in 2020, astoundingly, more than 75,000 people from around the world have participated in Ever Forward's intentional efforts to promote and celebrate personal authenticity and identity. The organization has provided resources for 500 educators, supporting more than 180,000 youth and adults in the U.S. and globally. You can find out more about Ashanti Branch and the Ever Forward Club by visiting www.everforwardclub.org.

Authenticity in the Workplace

The momentum behind identity development is also reflective of a larger movement of growing personal authenticity in the workplace. One of the best places to see this transformation is via LinkedIn, the world's largest social media platform for professionals. The platform has undergone a significant transformation, evolving from a space where individuals showcased their "work" personas to a platform that welcomes and encourages the expression of their "whole" selves. Professionals have seized this medium to build their personal brand through authentic storytelling. But even as individuals celebrate and feature their authentic selves as a social media movement, workplace environments are still evolving in their ability to establish authentic, safe, connected, and inclusive spaces for employees.

Embedded within this context, one of the most notable strategic endeavors emphasizing identity development as a vital career competency is observed in the realm of Diversity, Equity, and Inclusion (DEI) initiatives. An April 2023 *Forbes* article entitled "10 Reasons Why DEI Efforts Fail (And How to Ensure They Succeed)" identified "barriers to success not being resolved" as one of these top 10 reasons for such efforts falling short (YEC Expert Panel, 2023). The author described "that everyone has different barriers to success and that it's up to industry leaders to create safe spaces in their organizations where individuals can express their needs clearly and without feeling embarrassed or judged" (p. 3). Having a strong sense of self in the workplace will continue to be an indispensable competency and skill. Employees' individual voices and perspectives will continue to be the

68 C. SANTINI

backbone of how organizations build and maintain a positive and productive workplace climate and culture both now and in the future.

Identity Development and Storytelling

In 2016, while serving as the National Vice President of Programs for the After-School All-Stars, my team and I were preparing for a weeklong youth leadership experience called All-Star Leadership University. Taking place at the 4-H Center in Maryland, youth leaders from 19 cities across the country came together to continue discovering and activating their own leadership and advocacy skills. As we designed the program agenda, we understood that it would take collaboration to achieve our outcomes and objectives for the week. To this end, we enlisted the support of an exceptional non-profit organization: The Plus Me Project (PLUS ME). Focused on harnessing the art of personal storytelling to bolster the confidence of youth as they embark on pursuits of academic, vocational, and life aspirations, PLUS ME has impacted the lives of over 100,000 students spanning more than 300 underserved middle and high schools throughout Southern California.

I reached out to the organization's founder, Richard Reyes, to integrate storytelling as a leadership competency for young people. We were able to implement PLUS ME's My Story Matters journaling curriculum, creating a space and experience for youth to gain skills and knowledge in how to advocate for themselves and their communities through an intentional storytelling process. The journaling curriculum guides students through an effective process of reflecting upon and telling their own stories by focusing on the characters, settings, events, and lessons learned in their lives.

I had referenced LinkedIn's evolution, transitioning from a platform primarily centered on job recruitment and professional to a more human-centric virtual space, fostering the exchange of career journeys and personal career narratives. As more youth development professionals experience longer tenures in their careers, storytelling has also become an important competency to model for the youth they serve. Like PLUS ME's storytelling formula, it is imperative for staff to intentionally guide and equip youth with the ability to tell their own stories and that of others. Opportunities for storytelling competencies to have an impact in preparing youth for the future of work include:

- Integrating storytelling as part of an overall data strategy to build more compelling impact narratives.
- Leveraging storytelling as a foundational component of organizational fundraising.

Importance of Youth Workers in Preparing Youth for the Future of Work   69

- Storytelling as an advocacy tool to elevate and promote community voices.
- Personal storytelling as an effective way for individuals to be standout candidates in various selection processes such as job interviews and college applications.
- Storytelling to validate and elevate the value of lived experiences.

Initiatives spearheaded by organizations such as the PLUS ME Project represent just one example that youth developers can draw inspiration from, offering a structured approach to equipping youth with the aptitude to navigate the terrain of identity development and self-advocacy along their career pathways. Moreover, organizations can design their staff's professional development plans to intentionally address these emerging workforce readiness skills to include:

- Staff Reflection and Story Development: Youth practitioners reflect and document their professional journeys.
- Personal Narrative Presentations: Staff prepare and deliver presentations based on their reflections and personal stories.
- Connecting data and storytelling: Staff acquire the ability to present compelling impact narratives through the effective use of quantitative and qualitative data.
- Career Advancement: Integrate personal advocacy methodologies in your organization's performance review and promotions strategies.

The Value of Lived Experiences

Following in the footsteps of bringing our full and authentic selves to the workplace, recognizing practical lived experience as part of a professional acumen has also transformed the professionalism narrative. As the world of education continues to recover from the pandemic, the lived experiences of young people have become more important than ever. To this end, equipping young people with the ability to identify and leverage their lived experiences will enable youth to present themselves as competent in engaging with real-world workplace challenges and opportunities.

An example of this is a recent interview my 16-year-old daughter had with our local Starbucks. Although her work experience was limited to babysitting, she was able to leverage her experiences as an athlete on her cross-country team and the challenges of her AP classes when asked about her approach to working in a team environment, giving, and receiving criticism, working through challenging interpersonal situation, etc. It took a conversation anticipating potential interview questions to reflect on her experiences as a student and how those could cross over into a job interview. Our young people have experience.

Youth Engaged 4 Change (YEC; https://engage.youth.gov) is a resource center created by the Interagency Working Group on Youth Programs, a group within the executive branch of the U.S. government responsible for promoting healthy outcomes for all youth, published a piece on the Power of Lived Experiences (YEC, 2023) from the vantage point of a teenager. The blog piece underscores the importance of creating spaces and facilitating interactions that elevate youth's lived experiences.

> Understanding and valuing our "lived experiences" helps us grasp who we are as individuals and helps us communicate our experiences to the world. Young people are often viewed as inexperienced, but we already have a life full of lived experiences that have shaped who we are. Lived experiences inform the decisions we make, and they influence the way we see and think about the world around us. (Espinal, 2023, p. 1)

Engaging Lived Experiences in Youth

In my capacity as CEO of Mizzen Education (formerly Mizzen by Mott)—an organization committed to furnishing OST practitioners with free teaching and learning resources through our digital platform, alongside professional development experiences for educators—we've pinpointed the term "engagement" as a more precise descriptor for high-quality out-of-school-time programs. From our many interactions with both youth and practitioners, it is commonly known that the more youth-serving organizations listen to and implement recommendations from young people regarding the programs they offer, the higher the engagement and participation from youth. This feedback comes from youth being mostly on the receiving end of program experiences.

This presents an opportunity for organizations to engage youth in roundtables and focus groups. These types of "platform moments" enable youth to see themselves as meaningful contributors to the design of products and/or experiences in an era where consumer feedback has become a mainstay as to how companies and corporations design and continuously improve their products and services. Youth developers can take some of these practical steps to translate lived experiences into actionable steps in the design and delivery of their organization's programs.

1. Build a culture of reflection and feedback amongst the youth in your programs.
2. Establish youth as strategic stakeholders by defining and describing the form and function of roundtables and focus groups.
3. Create at least two feedback sessions per year, scheduling them during strategic times in the program year (summer, returning from winter-break, transition periods such as elementary-to-middle school or middle-to high school).
4. Aggregate results and hold "action-steps" session for youth to determine how to proceed with focus group/roundtable sessions data and/or outcomes.
5. Establish timelines for implementation.
6. Track and discuss progress/performance of agreed-upon next steps.

The ability for youth to be aware of and exercise their lived experiences is an important career pathway skill, as the action of giving and receiving feedback guides progress and innovation in what is known as the Feedback Economy, the strategy by which a business collects, analyzes, and leverages customer input to beat out their competitors in customer satisfaction. Lived experiences can be transformed into a powerful advocacy strategy that young people can add to their personal toolkit.

Modeling and Transferring the Value of Lived Experiences

Young people's ability to recognize and leverage the power of their lived experiences can be influenced by youth development professionals' ability to do the same. Due to the prioritizing of relationship-building within OST programs and the consistent practice of organizations hiring staff from within the communities they serve, youth development professionals stand to have a significant impact on youth from leaning into and leading with their life experiences. And this is not limited just to the world of youth development and education. An October 2022 article in *Inc. Magazine*, "Use Your Life Experiences to Your Advantage," the author quotes Dr. Lindsey Godwin in underscoring the value of our lived experiences: "What we have yet to fully harvest and recognize as an important element for cultivating success is the latent intelligence that comes from our lived experiences" (Kaplan, 2022). The article goes on to define lived experiences as Experiential Intelligence consisting of:

72   C. SANTINI

- Mindsets: attitudes and beliefs about yourself, other people, and the world
- Abilities: competencies that help you integrate knowledge, skills, and experiences to respond to situations in the most effective way possible
- Know-how: your knowledge and skills

Dr. Christopher Emdin, author and the Robert A. Naslund Endowed Chair in Curriculum Theory and professor of Education at the University of Southern California (and an esteemed mentor of mine in the work of social justice and equity in education) delivered a powerful Tedx Talk in 2013 out of Columbia University's Teacher's College entitled *Reality Pedagogy where he shared the Five Cs of Reality Pedagogy with one being "Cosmopolitanism* (Emdin, 2013). He defined it as a school's ability to include and integrate the places and people of a community into the curriculum and learning experience of said institutions of learning.

He described that life experiences of community members such as matriarchs, patriarchs, and other people of influence within such communities can positively impact the learning outcomes of young people. This serves as an opportunity for afterschool educators, whether they are seeking a career pathway as core day teachers or are looking to continue in their role as non-formal educators, to elevate and articulate the value of their lived experiences as part of the expertise they bring to the teaching profession.

Social and Emotional Learning and the Future Work Landscape

The year is 2018. Picture a board meeting presentation to a high-powered group of executives supporting a non-profit afterschool organization. The topic: social and emotional learning. Arnold Schwarzenegger is in the room as an honorary board chair for the After-School All-Stars. The following is announced to the group, "As you all know, we've been working on a program pilot to implement a national SEL curriculum. Today, I'd like to invite you all to participate in an SEL activity together."

That was me leading this experience in the middle of Arnold Schwarzenegger's offices. The moment I introduced the concept, all eyes turned to Arnold. The activity asked the audience to think of a skill that had contributed to their success and who they learned it from. I am happy to share that he was all over it. That Schwarzenegger smile was ear-to-ear as he recalled people who had influenced his work ethic and vision. Arnold understood the importance of connection and relationships in his career journey.

Importance of Youth Workers in Preparing Youth for the Future of Work   73

Throughout this chapter, my focus has been relationship-building, storytelling, identity development, and lived experiences. These components collectively constitute a paradigm shift in what are considered essential skills and assets needed for youth to experience future career success. The same can be said for the skills and competencies that make up social and emotional learning. I had the opportunity to present alongside some of my OST peers at a 2018 Afterschool Alliance presentation on SEL and Employability Skills. The session highlighted connections between SEL programming and the emerging skills needed to succeed in the workplace. The session included connections made by The Office of Career, Technical, and Adult Education (OCTAE) at the U.S. Department of Education between key employability skills and CASEL's SEL Competencies found in interpersonal and intrapersonal skills and cognitive competence.

Table 4.1

SEL Skills and Employability Skills

Applied Knowledge	Effective Relationships	Workplace Skills
Problem Solving Skills	Interpersonal Skills	Time Management
Critical Thinking Skills	Ability to Collaborate	Resource Management
Sound Decision-Making	Ability to Communicate Effectively	

Today's youth development professional has experienced one of the most dramatic changes in workplace culture over the last 100+ years prompted by the COVID-19 pandemic. Entire industries prioritized staff well-being and self-care as part of a general staff retention and workplace satisfaction strategy as highlighted in a statement by Sir Richard Branson in an *Inc.* magazine July 2023 article:

> I think being emotionally intelligent is more important in every aspect of life—and this includes business. Being a good listener, finding empathy, understanding emotions, communicating effectively, treating people well, and bringing out the best is critical to success. (Stillman, 2023, p. 1)

There exists a tremendous opportunity for practitioners to transfer skills listed above to young people participating in specific out-of-school-time experiences, such as entrepreneurship programs, career and college readiness initiatives, and youth leadership activities.

74 C. SANTINI

COLLABORATION:
A KEY 21st CENTURY SKILL AND COMPETENCY

Reviewing the various skills and competencies I have highlighted including relationship-building, storytelling, and identity development, one could argue that they all come together to develop what I consider being one of the most important tools in our career pathway building toolkit—collaboration.

Teaming up for Success: The Power of Collaboration

As education underwent a seismic shift towards virtual learning in response to the unprecedented upheaval triggered by COVID-19, my former team at After-School All-Stars embraced collaboration to best support our teaching staff across our organization. As our students and staff left their schools and hunkered down for the long haul of virtual learning at home, I turned to my colleagues at organizations like Alliance for a Healthier Generation, Common Threads, BOKS by Reebok and kid-grit, to design a virtual learning community aimed at supporting the health and wellbeing of staff as they prepared to meet the challenge of remote work and virtual learning. All these organizations came together to establish a community of practice entitled *Permission to Pause*. The goal was to create a virtual learning community where staff from across the organization could convene. Within this virtual realm, they could immerse themselves in a shared sense of community, forge connections, partake in virtual wellness activities, and gain invaluable insights and best practices in self-care. This multi-organization collaborative leveraged the talents and resources of various groups to produce high-quality content and engaging learning experiences for educators. Necessity became the mother of invention for us as we leaned on a virtual community of practice to increase our capacity and expertise as an organization to better support our staff.

During this same period, I observed many organizations turning their focus towards adapting and/or creating curriculum and lesson plans to better support staff in facilitating learning experiences in a whole new and unfamiliar setting—enrichment programming delivered through a laptop or tablet. Additionally, there were many examples of collaboration between organizations in sharing teaching and learning resources. One of the positive and lasting impacts of the pandemic was twofold—organizations sharing resources and the increased presence and implementation of virtual learning communities.

After joining Mizzen Education in 2021, I was excited about the prospect of supporting the out-of-school-time community through the very strategies and approaches that enabled programs to provide engaging learning experiences, even through a global pandemic. At the heart of our mission at Mizzen is the idea that partnership is foundational to quality; that great content and resources are built in collaboration with great organizations and educators; and that the out-of-school-time community has long been overdue for a streamlined hub and delivery system to ensure equitable access to said resources.

As Mizzen continues to explore ways to support youth development professionals in out-of-school-time, we have continued to hear from educators about the need to collaborate with their peers from other organizations and throughout the country. We have experienced this in activity and lesson plan design sessions with practitioners as they shared how the collaborative settings they participated in energized and inspired them to new levels of creativity. This feedback has guided our organization to look beyond our current model of educators accessing content, to one of creating virtual and in-person collaboration spaces where practitioners design content in real-time with one another. This includes opportunities for youth to build lessons, activities and curriculum alongside educators and their peers. This presents an opportunity for youth development professionals to model practical collaboration skills that are part of 21st century learning competencies that are known to contribute to ongoing progress and innovations across various industries. Collaboration skills and competencies have long been outlined and recommended as foundational to young people's career success. The Partnership for 21st Century Skills identified the knowledge, skills, and expertise students (https://files.eric.ed.gov/fulltext/ED519462.pdf) should master to succeed in work and life in the 21st century (Stillman, 2023).

The QuEST Model and Effective Skills Transfer

In reflecting on my transition to Mizzen, my ability to transfer learnings from one environment to another has played a significant role in my navigating differences between industries. Shifting from being a direct service provider in out-of-school-time to a resource provider offering digital solutions and professional development supports required my ability to transfer skills and competencies in collaboration and communication.

One such methodology that provides guidance on how to apply skills transfer approach was designed by The Forum for Youth Investment in 2014 (Smith, 2014). Their theory of change entitled the QuEST Model (**Qu**ality-**E**ngagement-**S**kills **T**ransfer) guides programs in identifying skill sets they want to cultivate in youth with the goal of equipping young people with the ability to transfer such skills to other areas of their lives (Smith,

2014). The American Camp Association has looked to the QuEST model as part of their continuous quality improvement (CQI) initiatives, including their formal skill-building activities, in partnership with the Forum's Weikart Center.

> As young people participate in high-quality camp programming, they learn new Skills, including social, emotional, and cognitive skills, and develop beliefs about their skills and abilities. With time and practice, those skills can Transfer outside of the camp setting to campers' everyday lives at school, work, and in the community. (Smith, 2014)

A Bright Future Ahead

I introduced a group of young professionals at the National Afterschool Association's (NAA) Convention in 2018 recognizing their efforts in leading, supporting and elevating the work of the afterschool field beyond their own organizations. The work of NAA's NextGen Leaders initiative highlights emerging young leaders who are active in the broader afterschool community (NAA Honors, 2023). In my opening statement during the 2018 convention, I shared my experience in stumbling onto this work called afterschool in 2002, not knowing where it would take me. I also acknowledged the group behind me as a new breed of OST professionals, with many intentionally seeking degrees and certificate programs designed to equip them with the technical and leaderships skills needed to pursue a career in youth development and related youth-based work. This points to a larger trend identified by the BOOST Conference (http://www.boostconference. org), an all-inclusive convening supporting global educators and youth development professionals. In 2023, the week-long conference had almost 3,000 participants, with 35% reporting as having a bachelor's degree and 25% indicating they had 6–10 years of experience working with youth programs (BOOST Conference, 2023).

This level of professionalization in the youth development community has equipped the OST field and related youth-based organizations to design and implement an array of program experiences aimed at intentional skill-building in young people. Initiatives such as mentoring programs, college and career readiness experiences, project-based learning, STEM pathways, leadership and advocacy cohorts, workplace internships, and other related projects will continue playing a key role in supporting youth's preparedness for a rapidly evolving economy.

What's not always captured in how effective the OST setting has been in equipping youth with the skills and competencies needed to succeed in an ever-changing workforce are the stories told by young people who have gone on to college and career success following their years in youth

Importance of Youth Workers in Preparing Youth for the Future of Work   77

development programs. One such theme I heard frequently was youth sharing that if it were not for their programs, they wouldn't have become the students or professionals they turned out to be.

"If it weren't for my program…"

"If it weren't for my program leader…"

"If it weren't for my camp…"

"If it weren't for that retreat…"

All these statements validate the ways youth development professionals have modeled a set of balanced skills young people can emulate and cultivate. These skills serve as a bedrock for young individuals to build their proficiency, purpose, and potential in their future endeavors—whether it is in their personal lives, academic pursuits, or future careers.

It is worth acknowledging that my ability to share these insights today owes much to the OST programs I have been a part of over the past two decades. Without their influence, I would not have the opportunity to share the insights that have been core to the work that has enriched not only the youth we are here to serve, but myself in kind.

For Additional Consideration

In the time it took to finalize this chapter, additional skills relevant to the future work landscape have emerged. This includes the designing and engineering of questions for interaction with generative artificial intelligence (AI). Skillsets such as the creation of prompts and sentence structures that guide and equip tools such as ChatGPT and other AI-powered writing and digital assistants depend on an individual's ability to use voice tone, context, audience, and calls to action to generate the best possible products as requested by the user. Avnish Yadav, contributing writer for Medium, expands on this skillset in its July 2023 article entitled ChatGPT Ultimate Prompting Guide (Yadav, 2023). Just another example of the fluid and dynamic elements of the modern workplace.

REFERENCES

BOOST Conference. (2023). http://www.boostconference.org/images/PDF/BOOST-Conference-Attendee-Demographics.pdf

Christopher, E. [TEDX]. (2013, April 23). *Reality pedagogy* [Video]. YouTube. https://youtu.be/2Y9tVf_8fqo

Espinal, I. (2022, June). *The power of lived experiences*. Youth Engaged 4 Change. https://engage.youth.gov/blog/power-lived-experiences

Gallup (n.d.). *Steps for a successful CliftonStrengths for Students Initiative.* https://www.gallup.com/education/352583/successful-cliftonstrengths-for-students-initiative.aspx

Galván, A. [TEDX]. (2013, January 19). *Insight into the teenage brain* [Video]. YouTube. https://youtu.be/LWUkW4s3XxY

Galván, A. [TEDX]. (2022, June 4). *The adolescent brain: A thriving look* [Video]. YouTube. https://youtu.be/G99wxwK-mG8

Garringer,M., Kupersmidt, J., Rhodes, J., Stelter, R., & Tai, T. (2015). *Elements of effective practice for mentoring.* https://www.mentoring.org/resource/elements-of-effective-practice-for-mentoring/, https://www.mentoring.org/wp-content/uploads/2021/06/Final_Elements_Publication_Fourth-2.pdf

Kaplan, S. (2022, October). Use your life experiences to your advantage. *Inc.* https://www.inc.com/soren-kaplan/life-experience-business-success.html

Love, S. (2022, November). *Continuous quality improvement.* American Camp Association. https://www.acacamps.org/article/camping-magazine/continuous-quality-improvement

NAA Honors. (2023, June). *Next generation of afterschool leaders.* National Afterschool Association. https://naaweb.org/news/643401/NAA-HONORS-2023-NEXT-GENERATION-OF-AFTERSCHOOL-LEADERS.htm

O'Neil, M., Volmert, A., Gerstein Pineau,M., & Levay, K. (2019). *Reframing developmental relationships: A frameworks message memo.* FrameWorks UK. https://www.frameworksinstitute.org/publication/reframing-developmental-relationships-a-frameworks-messagememo/, https://www.frameworksinstitute.org/wp-content/uploads/2020/06/FRAJ7033-SEARCH-MessageMemo-190718.pdf

Smith, C., & McGovern, G. (2014, September). *The QuEST Model.* The Forum FYI. https://forumfyi.org/wp-content/uploads/2019/12/Brief-QuEST-Model.pdf

Stillman, J. (2023, July 18). Richard Branson says EQ is more important than IQ for success. Science suggests he's right. *Inc.* https://www.inc.com/jessica-stillman/richard-branson-says-eq-is-more-important-than-iq-for-success-science-suggests-hes-right.html

The Data Team. (2018). A study finds nearly half of jobs are vulnerable to automation. *The Economist.* https://www.economist.com/graphic-detail/2018/04/24/a-study-finds-nearly-half-of-jobs-are-vulnerable-to-automation

Yadav, A. (2023, July). ChatGPT Ultimate Prompting Guide. *Medium.* https://medium.com/@avnishyadav25/chatgpt-ultimate-prompting-guide-2135d5c3d1bc

YEC Expert Panel. (2023, April). 10 reasons why DEI efforts fail (and how to ensure they succeed). *Forbes.* https://www.forbes.com/sites/theyec/2023/04/03/10-reasons-why-dei-efforts-fail-and-how-to-ensure-they-succeed/?sh=412cc4272696

What we're learning about developmental relationships. (2016). Search Institute. https://www.search-institute.org/developmental-relationships/learning-developmentalrelationships/

CHAPTER 5

POST-TRAUMATIC GROWTH IN OST

Creating Nurturing Conditions for Growth and Transformation in the Youth Development Workforce

Melea Meyer

INTRODUCTION

With broad acknowledgement of Adverse Childhood Experiences (ACEs) as an indicator that we must take a universally trauma-informed approach to youth programming, there have been vast capacity-building efforts to *address* trauma, *mitigate* its effects and identify the negative consequences of post-traumatic stress responses, but have we given enough attention to the phenomenon of Post Traumatic Growth (PTG)?

PTG, while not new, has been explored by scholars such as Dr. Shawn Ginright, Dr. Femi Vance, Lawrence Calhoun, Richard Tedeschi, Roxane Cohen Silver, Bonnie Green and Michael Zoellner. Nonetheless, conversations about PTG, and its implications are often overshadowed by the more well-known effects of Post Traumatic Stress Disorder (PTSD). In fact, the term PTSD has become a sort of shorthand for anything about which one might ruminate or experience general discomfort (Psychiatry.org, 2023).

Within California's PK–12 education ecosystem, a deficit-based approach to evaluation, assessment, and growth has been nurtured by an inequitable, hierarchical, and binary system that favors comparison over achievement,

---

Built for More: The Role of Out-of-School Time in Preparing Youth for the Future of Work,
pp. 79–94
Copyright © 2024 by Information Age Publishing
www.infoagepub.com
All rights of reproduction in any form reserved.

and consequences before growth. This approach results in a focus on the negative effects of trauma, permeating social-emotional learning, staff support, and overall organizational effectiveness within schools. Consequently, a direct focus on mitigating and responding to trauma and its negative effects is a natural emergence of this orientation.

Research has long been established that teachers' perceptions significantly affect student outcomes. According to Rosenthal and Jacobson (1968), teachers' expectations can have a significant impact on students' academic performance. Similarly, Jussim and Harber (2005) conducted a meta-analysis of over 500 studies, corroborating these findings.

In the Rosenthal and Jacobson (1968) studies, teachers were randomly assigned to two groups. The first group was told that their students were "bloomers," meaning that they were expected to show exceptional intellectual gains during the school year. The second group received no information about their students' potential.

At the end of the school year, the students in the "bloomer" group had significantly higher IQ scores than the students in the other group, which suggests that teachers' expectations can have a significant impact on students' performance on IQ tests.

In 2005, researchers Jussim and Harber conducted a meta-analysis of over 500 subsequent studies, which revealed that teachers' expectations positively correlated with students' achievement, even after controlling for students' prior academic indicators. This finding suggests that teachers' expectations may have a causal effect on students' academic performance. However, it is important to note that this evidence only establishes a correlation between teachers' expectations and students' achievement. Other factors, such as students' socioeconomic status, persistent stress environments or family background, also have an effect on youth development and learning. Nonetheless, when viewed broadly, these studies do collectively provide evidence that teachers' expectations can significantly impact student achievement. This invites educators to consider how our understanding of social-emotional outcomes related to trauma may change if youth workers, teachers, and educational leaders take a positive orientation towards the potential for growth inherent in trauma. To achieve this positive orientation, youth workers, educators, and support staff must also be included in the self-care and wellness equation.

The relentless focus on mitigating, preventing, and responding to trauma contributes to burnout among education workers and professionals. With each new class or cohort of students, the need to mitigate trauma is cyclical. This cycle of seeing the same conditions persisting year after year leads to teacher, principal, and caregiver burn-out. Typical responses to this problem include providing more training, or maybe hosting a staff appreciation day, or sending a team to a conference. While these approaches may provide a temporary reminder of one's purpose and community, such quick fixes lack the systemic approach that could have a profound impact. Beginning with the internal systems of the teachers and children themselves through not only learning opportunities but schedules and structures that support a whole person approach to wellness in schools may be a better solution to meet the needs of a collectively traumatized community.

Trauma is part of the human condition, and few lives are free from it. Our current global conditions call for a new kind of leadership that can respond effectively and holistically to the needs of their communities. By first listening to those communities and orienting one's awareness to the potential for positive outcomes, it may make a difference in outcomes. The existence of PTSD and PTG as psychological phenomena indicate that how individuals react to trauma affects the survivor's ability to restore equilibrium and lead productive meaningful lives (Calhoun & Tedeschi, 2013).

Educators, community-members, and school leaders are generally not adequately trained to manage the kinds of behavioral and mental health challenges prevalent in today's schools. However, offering hope and recommendations for how to orient their awareness towards the potential for growth that is inherent in trauma could shift the lens through which more students could be viewed. Instead of being regarded with pity or despair, they could be seen through the lens of their potential growth. Perhaps this shift could guide adults' decision-making to create more space for themselves and others to resist the perpetual cycle of trauma bonding inherent in "venting" and other escalating behaviors that help shape staff culture in schools. By embracing a resistance to vent, complain, or focus on the negative aspects of trauma, both adults and youth could more easily rest in the goodness of being human together.

Taking a deficit-based approach to lived experience, where trauma is seen as an obstacle to be accommodated without accounting for the potential for growth inherent within it, naturally progresses from a system focused on filling *learning gaps and* mitigating *learning loss*. It is the natural orientation of a paternalistic hierarchical system designed to inject learning into its students rather than bring out the best of what's already inherent in its learners and help that to grow and transform into new possibilities and expanded opportunities.

While only 3-8% of trauma survivors experience PTSD, several studies show that as many as 70% of trauma survivors experience PTG. With 8% of women and 4% of men estimated to be trauma survivors in the overall population, it is important to incorporate a new awareness of how to relate to and respond to those who may have experienced traumatic events (Calhoun & Tedeschi, 2013). With the growing prevalence of climate-change-induced natural disasters, and the global trauma experienced during the COVID-19 pandemic, growing awareness of how to support

82 M. MEYER

PTG is becoming a future-ready skill all leaders will need. It can help in aiding youth and adults to move through trauma, rebuild resiliency, connect, and create more purposeful communities; indeed, some might argue that the future depends upon it.

Given this context, how can we focus our workforce development efforts and understanding of human growth and development around PTG-*responsive and PTG-supportive* practices? The importance of reframing how we engage with youth is foundational to the success of the youth serving workforce as well.

The research presented in the chapter is the author's application of Paul Tedeschi and Lawrence Calhoun's framework and indicators for posttraumatic growth, as demonstrated in California's System of Support for Expanded Learning. Research findings and recommendations are the author's own.

The Authenticity Gap

A deficit -based approach to understanding youth development has long been considered as ineffective and continuing to follow it risks an intergenerational deficit of authenticity as well. Youth in our care, in our schools, neighborhoods, and programs can spot a fake pair of Jordans, a fake LV bag or a fake adult a mile away. And while many adults in our care system have a variety of ways to connect with youth, the trauma-informed and trauma-centered viewpoint can also lead to pity and empathic distress. Pity is a poor substitute for compassion and is easily recognized as disingenuous. Adults who are unable to show up authentically will be revealed quickly and dispatched (from a circle of trust) with ease.

By basing our orientation of youth experience on a negative predicate of damage and darkness, we limit the light we can shed on the talents and strengths our youth bring to our lives and communities. What could happen if we shift our attention towards the potential of growth through adversity? With such an orientation it is possible to create conditions that support that growth, rather than play the endless game of whack-a-mole by seeking to address all the varied sources and sustainers of childhood trauma, while the children sit aside and wait for opportunities because the adults are busy fighting invisible monsters among themselves.

While efforts should be made to remove these sources and sustainers of trauma, and space is needed to allow youth to process and move through the emotions that accompany childhood trauma, we can make concurrent efforts to take a strengths-based approach to youth experience by acknowledging the phenomena of PTG. By investigating PTG's potential effects on the systems we continue to build, perhaps adults can reorient

Post-Traumatic Growth in OST   83

their awareness towards a high achieving future for all youth and make transformative decisions based on that vision *with* and *alongside* the youth we are honored to serve. This transformation must begin with the adults themselves; by starting with a growing internal awareness of the potential effects of trauma (personally experienced or otherwise), youth workers can better engage authentically with youth and colleagues.

This chapter outlines and explores how leaders' awareness of PTG may help shape more supportive and nurturing conditions for our youth serving workforce, and in turn help to create more nurturing conditions for youth. These nurturing conditions are those that can foster the kinds of skills needed in the future workforce: adaptability, creativity, and the ability to collaborate within various and diverse global contexts.

I've heard of PTSD: What Is Post Traumatic Growth?

According to the National Institutes of Health (NIH), the concept of post-traumatic stress disorder (PTSD) began to appear in the public discourse prior to World War I in reports of soldiers who returned home "shell-shocked," with mentions of PTSD described in literature and oral traditions dating back centuries. It was only in the 1980s, after PTSD had emerged from the battlefield to the factories and machines of the industrial revolutions, to every television screen in every home, that PTSD became a household term (NIH, 2021). PTG, at this time, also began to emerge in the discourse of psychologists, and behavioral researchers Lawrence Calhoun and Richard Tedeschi began studying the phenomenon among college students, and then later in combat veterans.

Calhoun and Tedeschi (2013) define PTG as "positive psychological change that may occur as a result of the struggle with highly challenging life experiences" (p. 1). They claim that PTG is a common experience, and that most people who experience a traumatic event will report some degree of positive change. Through their extensive research and their inventory of post-traumatic growth (IPTG) for more than two decades, have identified five areas in which post-traumatic growth most commonly occurs:

1. Changed sense of self: People who experience PTG often report a changed sense of self and may feel stronger, more resilient, or more compassionate.
2. Changed relationships: PTG may lead to changes in relationships. People may feel closer to their loved ones, or they may develop new relationships with people who have shared similar experiences.

84   M. MEYER

3. Changed philosophy of life: PTG can also lead to changes in philosophy of life. People may develop a new appreciation for life, or they may find new meaning and purpose in their lives.

4. Changed values: PTG affects survivor's values. People may place more value on relationships, or they may become more aware of the importance of helping others.

5. Changed mindset or belief system: PTG may also lead to changes in one's belief system, or adherence to mental models. People may become more religious, experience a mindset shift, or they may develop a new sense of connection to the universe.

Calhoun and Tedeschi's (2013) work has been instrumental in the development of our understanding of PTG. Their research has helped to legitimize the experience of PTG, and it has provided a framework for understanding how and why people can experience positive change after a traumatic event. PTG does not take some special set of circumstances; it can occur in people of all ages, stages, orientations, races, and geographical origins.

By believing growth and transformation relies on special magic, or exceptional individuals, we limit our potential for learning which can emerge from the difficulties growth and transformation demand, and by limiting our understanding of youth and adult survivors as "traumatized individuals" we may be limiting the growth and transformation of our youth and our communities. Several religious and philosophical texts in the Eastern and Western traditions include stories of struggle that lead to great transformation. These stories exist to remind us that growth, and sometimes pain, is also part of the human condition (Vance, 2019). Acknowledging only the negative effects of trauma and helicoptering around survivors in efforts to mitigate effects and respond to stress and eliminate all discomfort, we limit the potential for growth. When we only see the trauma in a child, we limit their potential to imagine a world without it.

PTG can occur in any individual, regardless of age, gender, or background. However, it is more likely to occur in people who have strong social support networks and who have access to resources and opportunities for growth. Youth-serving professionals can play a vital role in creating the conditions that foster PTG in young people. By providing a safe and supportive environment, and by offering opportunities for young people to connect with others, youth-serving professionals can help young people to heal from trauma and to experience positive growth. PTG is not a linear process. It can occur in waves, and it can be unpredictable. However, it is a process that can lead to lasting positive change.

PTG can have a number of benefits for youth serving professionals and young people. If you know a young person who has experienced trauma they may carry the markers of dysregulation and they may also demonstrate:

- Increased personal strength: Young people who experience PTG often report feeling stronger and more resilient. They may feel more confident in their ability to handle challenges and to overcome adversity. They may also take more risks.
- New possibilities: PTG can open up new possibilities for young people. They may develop new interests and talents, and they may find new ways to connect with others. They may be impatient with others who cannot see the vision they imagine.
- Deeper appreciation for life: PTG can lead to a deeper appreciation for life. Young people may feel more grateful for the good things in their lives, and they may be more likely to focus on the positive. Sometimes this positive thinking is fleeting, and sometimes it is long lasting (Calhoun & Tedeschi, 2013).

From these characteristics emerge three questions for youth serving professionals:

- How can youth professionals facilitate youth opportunities to take risks safely? (Ginwright, 2017)
- How can youth-serving professionals help youth bravely communicate their vision for a better world?
- How can youth-serving professionals help youth reframe, reflect, and restore when gratitude is hard to come by?

How Can Youth-Serving Professionals Create the Conditions for PTG

In these three questions, there is one broad call to action: Youth-serving professionals can play a vital role in creating the conditions which foster PTG in young people. By providing a safe and supportive environment and offering meaningful opportunities for purpose and connection with others, youth-serving professionals can help young people to heal from trauma, create the conditions for communities of care, and promote transformative growth.

To get a better idea of some specific things youth-serving professionals can do to create the conditions for PTG, we asked young people for their input. Their ideas will illustrate the power of PTG, and the role youth-

86 M. MEYER

serving professionals can play in helping create the conditions for growth and transformation.

Quotes below are from interviews with youth from ASAPconnect's BOLD youth program and the author's experience conducting site visits at expanded learning programs in California. Offered for consideration below are youth perspectives on how adults can best support their growth and development:

- Creating a Safe and Supportive Environment:
  It is important to be able to accommodate people with different sorts of needs for different environments. For example, I experience difficulties in environments with distracting noises, colors, and other elements. (QA, 14)
  I like afterschool, and home-cooked lunch and recess with my friends. It feels like at home here. (MA, 7)
- Offering opportunities for Connection:
  Learning how to talk to each other and work together, these are the things that matter. If you can connect with other people like that, you are winning at life. (XN, 17)
  I like working with my kindergarten buddy because we get to know every grade level here and that feels more like a family. (DG, 12). What I love about my school is the library, because every time I go there, Ms. G has new books for me, and she always remembers what I like to read. (AE, 8)
  The [virtual statewide] youth advisory committee on mental health was different than I expected, they actually wanted to know our opinions, and I had more in common that I thought I would with the other kids, even the ones who were already in high school. (QA, 14)
- Promoting Self-Efficacy:
  At my school, we get to teach our younger learning buddies, and we also get to lead their recess games doing Playworks coaching. Sometimes the kids can really be annoying, they don't always listen, but then that helps me act better for my teachers. I don't want them to get so tired like I do, these kids tire me out! (AJ, 12)
- Helping Young People Find Meaning:
  At XXX school, we don't make fun of people for their mistakes, our teacher, MS. A has a mistake jar and every time she makes a mistake we cheer because that gets us closer to a pizza party.

So we learn to celebrate mistakes and that means we have less to worry about. (LB, 13)

Circles helped me be able to say things that I wouldn't have ever expected to say, because usually our adults at school just don't listen. But this was different. I could use my voice for the first time, and then I saw how it made a difference (YB, 16)

These perspectives, demonstrated by the inherent understanding and wisdom present in our youth, can help us better understand how to create conditions in which youth can thrive. The recommendations underscore the importance of incorporating youth voice and leadership in any school transformation efforts. The four key recommendations shared are:

1. Provide a Safe and Supportive Environment: One of the most important things youth-serving professionals can do is to provide a safe and supportive environment. This means creating a space where young people feel comfortable sharing their experiences and where they know they will be accepted and supported. It includes attending to the physical, emotional, and cultural quality of the environment.

2. Offer Equitable Opportunities for Connection: Young people who have experienced trauma often feel isolated and alone. Youth-serving professionals can help young people to connect with others by providing opportunities for them to participate in group activities, to connect with mentors, and to build relationships with caring adults. Cultivating cultural humility, respect, and curiosity, inviting youth collaboration, and maintaining awareness of potential biases, youth serving professionals can ensure that these opportunities are broadly offered and accessed.

3. Promote Self-Efficacy: Young people who experience trauma often feel powerless and helpless. Youth-serving professionals can help young people to develop a sense of self-efficacy by providing them with opportunities to succeed and by helping them to set and achieve goals. This means allowing youth space to make mistakes and take risks, while remaining a reliable resource and support if those risks and mistakes become unmanageable for the young person (Calhoun & Tedeschi, 2013).

4. Help Young People to Find Meaning: Young people who experience trauma often struggle to find meaning in their lives. Youth-serving professionals can help young people to find meaning by providing them with opportunities to reflect on their experiences and by helping them to connect their stories to a larger purpose.

Opportunities for meaningful interaction with adults representing diverse lived experiences and viewpoints, providing access to decision-makers in their communities, and lawmakers can ignite purpose and possibilities for youth that help them extend their thinking beyond current challenges or conditions (Calhoun & Tedeschi, 2013).

PTG in CA's System of Support for Expanded Learning

Implementing these recommendations, collaboration, alignment, and coherent systems of support can be most effectively established when centered around student needs. In order to find out if California's PK–2 educational leaders are ready to support this need, I sent out surveys to fifty educational leaders working in schools, community-based programs, County Offices of Education, and the California Department of Education. Fifty surveys were sent out, 25 were returned. Before addressing the surveys, it is important to consider the context within which the respondents are working.

California's schools are undergoing a vast transformation, supported by immense injections of funding and increased calls for collaboration and establishing authentic partnerships. The prevalence of state-wide trauma inherent in the struggles of wildfires, floods, and vastness of the state predates the idea that our state's leaders are no strangers to trauma, and yet the very culture of the Golden State signifies resilience. This study seeks to emerge as an understanding of how an orientation towards growth and positive development could change the results of our education system.

California is not the only state suffering alarming rates of Adverse Childhood Experiences (ACEs), but its diverse population, coupled with broad geographic and vast economic diversity, offers several opportunities for reflection and investigation. Despite billions of dollars of Title IV funding, the wounds represented in ACE's data show only very weak signals of healing.

Inherent in the idea of PTG is the potential for transformation. California's leaders are currently called to transform their schools, and in the process may find they must transform themselves. To effectively serve all students inclusively, educators should look deeply at a system that is built to get the results it has achieved. California Assessment data from 2022 shows us that:

1. The percentage of students who met or exceeded the proficient level on the CAASPP English Language Arts test was 36%, which is a decrease from the 2021 percentage of 38%.

2. The percentage of students who met or exceeded the proficient level on the CAASPP mathematics test was 34%, which is also a decrease from the 2021 percentage of 36%.
3. The achievement gap between white students and students of color remained relatively unchanged in 2022. White students were more likely to meet or exceed the proficient level on both the CAASPP English Language Arts and mathematics tests than students of color.
4. The achievement gap between students from high-income families and students from low-income families also remained relatively unchanged in 2022. Students from high-income families were more likely to meet or exceed the proficient level on both the CAASPP English Language Arts and mathematics tests than students from low-income families (California Department of Education, 2022).

Since the beginning of national assessment data tracking, these results have marginally shifted, with the only significant increase occurring for any student groups occurring when significant litigation required it, as in the case of *Mendez vs. Westminster* (1947).

Compounding this complex reality, teachers are experiencing the long-term effects of their own ACEs. A 2016 study cited by the CDE found 61% of teachers in California reported at least one ACE. The study found that teachers who reported ACEs were also more likely to experience burnout, depression, and anxiety (CDE, 2018).

This report highlights some of the strategies currently in place to address the issue of ACEs, raise achievement levels, and avoid teacher burnout in California's schools. These include:

- Increasing awareness of ACEs among teachers and administrators.
- Providing high dosage tutoring for students and professional development for staff.
- Providing training on how to identify and support students who have experienced ACEs.
- Providing resources and support services for teachers who have experienced ACEs.
- Creating a more supportive and healthy work environment for teachers.
- Facilitating home visits and family support by partnering with social services.

90   M. MEYER

While these recommendations hold potential, implementing them requires considerable coordination, collaboration, and focus. Successful implementation of these recommendations will require a workforce of trauma counselors, trained tutors, and effective trainers, placing a strain on educator and school leader capacity. The reality of stretched capacities among educational institutions, community-based organizations, and technical assistance providers poses significant challenges in fully realizing these recommendations.

Amidst these challenges, a potentially simpler yet transformative solution emerges—rather than addressing only what we are doing, looking more closely at how we, as educators and leaders, are being.

In an effort to prevent burnout and promote PTG rather than PTSD, we can grow our awareness of how PTG is represented in our system and reflect on these implications. The surveys and study referenced earlier in this chapter emerged a new understanding of the prevalence of PTG among California's System of Support for Expanded Learning and is one example of this kind of systemic reflection in action. By calling out the positive indicators of growth and transformation, we may find ourselves oriented with more hope towards the future. Without hope, youth workers cannot give youth the space they need to imagine a future beyond our wildest dreams, one they are due to inherit.

Figures 5.1 shows the percentage of responses to 21 questions designed to establish the prevalence of PTG in California's PK–12 education system leaders. From the survey data, it is clear to see a high prevalence of PTG across all questions, barring the last two ("I developed a new plan" and "I developed new interests").

As seen in Figures 5.1 and 5.2, among survey respondents, 80% or more self-reported high levels of PTG in at least two of the five domains of PTG: faith/ trust in oneself, and compassion for others. The two qualities: com-

Figure 5.1

Prevalence in System Leaders

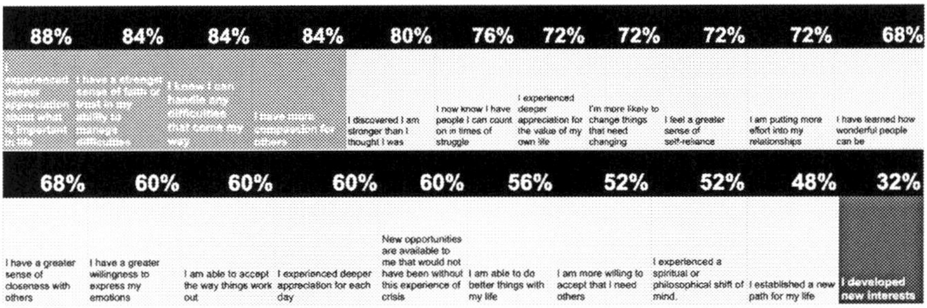

passion and confidence are nice-to-have qualities for leaders of any kind; for state, regional, and county-wide leaders in education, during a time of exceptional volatility and potential for transformation, these qualities are essential. On the other end of the spectrum of responses, the lowest rated indicators of PTG represented in the data were in the domain of PTG related to developing new interests or finding a new purpose. This aligns with the lived experiences expressed in the sample. When asked to check which lived experiences best reflected their own self-perception, 90% of respondents stated, "I have a sense of purpose that guides my decision-making" and "I chose a career in education so that I could make a difference."

Prior to the survey, respondents had a preexisting strong commitment to a path for their lives and interests to support that path, so it follows that this would be the lowest rated question in the inventory. This data suggests that, with a foundational purpose, PTG may be evident in a balance of confidence and compassion; two characteristics to seek out in youth serving professionals. These qualities are also worth cultivating in our classrooms, boardrooms, and dining rooms, and if an orientation towards growth and transformation can encourage this, then it is worth considering.

Survey respondents were also asked to think about what kinds of external conditions affect their decisions as a leader. Their responses indicated that ACEs and systemic bias are on California's P–12 leaders' minds when making decisions. This shows education leaders in California may be aware of the issues which can lead to negative student outcomes. Adding to recognition and awareness of PTG combined with the confidence to act with compassion may prove to be transformational.

PTG as a Lens Through Which to Envision a Transformation for Youth Programs

Understanding the coexistence of PTG and PTSD is essential when investigating post-traumatic growth. PTG Researchers Calhoun and

Figure 5.2

ACEs and Systemic Bias on Leaders

80% of respondents chose 4 or 5 out of 5 when asked	**76%** of respondents chose 4 or 5 out of 5 when asked	**56%** of respondents chose 4 or 5 out of 5 when asked
To what degree do **Adverse Childhood Experiences** affect your decision-making as an educational leader?	To what degree does the consideration of **systemic bias** affect your decision-making as an educational leader?	To what degree does **climate change** affect your decision-making as an educational leader?

92 M. MEYER

Tedeschi, who have studied PTG in combat veterans for decades, have several recommendations for helping trauma survivors to orient more toward their PTG and shift one's orientation when PTSD takes over. One such recommendation most relevant to youth serving professionals is what Calhoun and Tedeschi call the "expert companion" (Calhoun & Tedeschi, 2013).

Despite the name, the requirements for being an expert companion are quite simple: one must be an expert at simply being there for their friend, loved one, client, constituent or community member who is recovering from a personal crisis or trauma. Holding space for a survivor's pain, confusion, discomfort, and self-doubt, and asking questions can bring awareness back to one's purpose, faith, or source of strength. The expert companion can help a trauma survivor through the pain of PTSD to a condition more indicative of PTG. Being an expert companion does not mean denying or refuting the experience of trauma, or even the potential negative effects the survivor may be experiencing. Expert companionship means sitting with the survivor, letting them know they are not alone, and reminding them of their purpose. In some cases, it may also mean staging interventions that can be lifesaving and persevering for the long-term recovery process that may ensue.

Shifting from a deficit-based approach to a strengths-based approach of creating generative conditions offers the potential for transforming the discourse surrounding youth and community development work. Rather than addressing or responding to trauma, we can create conditions for growth that help youth and the adults who provide programming in their communities to connect to their purpose, strengths, and each other with the goal of sustaining resilient communities that are growing through trauma and creating new possibilities.

PTG is a crucial element foundational to visualizing and creating a world fit for our children to inherit. One way to create these conditions is by cultivating networks of expert companions who can hold space and manage the creative tension of PTG and envision potential that may be hidden in the shadows created by the negative effects of trauma (Silver & Updegraff, 2013).

CONCLUSION

Looking Towards Growth and Transformation

PTG is a positive psychological change which can occur as a result of struggling with significant life challenges and coming through them with new perspectives. It is characterized by:

- increased personal strength,
- new possibilities,
- stronger ties to community,
- a sense of purpose, and
- deeper appreciation for life.

To support the development of these characteristics, youth serving professionals can play the role of "expert companion" by holding space for the growth and development that occurs simultaneously with struggle while also providing resources and support which can mitigate any negative effects of conditions the youth or youth serving professionals may otherwise have no ability to control.

To promote their growth and transformation, youth need generative leaders who can create conditions which provide fertile foundations for positive development. With opportunities to expand self-awareness, make meaning out of their experiences, and develop confidence in themselves and their community, youth can build resilience and hope for the future. With these characteristics, strong identity, increased achievement, goal-setting and steady career-development follow naturally. Youth-serving professionals can play a vital role in creating the conditions that foster PTG in young people.

By providing a safe and supportive environment, by offering opportunities for young people to connect with others, and creating opportunities for meaningful engagement, generative leaders in youth-serving organizations can help young people to heal from trauma and to experience positive growth. As expert companions, youth serving professionals can hold space for that growth from a strengths-based orientation and support the next generation to uncover the inner resources that can sustain families and communities into an uncertain future.

REFERENCES

Calhoun, L. G., & Tedeschi, R. G. (2013). *Transformed by trauma: The power of positive change.* Oxford University Press.

California Department of Education. (2022, March 28). *CAASPP Test Results—CAASPP Reporting.* https://www.cde.ca.gov/ta/tg/ca/caaspp_reporting.asp

California Department of Education. (2018). *Adverse childhood experiences: A call to action for California.* https://www.cde.ca.gov/ls/ex/fundingop.asp

Ginwright, S. (2017). *The four pivots: A framework for social change.* AK Press.

Jussim, L., & Harber, K. D. (2005). Teacher expectations and student achievement: A meta-analytic review. *Psychological Bulletin, 131*(2), 459–499. https://doi.org/10.1207/s15327957pspr0902_3

94 M. MEYER

Psychiatry.org. (2023). *What is post-traumatic stress disorder (PTSD)?* Psychiatry.org. Retrieved April 9, 2023, from https://www.psychiatry.org/patients-families/ptsd/what-is-ptsd

Rosenthal, R., & Jacobson, L. (1968). *Pygmalion in the classroom: Teacher expectation and pupils' intellectual development.* Holt, Rinehart and Winston.

Silver, R. C., & Updegraff, J. A. (2013). *Searching for and finding meaning following personal and collective traumas.* American Psychological Association.

Vance, F. (2019). *The role of spirituality in the lived experiences of Black women who have experienced intimate partner violence: A phenomenological study* [Doctoral dissertation, University of Southern California]. ProQuest Dissertations & Theses Global. (13912467)

CHAPTER 6

HIGHER EDUCATION AND YOUTH WORK
Opportunities for Expanding the Field

Nancy L. Deutsch and Melissa K. Levy

INTRODUCTION

Skillfully and authentically executed youth work—wherever youth can be found—is one of our most critical means for countering harm, resolving conflicts, and catalyzing meaningful societal change. Through the support and development of our nation's most valuable resource, our youth, youth workers are fostering current and future leaders and innovators around climate change, racial justice and reconciliation, and other global threats which affect human well-being. Despite the importance of youth work in shaping the social and economic fabric of our country, youth workers are notoriously and frequently undervalued and inadequately compensated. This issue extends from childcare workers to out-of-school time (OST) program staff, with the people who care for and cultivate the talent of young people often relegated to the margins of the workforce. Furthermore, it is not just the workforce that tends to marginalize youth work. Institutions of higher education, despite their marketing efforts to educate the next generation of leaders and innovators, typically do not prioritize youth work within their curricula. Despite growing pressure on colleges and universities to meet the needs of the work force more directly, youth work is seldom a focus in higher education.

Built for More: The Role of Out-of-School Time in Preparing Youth for the Future of Work,
pp. 95–120
Copyright © 2024 by Information Age Publishing
www.infoagepub.com
All rights of reproduction in any form reserved.

Within this chapter, we present our perspective on the current status of youth work and our thoughts about, and experiences with, embracing youth work in higher education. Throughout our discussion, we highlight underlying theories that inform the field of youth development and underscore the essential skills and competencies needed for successful youth work. We propose that institutions of higher education can support and advance the shared aims of youth work and colleges/universities by infusing youth work principles into a variety of disciplines and youth-related employment sectors. This approach would serve to broaden the impact of youth work and enhance the youth development workforce's reach. By bringing an expanded view of youth workers to higher education, we can shepherd youth development principles into all spaces where young people learn and grow. This, in turn, would develop and build a generation of college students—many of whom keenly relate to youth because of their own status as youth—who see working with and advocating on behalf of youth as part of their purpose.

What Is Youth Work?

What constitutes youth work is somewhat contested and has been interpreted in varying ways. According to Dana Fusco (2016), a prominent youth work scholar, youth work is "an informal education strategy." This definition aligns with the characterization provided by Hurley and Treacy (1993) as "the social education of young people in an informal context" (Fusco, 2016, p. 1). For Fusco, part of the aim of this social and informal education is to empower and support youth to become changemakers who themselves work towards a more equitable and just world. In a similar vein, Howard Sercombe (2015), echoes this definition, writing:

> Youth work is characterized by its attempt to restore a sense of agency for young people and to work with them within their social context to negotiate their ambiguous and often prejudiced economic and political status ... sometimes a product of the initiative of young people themselves, sometimes an intervention in order to mitigate social damage or distress. (p. 25)

In recent years, the term "youth work" has often been replaced in our parlance by variations of "youth development," a phrase that reflects psychologists' research and theoretical conceptions of adolescence. The youth development frame—specifically Positive Youth Development (PYD), which will be further discussed below—gives youth work the aim of supporting young people to thrive by building the strengths and assets present in themselves and their environments. This frame has been criticized, however, for providing "little contextualization for the sociopolitical and economic factors that play a role in family, school, and community wellbeing" (Fusco, 2016, p. 41) and for ignoring the impact of power and privilege on youth outcomes (Gonzalez et al., 2020). Fusco argues that the youth development frame's scant attention to sociological factors and elements leads to a focus on individuals within micro-contexts without providing a "methodology for community action and activism" (p. 41).

Conversely, stances predicated on the need to counter oppressive systems position youth work's focus on models and actions aiming for systemic change. This tension between theoretical models of PYD and action-oriented approaches to youth work is not surprising, given PYD's origins. Whereas field-based approaches to positive youth development arose from practitioners working in programs with young people, its academic development within psychology was a reaction to the traditional deficit-based view of adolescents. These disciplinary roots have shaped the individual, albeit ecological, lens that PYD brings to youth work. Nevertheless, PYD and systemic change efforts need not be mutually exclusive; scholars and practitioners committed to both paradigms have married the values inherent in each approach in their recommendations for how to support youth thriving (e.g., Aspen Institute, 2019; Gonzalez et al., 2020). Some of these combined approaches will be discussed in the section below on grounding developmental frames of youth work.

The potential for youth work to take place in myriad places and ways is evident. Yet the same diversity that allows for youth development to occur in different forms and formats also poses a barrier to youth work being seen as a "unified profession" (Borden et al., 2020, p. 270). Indeed, Lynne Borden and colleagues (2020) found a "huge variability across the nature, setting, and participants in youth programming ... [leading to a lack of] recognition as an integrated field" (p. 270). Typically, we tend to think of youth work as taking place in OST programs. Youth development practices do tend to diverge from the traditional banking model of schooling, whereby children are viewed as empty vessels in which to pour knowledge (Freire, 1970). Nevertheless, it is essential to acknowledge that youth work can also take place within K–12 spaces, facilitated by teachers and other school personnel playing a vital role in this regard. In line with this observation, some scholars and practitioners have advocated for an expansion of the definition of youth work. They point out that in addition to youth development organizations, youth work can and does exist within the domains of education, social services, healthcare, mental health services, as well as sports and recreation, civic institutions such as museums and libraries, faith-based organizations, and even some businesses (Aspen Institute, 2019; Sercombe, 2015).

Broadening the definition of what happens in these varied settings as youth work not only expands the definition of youth worker, but it changes our expectations about where young people should be able to access the opportunities and supportive relationships that promote positive development (Aspen Institute, 2019). Recognizing the importance of every young person having access to a web of supportive adults (Varga & Zaff, 2018), this expansion of youth work brings more adults into the fold as part of youth's support systems. These adults offer a wide range of types of social support that are critical for the well-being and thriving of young people.

The wide array of locations that are potential settings for youth development, along with the diversity of professions and academic disciplines that could be informed by youth work principles, extends the potential reach and impact of youth development as a field. Additionally, it broadens the potential power and collective influence of youth workers across sectors, widening the network of those who advocate on behalf of both youth and youth workers. Yet, in the United States, we have traditionally limited our focused attention on youth work and youth development to out-of-school time programming, especially the after-school space. Unfortunately, due to our nation's lamentable lack of regard for careers working with youth, this narrow focus subsequently lessens the influence of youth work principles in other spaces and through other mechanisms that reach youth.

Among the challenges to the aim of advancing youth work is the lack of value we place on youth work and the lack of support we provide for youth workers (Borden et al., 2020). Political analyst and journalist Ezra Klein (2023) reflected what those of us in fields related to youth know from our own experiences when he stated:

> Anything and everything with children [is the most undervalued work in the U.S.]. Being a social worker who works with children, being a teacher, being somebody who is a guardian in the foster care system, given how important that work is, it is badly compensated.... We just really undervalue things with children. We talk about how the children are our future. And we treat them, in many ways, like an afterthought. And we certainly treat the people who are in charge of helping them as an afterthought. (Klein, 2023)

As a result of this low regard, students may hesitate to pursue youth work as a career. This disconnect between the importance of adults who work with children and youth and our valuing of them highlights the urgent need for a shift in societal perception of and support for those dedicated to the welfare and development of young people.

The pursuit of youth work by students in higher education is limited by various factors over which higher education has different degrees of control and influence. College enrollment, in general, has declined over the past decade. Despite some post-pandemic increases in enrollment in 2022, fewer students overall are pursuing higher education (National Student Clearinghouse Research Center, 2019, 2023). Financial considerations can prevent both (1) undergraduate college students from pursuing youth work, and (2) already minted youth workers from elevating their practice through relevant coursework at institutions of higher education. Increased college costs may contribute to college students and their families desiring career pathways that are more likely to yield salaries that facilitate paying off student loans. Likewise, the low pay associated with youth work does not provide excess resources for financing expensive college classes.

When we constrain our thinking about our target audience to only those working with youth after school, we squander the opportunity to attract people who care deeply about youth and other social issues. Within higher education settings, disciplinary siloes tend to be robust and structure the experiences of students. If we are to infuse youth work principles more broadly across the sectors that serve young people, including formal educational settings, out-of-school settings, health and human services, and policy and politics, higher education professionals must think more creatively about how, what, and to whom we teach.

Expanding the scope of the intended audience, encompassing those whom we wish to have learn about the principles that underlie youth work, will extend our influence beyond the micro-level of youth work (field based) to the macro-level (systemic). To achieve this, we must both (1) attract those potential students whose passions are at the macro-level, and (2) educate those individuals drawn to "hands-on" youth interaction about the larger contexts. In addition, both populations of students need to understand the value and influence of the other domain on youth to maximize the reach of youth work principles.

By building and fostering connections between students who are planning to work across the different domains and levels of young people's lives, we are better equipping them to disseminate youth work principles throughout the varied ecosystems of youth's developmental experiences. While the status of youth work as a profession and as a field, closely aligned with inadequate financial compensation, remains a factor to contend with, broadening the reach of youth work concepts into non-traditional realms can lessen the constraints prompted by traditional hierarchies in which K–12 schooling trumps out-of-school time and most collegiate disciplines trump youth studies and education. In this model, students who may be deterred by status and pay can still pursue youth work education as part of their training in disciplines associated with higher status and pay than education and youth work.

What Makes for Effective Youth Work: Guiding Frameworks

The multiple frameworks that guide approaches to youth work share an assets-based lens that centers the strengths of young people and the role of supportive environments and relationships in fostering opportunities for young people to thrive. Higher education has a crucial role to play in making these frames, and the concepts that underlie them, common knowledge across disciplines that intersect with youth work. Below, we synthesize key tenets of some of the major frameworks, identifying shared values and concepts that should inform the curriculum in youth-related higher education fields. We separate these frames into two categories: frames focusing on the development of individuals and frames focusing on the relationships and contexts that support youth. We close the section with a discussion of the role of young people themselves within these frames. While this review is not comprehensive, it aims to highlight and underscore key concepts that are necessary for understanding the competencies and skills that higher education should seek to foster in students who want to work with young people.

Before delving into the frames guiding youth development, it is important to define what we mean by the term "youth." "Youth" is often used somewhat synonymously and interchangeably with "adolescents." However, the United Nations (n.d.) defines youth more specifically as those between the ages of 15–24, whereas Merriam-Webster Dictionary (n.d.) defines youth as the time between childhood and adulthood (i.e., adolescence). Adolescence, in itself, is a developmental period that is influenced by biological, physiological, and social factors. There is evidence that the human brain experiences a second "critical window" of rapid change and development during the adolescent years, roughly spanning ages 10 to 25 (National Academies of Sciences, Engineering, and Medicine, 2019). The window of what American society has considered adolescence has expanded and shifted as we have learned more about the neurological changes that occur in the brain during this period of life. In addition, as the average age of onset of puberty has declined, our definition of the onset of adolescence has similarly become younger. At the same time, social forces in the industrialized west have contributed to the longer time span of adolescence. The historical increase in the number of young people attending college as well as changes in the workforce and economic sector, which have tended to increase the years in which an individual is dependent on their family of origin, has lengthened adolescence into what has been thought of as the early adult years.

Other social forces, such as digital technology and social media, have also influenced who sees themselves, and who society sees, as adolescents.

Consequently, when we think about youth work and youth development, it is imperative to acknowledge who is encompassed by the term "youth" and how that is defined by a combination of physical and social influences. This understanding helps us appreciate the complexity of working with young individuals and the need for adaptable and multifaceted approaches within youth-serving sectors.

Developmental Frames

Among the well-known frames in the field of youth development are variations of the Positive Youth Development (PYD) model (Benson et al., 2006). Indeed, PYD has become shorthand for approaches that are based on a strengths-based view of youth. Two prominent models have been particularly prevalent in the literature, the 5 C's model (Geldhof et al., 2015) and the Developmental Assets Framework (Benson et al., 2011). While these models are different in their details, they share an emphasis on the dynamic and contextual nature of youth development, the importance of interactions between individuals and their environments, and the role of adolescents in contributing to their own developmental pathways (Lerner et al., 2011). Measures exist for both frames to assess the presence of the associated constructs and the relationship between those constructs and other outcomes.

The 5 C's model of PYD was empirically developed and examined in research conducted with participants of a popular, national youth development program: 4-H (Bowers et al., 2015). The 5 C's model defines adolescent thriving as characterized by five areas of outcomes: Confidence, Competence, Character, Caring, and Connection. Youth are most likely to develop in these five areas when the resources available in their environments provide opportunities for them to demonstrate and build on their strengths, while also offering support for their individual needs. The presence of these five C's not only promotes individual youth thriving but leads to a sixth C: youth Contribution to their communities (Geldhof et al., 2015).

The 5 C's model was further expanded by Gonzalez and colleagues (2020) to include a 7th C: Critical Consciousness. This critical positive youth development model (CPYD) situates youth within systems of oppression, reflecting theories such as Coll's integrative model of child development (Coll et al., 1996), which examine the role of discrimination, segregation, racism, and other forms of oppression in shaping youth experiences. Importantly, such models also center on the role of adaptive culture in shaping competencies and coping processes for young people who have to navigate life within oppressive systems. Reflecting these legacies, Gonzalez and colleagues (2020) center critical consciousness as a core competency that supports young people in not only recognizing and navigating, but challenging, oppressive systems. In CPYD, the presence of the 5 C's supports the development of critical reflection and political efficacy. These in turn promote critical action, which leads to contribution. CPYD requires the adults who work with young people to think in a systems way about youth development and to themselves engage in, and model, critical reflection, and action (Gonzalez et al., 2020).

The *Developmental Assets Framework,* developed by researchers at the Search Institute (Benson et al., 2004; Benson et al., 2011) is founded on the idea that "healthy development" requires the presence of "nutrients" (assets) that serve to both promote positive outcomes and prevent risk. Drawing from concepts such as resilience and empirical research from developmental psychology, the developmental assets frame emphasizes the importance of the contexts of young people's lives. The model identifies a total of 40 assets, divided into two categories: 20 external assets (residing in a youth's environments) and 20 internal assets (residing within a youth).

The external assets are grouped into four categories:

1. Support: Emphasizing the importance of having caring adults, positive role models, and a support system.
2. Empowerment: Highlighting the need for young people to be given opportunities to contribute and take on leadership roles.
3. Boundaries and Expectations: Focusing on the establishment of clear rules and consistent expectations, which provide structure and guidance.
4. Constructive Use of Time: Recognizing the value of young people being engaged in activities that are both enjoyable and enriching.

The internal assets are grouped into four categories as well:

1. Commitment to Learning: Emphasizing the importance of educational engagement and a desire to achieve.
2. Positive Values: Focusing on the development of moral and ethical principles.
3. Social Competencies: Highlighting the need for interpersonal skills and a capacity to build positive relationships.
4. Positive Identity: Centering on self-esteem and a sense of purpose and identity.

The authors of this framework assert that these general categories of assets are universal; however, they acknowledge that culture and context play a significant role in how assets are expressed. Thus, there is no one-size-fits-all approach to ensure the presence of these assets; how assets are promoted will differ across communities (Benson et al., 2006).

In 2022, the University of Virginia's Youth-Nex Center convened a national group of researchers and practitioners to develop a synthesizing framework for positive youth development. The aim of this project was to review the existing literature for commonalities in content to create a shared language for describing a "thriving adolescent." The outcome of this effort is the Portrait of a Thriving Youth (Youth-Nex, 2023) which provides "a collective and broadly understood vision of what thriving youth might be and do, as individuals and as part of their communities" (Youth-Nex, 2023, p. 4). The Portrait defines six domains of adolescent learning and development grounded in the science of adolescence:

1. Health (Physical & Mental): establishing healthy physical behaviors and developing psychological and social well-being.
2. Cognition: Acquiring the skills, knowledge, and abilities to achieve goals and objectives.
3. Identity: Exploring identities and figuring out who they are now and who they want to be.
4. Meaning & Purpose: Exploring how to meaningfully connect with and contribute to the world around them.
5. Emotion: Identifying emotions and how to manage them in positive ways.
6. Social: Developing trusting and reliable relationships and navigating diverse social contexts.

Each domain contains a set of knowledge, skills, and competencies needed for positive development in that domain. The intent is to ensure that every youth has access to settings that provide opportunities to develop knowledge, skills, and competencies within each domain. The Portrait is meant to support practitioners, policymakers, and researchers across youth-serving sectors as they make decisions related to resources and support for youth.

Contexts and Relationships

In addition to the developmental science-based frames described above, it is essential to acknowledge the importance of environments. We now turn our attention to frames which focus on environments, specifically, the characteristics of developmentally supportive relationships and contexts. These frames are important for youth workers to understand, as they describe conditions that adults can nurture and actions they can take in their own relationships with youth to promote positive development.

With the rise of the positive youth development frame informing both practice and research, the National Research Council (NRC, 2002) was charged with conducting a review of literature on community-based programs and interventions. The objective was to begin to inform and develop a common framework for understanding the conditions that support youth development. The committee included in their review the empirical and theoretical literature on youth programs and adolescent development as well as expertise from field-based practitioners. Through this process, the NRC identified eight features of settings that support positive youth development:

1. Physical and Psychological Safety: Ensuring that young people feel secure and protected in their environment.
2. Appropriate Structure: Providing a level of organization and routine that allows for predictability and stability.
3. Supportive Relationships: Fostering connections with caring and trustworthy adults.
4. Opportunities to Belong: Creating a sense of inclusion and community where young individuals feel like they belong.
5. Positive Social Norms: Encouraging behaviors and attitudes that promote pro-social values and respect.
6. Support for Efficacy and Mattering: Helping young people believe in their own abilities and that they are valued by others.
7. Opportunities for Skill Building: Offering chances for young individuals to acquire and develop skills that are relevant and valuable.
8. Integration of Family, School, and Community Efforts: Coordinating efforts across these various spheres to create a comprehensive support network for youth.

These eight features continue to guide much of the field of youth development, and their influence can be seen in the key competencies of youth workers, discussed below. Understanding and applying these principles can significantly contribute to the creation of supportive environments and relationships that nurture positive youth development.

Whereas the presence of supportive relationships is one feature of supportive environments noted by the NRC (2002), several models exist which expand on the key features of supportive youth-adult relationships themselves. The presence of a network of supportive relationships, termed a *web of support*, can serve both promotive and protective functions for youth (Varga & Zaff, 2018). However, it is not merely the presence of adults that matters; those adults must interact with youth in ways that promote positive development.

The Search Institute's *Developmental Relationships* frame (Scales et al., 2022) focuses on what adults *do* in relationships with youth that contributes to strong, supportive relationships and positive youth outcomes. According to the model, developmentally supportive relationships are comprised of five key elements:

1. Expressing Care: Demonstrating genuine concern and empathy for the well-being of youth.
2. Challenging Growth: Encouraging and motivating young people to strive for personal growth and development.
3. Providing Support: Offering practical assistance and guidance when needed.
4. Sharing Power: Involving young individuals in decision-making processes and giving them a sense of agency.
5. Expanding Possibilities: Helping young people explore new opportunities and envision a broader range of possibilities for their future (Search Institute, n.d.).

A specific type of youth-adult relationship, *youth-adult partnerships* (YAPs), wherein youth and adults work together on community change via relationships that are characterized by mutuality and shared decision making (Camino, 2000), has gained traction in the last two decades in community organizations (Zeldin et al., 2005). While YAPs have also been recommended for use in schools (Mitra, 2009), they are not as well established, and may encounter greater resistance in formal educational settings. Relationships founded on principles of mutuality and care can foster settings wherein youth and adults trust and respect each other and, thereby, where youth feel a sense of belonging and purpose. It is critical that individuals preparing for careers in youth work understand the components of developmental relationships and the types of actions that support such relationships.

Critical Understandings of Settings and Systems

Yet, we know that neither developmental assets nor developmental relationships are distributed equitably across youth. For all young people, including but not exclusively those who have been historically and/or structurally marginalized, supportive relationships and contexts should not merely teach how to navigate oppressive structures but should engage youth in changing them. Frameworks such as Torie Weiston-Serdan's (2017) *Critical Mentoring* and Sean Ginwright's (2010, 2015) *Radical Healing*, as well as Gonzalez and colleagues (2020) CYPD, discussed above, emphasize the importance of providing young people with settings and relationships that actively address and dismantle systemic issues that impact their lives.

Weiston-Serdan (2017) contends that formal mentoring programs are too often rooted in mainstream approaches that focus on changing the individual rather than the systems that perpetuate the inequality. Weiston-Serdan argues for mentoring relationships that are culturally responsive, youth centric, and in which adults not only become institutional agents and opportunity brokers but also engage with youth directly in naming and dismantling oppressive structures.

Similarly, Ginwright (2010, 2015) notes that for social change to occur, there must be hope, but that communities and youth who have experienced structural oppression and marginalization must heal before they can hope. Thus, he argues, it is necessary for youth organizations and schools to become spaces wherein radical healing (Ginwright, 2010) builds the capacity of young people and promotes healing justice (Ginwright, 2015). Radical healing is not only restorative but also explicitly collective and political, which differentiates it from traditional approaches to social-emotional development that have grown common in both formal and informal educational settings. Spaces in which radical healing occurs prepare young people for engagement in social change, strengthening them to be active agents in their environments.

Youth's Agency in Their Own Development

The field of positive youth development has consistently emphasized the active role youth take in their own development (Benson et al., 2006; Lerner et al., 2011). In addition to the centering of youth within developmental theories, there is also increasing focus within youth work on the importance and power of youth voice. This can be seen in the growth of youth councils within local governments (Cushing & van Vliet, 2017), youth advisory boards within organizations (Roholt & Mueller, 2013), and Youth

Participatory Action Research (YPAR) as both a method of scholarship and a tool to promote positive development (Ozer, 2017).

Yet the charge to increase opportunities for young people to be active participants in their environments is not new; it is a long-standing and foundational tenet of youth work. In 1992, Roger Hart (1992) introduced a frame to help people visualize what different levels of participation in programs look like: the *ladder of participation*. The ladder presents eight levels at which youth might participate in programs or projects, ranging from manipulation and tokenism to being consulted, initiating projects, and sharing in the decision making with adults. This model has demonstrated staying power, even as its creator has reflected on its limitations (e.g., suggesting a stage-like development of youth's abilities to participate, basis in Western ideas of child development; Hart, 2008).

More recently, Wu and colleagues (2016) developed a rubric to assess authentic youth engagement in programs and settings. The rubric includes four dimensions, each comprised of a series of indicators:

1. Authentic Decision Making: Youth are involved in meaningful decisions related to programs and policies.
2. Natural Mentors: Adults intentionally support youth development through nurturing relationships.
3. Reciprocity: Youth and adults work together as equal partners.
4. Community Connectedness: Young people are actively engaged in their communities.

The inclusion of young people in decisions about the programs and policies that affect them has been argued to be not only beneficial for youth developmentally but also to lead to better decisions and services. Additionally, involving youth in decision making has the potential to benefit society as a whole by fostering civic engagement (Head, 2011; Zeldin et al., 2003). *Youth Participatory Action Research* (YPAR) brings this idea into our methods of research, engaging youth in the process of examining and reporting on the issues that impact them (Ozer, 2017).

WHAT COMPETENCIES DO YOUTH WORKERS NEED? FRAMEWORKS FOR PRACTICE

The frameworks presented above provide important background knowledge for youth workers. Translating those frameworks into key competencies and dispositions people need to be effective youth workers is critical. However, developing shared competency frameworks within the out-of-school sector has been challenging due to the diverse nature of the field, of the age groups served, and the various settings of service, among other factors (Starr et al., 2009; Vance, 2010). Despite these challenges, competency frameworks are important to guide standards of practice and professional development (Starr et al., 2009; Vance, 2010). In addition, a common set of competencies can serve to build a shared identity across sectors that advances the professionalization of the workforce (Starr et al., 2009; Vance 2010). Identifying shared competencies to guide education and training of those who are interested in a wide array of youth work is particularly important given the diverse backgrounds of youth workers and the lack of required credentials for youth work jobs (Vance, 2010). Competency frameworks also serve as guidance for the knowledge and skills that institutions of higher education should attend to in programs for students who want to work with and on behalf of youth.

Two prior reviews of youth worker competency frameworks have been conducted (Starr et al., 2009; Vance, 2010) which present syntheses and comparisons of the key concepts from 23 different frameworks (14 in one, 11 in the other, with 2 frameworks appearing in both reviews). These frameworks represent efforts from states, cities, federal agencies, youth development and advocacy programs, and professional development, research, and policy organizations. There are eight overarching areas that appear in the majority of frameworks reviewed across both studies. Notably, *knowledge about child and youth development*, *connections with families and communities*, and *professionalism* each appeared in all but two of the frameworks examined. Other common competencies across the frameworks in both reviews were *providing guidance*, *program management*, *supporting the physical health and safety of youth*, *cross-cultural competence*, and *curriculum* (Starr et al., 2009; Vance, 2010).

In addition, the competencies of *communication* (Vance, 2010) and *environment* (Starr et al., 2009) may reflect similar skills and overlap to some extent, as environmental competency appears to be defined as being able to foster supportive environments with and for youth, which could itself rest on a staff member's ability to communicate effectively with young people. Vance (2010) identified two additional competencies when only frameworks that focused on school age youth (versus also counting those with a focus on youth over 18) were included in the review: *cognitive*, and *social*. These competencies appear to be developmentally oriented, addressing the specific needs of school aged youth for support in these domains of development.

The Mott Foundation's *Core Competencies for Afterschool Educators* (CCAE) establishes a comprehensive set of skills that youth workers need to implement high-quality programming. Recognizing the diversity of backgrounds among youth workers, the Mott Foundation (2009) points out the importance of having such a set of competencies to guide professional development. The CCAE includes both a set of principles for professional development and reflection questions for decision makers about their own beliefs and programs. Each of the five competencies includes a series of indicators and observable behaviors for each indicator that can guide both the growth and assessment of youth workers.

1. Ability to relate to and work well with diverse children and youth: This competency emphasizes supporting positive relationships and promoting a sense of physical and emotional safety among young people.
2. Facilitating youth's learning of new knowledge and skills: Youth workers are expected to create a learner-centered environment and design activities that align with program goals.
3. Engaging respectfully with important adults in the youth's life: This competency highlights the importance of involving and collaborating with key adults who play a role in a young person's development.
4. Commitment to personal growth, development, and professionalism on the job: Youth workers are encouraged to continuously enhance their own skills, knowledge, and professionalism.
5. Implementing program policies and operations to meet program goals: This competency focuses on the ability to effectively carry out program policies and operations to achieve program objectives.

Additionally, the CCAE includes competencies tailored for supervisors to ensure leadership and effective oversight within youth programs.

More recently, the National Afterschool Association published its updated *Core Knowledge, Skills, and Competencies for Afterschool Professionals* (CKSC; National Afterschool Association, 2021). This revised framework incorporates new content to address diversity, equity, inclusion, and anti-racism. The current CKSC "describes the dispositions, knowledge, skills, and competencies individuals need to provide high-quality OST programming, support the learning and development of children and youth, and advance equity, particularly for those who have been historically excluded" (National Afterschool Association, 2021, p. 4). The 10 knowledge content areas of the framework include:

1. Child/youth growth and development;
2. Learning environments and curriculum;
3. Child/youth observation and assessment;

4. Relationships and interactions with children and youth;
5. Youth engagement, voice, and choice;
6. Equity and inclusion;
7. Family, school, and community relationships;
8. Safety and wellness;
9. Program planning and development, and;
10. Professional development and leadership.

Within each area, skills and competencies are grouped into identify, apply, and amplify, to reflect how practitioners can learn and demonstrate their competencies over time: by learning about the skills, by demonstrating them in practice, and by supporting the development of the skills in their colleagues.

The CKSC frame also includes a set of dispositions needed for effective youth work. These include dispositions such as being curious about how youth grow and learn, appreciating the role of families, schools, and communities in youth development, being self-reflective, valuing creativity, flexibility, valuing diversity, resilience, embracing continual learning, embracing self-care so as to be able to care for others. These competencies, and the description of the developmental pathways of the competencies, provide a useful blueprint for higher education programs to include as learning objectives for students in the vast array of fields that have relevance for and impact on youth.

Educating the Next Generation of Youth Workers and Youth Advocacy-Minded Adults

Throughout this chapter, we have encouraged institutions of higher education to think broadly about to whom the tenets of youth work are relevant. By thinking beyond the traditional direct-service model of youth work in out-of-school settings, colleges and universities can help build a future where professionals across multiple systems that impact youth share a commitment to and a frame for understanding the positive development of young people. Imagine a world where pediatricians, lawyers and police officers in the juvenile justice and family law systems, policymakers in departments of education, and community planners within city governments all understood and valued the core developmental assets of youth and were committed to fostering environments where youth needs and competencies were at the center. Below, we dis-

Higher Education and Youth Work   111

cuss the core sets of knowledge, skills, and dispositions that we believe institutions of higher education should include across the programs that serve students who may work with, on behalf of, and in areas that impact youth. We propose that by focusing on educating a cohort of youth-advocacy minded adults, we build the competencies of youth workers as well as a broader social environment that values, supports, and amplifies their work across systems.

There are multiple ways that institutions of higher education can offer educational opportunities for current and future youth workers and advocates for youth. Borden and colleagues (2020) suggest that the field should develop credentialing programs for youth work, and institutions of higher education are a natural place for such programs to reside. Credentialing programs could be directed at currently working youth development professionals as well as traditionally aged college students who might be interested in youth work in the future. In addition to specific credentialing programs, many of the core skills and sets of knowledge needed for effective youth work are broadly applicable across disciplines and could easily be incorporated into traditional college majors and courses.

Of course, traditionally aged college students are themselves youth. Thus, the frameworks presented above are not only background knowledge for the students in higher education. These frameworks can also guide colleges and universities in how they think about their own students. The Portrait of a Thriving Youth, therefore, can serve as a planning document for institutions of higher education in thinking about how they are providing opportunities and resources for students across the six domains of development. As we are educating students to work with and on behalf of young people, we need to also ensure that we are meeting their own developmental needs. Institutions of higher education are themselves communities in which young people are growing and developing. Yet we seldom think about student affairs professionals as youth workers. Taking this "meta" view—of college students as both still-developing youth and emerging youth workers and advocates—broadens how institutions of higher education approach our work.

Mirroring some of the frameworks discussed above, we outline the sets of knowledge, skills, and dispositions that we believe are key for successful youth work and advocacy. Some of these are content-specific and are best addressed via courses within specific disciplines (e.g., developmental psychology). However, many of these areas, especially the skills and dispositions, are broadly applicable to 21st century workforce demands, and could be infused across curriculum in a variety of disciplines and types of courses.

Skills and Dispositions

Self-understanding and awareness. In order to effectively work with young people, one must be self-aware and able to reflect on one's own position in the world. This includes an awareness of bias and power, an understanding of intersectional identities, and how one's own social position may shape relationships. A sense of confidence and competence in one's self and abilities is important, but so is humility and openness to others' experiences and opinions. Many people are drawn to youth work because of their core values and belief systems. Understanding how this shapes one's behaviors and actions is important; so is being adaptable and having a growth-mindset about one's skills and abilities. Although Americans tend to be socialized to prioritize and value independence, we believe that it is critical for people who work with youth to value and act in ways that promote interdependence. The evidence of the importance of webs of support for young people (Varga & Zaff, 2018) reinforces the idea that adults who appreciate the value of interconnectedness may be especially well-suited to fostering supportive environments for youth. Finally, given the high turn-over rates in youth-serving professions, and the increasing levels of mental health needs reported among youth (Murthy, 2021), it is imperative that people going into youth serving professions be well-versed in the importance of and techniques for self-care, or as we have heard it called, self-preservation. It is an old but true adage that one has to put on one's own oxygen mask first.

Social awareness and understanding. In addition to having a solid self-awareness, it is also necessary for those working with or on behalf of youth to have a strong set of social and *interpersonal* skills and dispositions. This begins but does not end with having a relational orientation and anchoring one's work in relationships. It also includes key social skills, such as collaboration, communication, and the ability to work across differences. The ability to foster trust with other people, a sense of authenticity and intentionality in one's work, and a deep respect for young people are additional dispositions needed by potential youth workers. Research on youth's relationships with youth workers and other important adults in their lives indicates that adults who successfully foster strong and trusting relationships with youth do so intentionally (Deutsch et al., 2020; Griffith & Johnson, 2019).

In addition to the skills and dispositions that help build solid interpersonal relationships, an understanding of social structures and of other people's identities and positionings within those systems are important. Understanding the role of structures and systems in social inequities is important for nurturing in youth not an ability to adapt to inequity, but the capacities to change inequitable systems. These competencies empower youth workers to be advocates for positive change in the lives of young people and the systems that affect them.

Knowledge

Developmental knowledge. Building a strong foundational knowledge of child and adolescent development is a universal area of agreement among the various frames identifying key competencies for youth workers. We see the developmental knowledge needed for youth work as falling into three areas: key theories of development, developmental stages and trajectories, and domains of development. Within key theories of development, students who are planning for careers working with or on behalf of youth would benefit from understanding socio-ecological developmental frames that emphasize the ways in which contexts influence and impact developmental trajectories and outcomes. The key tenets of positive youth development, noted earlier in the section on guiding frameworks, are also important for emphasizing not only the assets-based approach that youth work is grounded in, but also the key principles that have shaped the field. Finally, we think that a specific understanding of stage-environment fit (Eccles et al., 1997) and similar frames that emphasize the importance of alignment between developmental needs and environments can help youth workers apply their developmental knowledge to their practice more concretely. This is complemented by understanding the main developmental pathways of childhood, adolescence, and emerging adulthood. Knowing the ways in which core domains, including identity, social-emotional, cognitive, and physical development progress across these stages of growth is critical.

Contextual knowledge. Given the importance of the social environment to youth development, it is important that youth workers develop knowledge of both the micro and macro contexts in which the youth they will be working with are living. This means having knowledge of the local community, including its history and the cultures of community members. While institutions of higher education cannot predict all the local communities in which their students will eventually be working, educational institutions can habituate students' learning about the community in which one is living and develop students' skills in learning about, connecting with, and valuing local knowledge and histories. In addition, attuning students to the more macro forces shaping youths' lives, including policy and political systems, historical forces, and cultural beliefs and norms, sets future youth workers up to be able to engage with young people in meaningful ways to not only support individual development, but collective change.

THE YOUTH AND SOCIAL INNOVATION MAJOR

At the University of Virginia, we have pursued the aim we have outlined in this chapter—of disseminating youth work principles more broadly—through the creation and ongoing evolution of an undergraduate major at the School of Education and Human Development: Youth and Social Innovation (YSI). The program intends to attract students interested in impacting youth at all levels, from direct work with youth to policymaking and research, to collaboration with diverse communities. Influenced by faculty with backgrounds in developmental psychology, education policy, clinical & school psychology, and educational foundations (history, sociology, anthropology, etc.), the YSI major's learning objectives include being able to:

Demonstrate an understanding of the dynamic processes of the biological, social, emotional, and cognitive development of youth, with a focus on how youths' assets and school/community settings influence youth outcomes.

Demonstrate an understanding of how regulations and rules that affect schools and organizations serving youth are developed, and the effects of those policies on youth outcomes.

Develop a repertoire of, understand, and design social innovations for youth, which enhance youth development through systematic approaches to developing and refining youth experiences and programs, with attention to what works for different youth in diverse settings and contexts.

Collaborate with peers, youth, and other partners/stakeholders to determine and then work toward desired youth outcomes.

Demonstrate an understanding of how to interact with youth and service settings in diverse cultural contexts.

Demonstrate the ability to be an informed professional and/or scholar in youth development through thoughtful self-reflection, effective verbal and written communication, culturally sensitive practice, and ethical conduct.

These learning objectives reflect what our faculty believes to be foundational for effective and ethical youth work practice.

To achieve these learning objectives, we have constructed a curriculum that incorporates content knowledge and applied experiences. Coursework exposes students to key academic content in youth development, youth policy, research skills, and Design Thinking. Students both learn curricular content about and participate in

Higher Education and Youth Work 115

community engagement. In several of their courses, students work collaboratively with their peers on team projects. In their yearlong capstone experience, they work in teams of their peers with a community or university partner on a project that aims to benefit youth. Additionally, every student chooses an applied experience working directly with youth, interning with an individual or organization doing work related to youth, or conducting youth-relevant research with faculty.

Since the YSI major's inception in 2014, affiliated faculty—informed by student and alumni feedback and our own emergent understandings—have shaped different pathways within the major to support students' varied interests and career pursuits ranging from working with youth to influencing the direction of systems that impact youth. These pathways represent a variety of types of careers, from working with young people in schools to serving youth in clinical or informal educational settings to working on behalf of youth by informing policy or conducting research. We believe that the learning objectives above are applicable, and foundational, regardless of which career path a student chooses. Students can choose a concentration or choose electives across the five different concentrations offered through the major: Applied Child and Youth Development; Education, Culture, and Society; Policy and Data Analysis; Program Design; and Youth Mental Health. Interest-area electives provide opportunities for students to carve out their own pathways.

Our alumni, still small in number and early in their careers, have followed diverse career paths. In addition to pursuing careers as youth workers and teachers, YSI graduates have also gone on to pursue careers in counseling and clinical mental health work, policy, government, law, and roles in the non-profit sector, often focused on children and families, higher education and student affairs, and careers in youth-related research. The diversity of pathways reflects the program's commitment to equipping students with essential competencies to make a positive impact on the lives of young people, regardless of their chosen career trajectory.

CONCLUSION

Higher education needs to be a key player in the field of youth development—through broadening and expanding the disciplines and career pathways to which key principles, knowledge, and competencies related to youth work are seen as applicable. Young people's critical role in the future of society calls for serious investment in educating college students broadly in the assets-based principles of youth work. Infusing the theories, skills, and dispositions that are needed for successful youth work into broad sets of courses within traditional college curriculum is one means by which higher education can impact the field. We presented an example of an undergraduate program at the University of Virginia that has picked up this charge. But more such programs are needed.

A second strategy involves incorporating the underlying tenets and knowledge base of youth development into the curriculum of traditional majors. For example, a history curriculum could include a study of the history of youth as a concept and the ways in which socio-historical forces have shaped ideas about adolescence. A political science class could examine the role of youth voice and activism in political movements. Such efforts can help expand where we see youth work occurring, create a more coherent professional identity for those engaged in youth work, and build networks across people who are working with and advocating for young people in ways that increase the power of the field.

Yet institutions of higher education also have an opportunity to use their resources to expand educational offerings to the existing youth development workforce. Through new types of credentialing programs, such as digital badges and certifications, colleges and universities can create new professional development opportunities and build pathways for career advancement, which itself can help foster professionalization. Finally, those of us who work at colleges and universities can align ourselves with youth workers.

Many of the students we work with are themselves still youth. And before they showed up in our classrooms, it was our kindred spirits in formal and informal educational settings who were supporting their development. Higher education has tremendous potential to be a partner to and amplifier of youth work. After all, at its heart, youth work is about *valuing* young people. Higher education is a key setting for the development of a value system and the gaining of skills to enact that value system through our work and civic engagement. Imagine if our higher education system imparted key principles of respect and value for youth, and transmitted skills to work with and on behalf of young people. This feels like a goal that is worthy of pursuit.

REFERENCES

Aspen Institute, National Commission on Social, Emotional, & Academic Development (2019). *From a Nation at Risk to a Nation at Hope.* https://learningpolicyinstitute.org/media/3962/download?inline&file=Aspen_SEAD_Nation_at_Hope.pdf

Benson, P. L., Mannes, M., Pittman, K., & Ferber, T. (2004). Youth development, developmental assets, and public policy. *Handbook of adolescent psychology*, 781–814. https://doi.org/10.1002/9780471726746.ch25

Benson, P. L., Scales, P. C., Hamilton, S. F., & Sesma, A., Jr. (2006) Positive youth development: Theory, research, and applications. In R. M. Lerner (Ed.), *Theoretical models of human development* (pp. 894–941). John Wiley & Sons. https://doi.org/10.1002/9780470147658.chpsy0116

Benson, P. L., Scales,P. C., & Syvertsen, A. K. (2011). The contribution of the developmental assets framework to positive youth development theory and practice. In R. M. Lerner, J. V. Lerner, & J. B. Benson (Eds.), *Advances in child development and behavior* (Vol. 4, pp. 197–230). Academic Press. https://doi.org/10.1016/B978-0-12-386492-5.00008-7

Borden, L. M., Ballard, J., Michl-Petzing, L., Conn, M., Mull, C. D., & Wilkens, M. (2020). Foundations for the future: Building an integrated, cohesive field of youth development. *Journal of Youth Development*, *15*(1), 266–286. https://doi.org/10.5195/jyd.2020.937

Bowers, E. P., Geldhof, G. J., Johnson, S. K., Hilliard, L. J., Hershberg, R. M., Lerner, J. V., & Lerner, R. M. (Eds.). (2015). *Promoting positive youth development: Lessons from the 4-H study*. Springer.

Camino, L. A. (2000). Youth-adult partnerships: Entering new territory in community work and research. *Applied Developmental Science*, *4*(S1), 11–20. https://doi.org/10.1207/S1532480XADS04Suppl_2

Coll, C. G., Crnic, K., Lamberty, G., Wasik, B. H., Jenkins, R., Garcia, H. V., & McAdoo, H. P. (1996). An integrative model for the study of developmental competencies in minority children. *Child Development*, *67*(5), 1891–1914. https://doi.org/10.1111/j.1467-8624.1996.tb01834.x

Cushing, D. F., & van Vliet, W. (2017) Children's right to the city: the emergence of youth councils in the United States. *Children's Geographies*, *15*(3), 319–333. https://doi.org/10.1080/14733285.2016.1244602

Deutsch, N. L., Mauer, V. A., Johnson, H. E., Grabowska, A. A., & Arbeit, M. R. (2020). "[My counselor] knows stuff about me, but [my natural mentor] actually knows me": Distinguishing characteristics of youth's natural mentoring relationships. *Children and Youth Services Review*, *111*, 104879. https://doi.org/10.1016/j.childyouth.2020.104879

Eccles, J. S., Midgley, C., Wigfield, A., Buchanan, C. M., Reuman, D., Flanagan, C., & Mac Iver, D. (1997). Development during adolescence: The impact of stage–environment fit on young adolescents' experiences in schools and in families In J. M. Notterman (Ed.), *The evolution of psychology: Fifty years of the American Psychologist* (pp. 475–501). American Psychological Association. https://doi.org/10.1037/10254-034

Fusco, D. (2016). History of youth work: Transitions, illuminations, and refractions. In M. Heathfield and D. Fusco (Eds.) *Youth and Inequality in Education* (pp. 36–50). Routledge.

Freire, P. (1970). *Pedagogy of the oppressed*. Seabury Press.

Geldhof, G. J., Bowers, E. P., Mueller, M. K., Napolitano, C. M., Callina, K. S., Walsh, K. J., Lerner, J. V., & Lerner, R. M. (2015). The five Cs model of positive youth development. In E. P. Bowers, G. J. Geldhof, S. K. Johnson, L. J. Hilliard, R. M. Hershberg, J. V. Lerner, & R. M. Lerner (Eds.), *Promoting Positive Youth Development: Lessons From The 4-H Study* (pp. 161–186). https://doi.org/10.1007/978-3-319-17166-1_9

Ginwright, S. A. (2010). Peace out to revolution! Activism among African American youth: An argument for radical healing. *Young, 18*(1), 77–96. https://doi.org/10.1177/110330880901800106

Ginwright, S. (2015). *Hope and healing in urban education: How urban activists and teachers are reclaiming matters of the heart.* Routledge.

Gonzalez, M., Kokozos, M., Byrd, C. M., & McKee, K. E. (2020). Critical positive youth development: A framework for centering critical consciousness. *Journal of Youth Development, 15*(6), 24–43. https://doi.org/10.5195/jyd.2020.859

Griffith, A. N., & Johnson, H. E. (2019). Building trust: Reflections of adults working with high-school-age youth in project-based programs. *Children and Youth Services Review, 96*, 439–450. https://doi.org/10.1016/j.childyouth.2018.11.056

Hart, R. (1992) *Children's Participation: From Tokenism to Citizenship.* UNICEF Innocenti Essays, No. 4, Florence, Italy: International Child Development Centre of UNICEF.

Hart, R. A. (2008). Stepping back from 'The ladder': Reflections on a model of participatory work with children. In A. Reid, B. B. Jensen, J. Nikel, & V. Simovska (Eds.), *Participation and learning: Perspectives on education and the environment, health and sustainability* (pp. 19–31). Springer.

Head, B. W. (2011). Why not ask them? Mapping and promoting youth participation. *Children and Youth services review, 33*(4), 541–547. https://doi.org/10.1016/j.childyouth.2010.05.015

Hurley, L., & Treacy, D. (1993). *Models of youth work: A sociological framework.* Irish Youthwork Press.

Klein, E. (Host). (2023, July 25). Biden, psychedelics, Twitter, my new book—and so much more [Audio podcast episode] In The Ezra Klein Show. *The New York Times.* https://www.nytimes.com/2023/07/25/opinion/ezra-klein-podcast-transcript-ama-2023.html

Lerner, R. M., Lerner, J. V., Lewin-Bizan, S., Bowers, E. P., Boyd, M. J., Mueller, M. K., K. L. Schmid, & Napolitano, C. M. (2011). Positive youth development: Processes, programs, and problematics. *Journal of Youth Development, 6*(3), 38–62. https://doi.org/10.5195/jyd.2011.174

Merriam-Webster Dictionary. (n.d.). *Youth.* Retrieved August 24, 2023, from https://www.merriam-webster.com/dictionary/youth

Mitra, D. L. (2009). Collaborating with students: Building youth-adult partnerships in schools. *American Journal of Education, 115*(3), 407–436.

Mott Foundation. (2009). *Core competencies for afterschool educators.*

Murthy, V. H. (2021). *Protecting youth's mental health: The U.S. Surgeon General's Advisory.* United States Office of Health and Human Services. https://www.hhs.gov/sites/default/files/surgeon-general-youth-mental-health-advisory.pdf?null

National Academies of Sciences, Engineering, and Medicine (NASEM) (2019). *The promise of adolescence: Realizing opportunity for all youth*. The National Academies Press. https://doi.org/10.17226/25388

National Afterschool Association. (2021). *Core knowledge, skills, and competencies for afterschool professionals*. https://cdn.ymaws.com/naa.site-ym.com/resource/collection/F3611BAF-0B62-42F9-9A26-C376BF35104F/NAA_Core_Knowledge_Skills_Competencies_for_OST.pdf

National Research Council. (2002). *Community programs to promote youth development*. National Academies Press.

National Student Clearinghouse Research Center (2019). *NSC Blog: Fall enrollments decline for 8th consecutive year*. https://www.studentclearinghouse.org/nscblog/fall-enrollments-decline-for-8th-consecutive-year/

National Student Clearinghouse Research Center. (2023). *Overview: Spring 2023 enrollment estimates*. https://nscresearchcenter.org/wp-content/uploads/CTEE_Report_Spring_2023.pdf

Ozer, E. J. (2017). Youth-led participatory action research: Overview and potential for enhancing adolescent development. *Child Development Perspectives*, *11*(3), 173–177. https://doi.org/10.1111/cdep.12228

Roholt, R. V., & Mueller, M. (2013). Youth advisory structures: Listening to young people to support quality youth services. *New Directions for Youth Development*, *2013*(139), 79–100. https://doi.org/10.1002/yd.20070

Scales, P. C., Roehlkepartain, E. C., & Houltberg, B. J. (2022). *The elements of developmental relationships: A review of selected research underlying the framework*. Search Institute Research Review.

Search Institute. (n.d.). *Developmental relationships help young people thrive*. Retrieved July 20, 2023, from https://tinyurl.com/mentza48

Sercombe, H. (2015). Youth in a global/historical context: What it means for youth work. In *Youth Work and Inequality in Education*, 19–35.

Starr, B., Yohalem, N., & Gannett, E. (2009). *Youth worker core competencies: A review of existing frameworks and purposes*. Next Generation Youth Work Coalition.

Vance, F. (2010). A comparative analysis of competency frameworks for youth workers in the out-of-school time field. *Child and Youth Care Forum*, *39*(6), 421–441. https:// doi.org/10.1007/s10566-010-9116-4

Varga, S. M., & Zaff, J. F. (2018). Webs of support: An integrative framework of relationships, social networks, and social support for positive youth development. *Adolescent Research Review*, *3*, 1–11.

United Nations. (n.d.). *Global issues: Youth*. Retrieved August 24, 2023, from https://www.un.org/en/global-issues/youth

Weiston-Serdan, T. (2017). *Critical mentoring: A practical guide*. Stylus.

Wu, H. C. J., Kornbluh, M., Weiss, J., & Roddy, L. (2016). Measuring and understanding authentic youth engagement: The youth-adult partnership rubric. *Afterschool Matters*, *23*, 8–17.

Youth-Nex. (2023). *Portrait of a thriving youth*. https://education.virginia.edu/research-initiatives/research-centers-labs/youth-nex/youth-nex-initiatives/portrait-thriving-youth

Zeldin, S., Camino, L., & Calvert, M. (2003). Toward an understanding of youth in community governance: Policy priorities and research directions. *SRCD Social Policy Report, 17*(3), 1–20.

Zeldin, S., Camino, L., & Mook, C. (2005). The adoption of innovation in youth organizations: Creating the conditions for youth-adult partnerships. *Journal of Community Psychology, 33*(1), 121–135.

CHAPTER 7

SUPPORTING THE YOUTH FIELDS WORKFORCE

Lessons Learned From the Power of Us Workforce Survey and the Field

Jill Young and Rebecca Goldberg

INTRODUCTION

Young people encounter many different adults across the settings and systems where they live, learn, work, and play (National Commission on Social, Emotional, and Academic Development, 2018). The science of learning and development provides insights into creating and sustaining equitable experiences and opportunities for youth to learn, develop, and thrive (Cantor et al., 2019; Osher et al., 2019; Osher et al., 2020). Relationships and contexts possess the potential to deeply shape youth experiences and opportunities (National Commission on Social, Emotional, and Academic Development, 2018; Osher et al., 2020). All adults, in all settings and systems, have the power and the potential to shape and support youth success (Osher et al., 2020).

The adults young people interact with outside the classroom include childcare providers, mentors, librarians, sports coaches, afterschool professionals, summer camp counselors, summer employment coordinators, and many more. These adults work in a variety of programs and contexts collectively referred to as the "youth fields workforce," encompassing youth-serving professionals and volunteers who engage with youth for a

---

Built for More: The Role of Out-of-School Time in Preparing Youth for the Future of Work,
pp. 121–137
Copyright © 2024 by Information Age Publishing
www.infoagepub.com
All rights of reproduction in any form reserved.

variety of programmatic purposes and influence young people's learning and development.

Given the key role the youth fields workforce plays in shaping young people's experiences outside of the traditional school day, it is important to support the workforce in developing their own knowledge and skills. Investing in professional development and other learning opportunities for the youth fields workforce can help retain high-quality, skilled staff (Borden et al., 2020; Cooper, 2013).

In this chapter, we aim to:

- Provide a succinct overview of the youth fields workforce and its professional development needs;
- Describe the American Institutes for Research's (AIR) recent effort to learn more about the youth fields workforce and their professional development needs through the Power of Us Workforce Survey;
- Elevate current efforts and lessons learned from various organizations who aim to support the youth fields workforce in preparing young people for the future of work; and
- Share key takeaways and recommendations for where the field can go next.

WHAT WE KNOW ABOUT THE YOUTH FIELDS WORKFORCE AND PROFESSIONAL DEVELOPMENT

The adults who work with youth outside of the regular school day work in a variety of roles and sectors. Members of the youth fields workforce serve as summer camp counselors, sports coaches, music teachers, museum educators, youth librarians, and afterschool program staff (Power of Us Survey, 2023). They work and volunteer during after-school, weekends, and summers, in programs across school and community-based settings (Borden et al., 2020). This diverse group may be full-time or part-time staff, volunteers, teens, or parents, often living in the communities they serve (Blattner & Franklin, 2017; Peter, 2009). They also vary in their age, background, level of education, and prior experience (Hall et al., 2020). They develop and implement content and relationship rich learning experiences for youth of all ages and various focus areas. Nonetheless, the youth fields workforce may experience multiple barriers to accessing high-quality jobs, exemplified by "high turnover rates, poor compensation and benefits, limited opportunities for upward mobility, and unstable funding" (Vance, 2010, p. 422). Though many members of the youth fields workforce identify with their program's goals, many other members see their jobs as

Supporting the Youth Fields Workforce   123

transient because of the many barriers they face in accessing viable career pathways (Blattner & Franklin, 2017).

Research concerning out-of-school time (OST) demonstrates that high-quality programs can provide safe and supportive contexts wherein youth can build skills, explore interests and potential careers, and develop relationships (Durlak et al., 2010; Naftzger et al., 2018; Naftzger et al., 2020; Vandell et al., 2007; Vandell et al., 2022). The key ingredient to high-quality programs and positive youth outcomes is the skilled staff who design and implement the programs (Bodilly & Beckett, 2005; Robideau & Santl, 2020). Therefore, investing in the development of the knowledge and skills of the youth fields workforce is critical to high-quality programs and retaining skilled and high-quality staff (Borden et al., 2020; Cooper, 2013). Members of the youth fields workforce serve in a variety of roles and settings and bring diverse types of expertise and backgrounds to the job. This diversity in the workforce is a strength, but also a challenge. Since it is difficult to define the role of members of the youth fields workforce and identify the knowledge, skills, and abilities they require, it is challenging to adequately support them with professional development and career pathways (Borden et al., 2020; Hall et al., 2020; Vance, 2010). The youth fields workforce requires the knowledge and skills to design and implement high-quality programs. Such knowledge and skills include building developmental relationships with youth; creating program climates which are physically and emotionally safe; supporting developmentally appropriate skill-building activities; and engaging youth in authentic and meaningful opportunities (Borden et al., 2020).

Professional development emerges as a pivotal strategy for supporting the youth fields workforce (Blattner & Franklin, 2017; Bradshaw, 2015; Cole, 2011; Cooper, 2013). Professional development can take several forms, such as onetime workshops and trainings, conferences, ongoing series, mentorship and coaching, professional learning communities, technical assistance, professional memberships, and college coursework (Peter, 2009; Vance et al., 2016). Effective professional development can improve program quality and activities as well as program approaches, such as contributing to the creation of safe and supportive program climates and developmental youth-adult relationships (Blattner & Franklin, 2017). Moreover, professional development can also provide several benefits to the youth fields workforce members, including "staff retention, improved health and safety, reduced stress, leadership succession, better use of resources, improved program quality, reduced hiring and orientation costs, improved job satisfaction, and more rapid and successful organizational change" (Garst et al., 2014, p. 2). However, professional development may not be accessible to all of the youth fields workforce members due to limited staff hours or lack of funding (Wiedow, 2018)

Additionally, organizations that dedicate time and money to professional development for staff and volunteers may not be able to provide follow-up supports to help them apply their learning to practice (Akiva et al., 2016; Wiedow, 2018). When staff and volunteers do not feel supported, turnover escalates, as does the need to hire and train new staff (Shanahan & Sheehan, 2020).

POWER OF US WORKFORCE SURVEY

About the Power of Us Workforce Survey

Ensuring adequate training and support for the youth fields workforce is paramount so they are equipped to provide high-quality experiences which help young people thrive. The most recent nationwide research on the youth fields workforce was conducted in 2005 (the Cornerstones for Kids' "Next Generation" studies). However, much has changed in the field over the last two decades. The number of youths participating in programs and the number of adults working in these programs have grown. Collaborative professional networks, such as statewide afterschool networks, are increasingly working together to serve young people through cross-sector systems and initiatives (Henig et al., 2016). Professional development for the youth fields workforce must consider and reflect the current demographics, experiences, challenges, and trajectories of the field. Furthermore, the COVID-19 pandemic has significantly impacted the youth fields workforce, leading to many youth-serving organizations having to furlough staff or reduce budgets (Afterschool Alliance, 2022). The youth fields workforce has also experienced additional stress due to health risks of working in programs as well as first- and secondhand trauma related to the pandemic (Woodberry-Shaw et al., 2020). Effects of the pandemic persist and linger; recruiting and retaining staff remains difficult for many youth-serving organizations as they try to combat staff burnout and higher program costs (Afterschool Alliance, 2023).

The American Institutes for Research (AIR) developed the Power of Us Workforce Survey to enhance the understanding of today's youth fields workforce and collect data which could be used to support research, policy, and practice. The core objective of the Power of Us Workforce Survey is to provide current, relevant, and reliable information about the workforce: who they are, what they do, where they work and have worked, their professional identities, pathways to and within their career, their competencies, and the professional supports they receive and need.

For the survey's purpose, AIR defined the workforce as youth-serving professionals and volunteers in the youth fields who work with young

Supporting the Youth Fields Workforce   125

people in any capacity outside of the traditional school day. Examples include summer camp counselors, sports coaches, music teachers, museum educators, youth librarians, and afterschool program staff. AIR included in the survey both individuals who currently work or volunteer in the field and individuals who were formerly in the field, particularly those who left their organization because of the economic and societal effects of the COVID-19 pandemic. AIR also included in the survey individuals working across the youth fields in diverse sectors, such as childcare programs, community-based out-of-school time programs, mentoring programs, juvenile and social justice programs, summer youth employment programs, youth-serving workforce development programs, among others.

Emerging Findings From the Power of Us Workforce Survey

AIR launched the Power of Us Workforce Survey in February 2022 and concluded data collection in March 2023. For the purposes of this chapter, we highlight preliminary and emerging findings from current workforce members focused on professional development, including the type of opportunities they participate in or use, how they access professional development, and what would improve the professional development opportunities available to them.

The survey indicated that most respondents reported they have access to professional learning, including training, courses, and tools, either through their organization, through other organizations where they do not work, or through the internet. Survey respondents also shared the top five types of professional learning opportunities they participate in or use through various resources:

1. Virtual trainings and workshops
2. In-person trainings and workshops
3. Webinars
4. Conferences or institutes
5. Courses

To a lesser extent, respondents also indicated their participation in or use of books, tools, and other resources, alongside engaging in professional networking, professional learning communities, coaching, and shadowing.

Survey respondents also shared their insights on what they thought would improve the professional learning opportunities currently available to them. The top five areas for improvement include:

1. Resources (e.g., funding, materials) to participate or use the learning.
2. More professional learning offered through their organization.
3. Professional learning offered at convenient times.
4. Time off to participate in or use the learning.
5. Professional learning offered at convenient locations.

Additionally, respondents also indicated the following would improve professional development learning opportunities: professional learning offered more frequently, organizational support for the implementation of the learning, topics relevant to their specific role, topics on knowledge or skills they do not already have, and a broader range of topics.

EMERGING LESSONS FROM THE FIELD

Many youth organizations offer programs and services which are designed to equip young people with work experience, prepare them to succeed in jobs, and support them in exploring potential career paths. Some organizations' missions may explicitly focus on preparing young people for the future of work and evolving job landscape, but it is not uncommon that general youth-serving organizations also serve this role. Many organizations endeavor to support their workforce through professional development and other supports. This section highlights and includes several examples from the field of how organizations are supporting their staff to effectively and successfully prepare young people for the future of work.

Girls Inc.

For nearly 160 years, Girls Inc. has offered programming and mentoring opportunities during and afterschool to young women across the country. Operating with nearly 80 affiliates and more than 1,500 sites in 350 cities, Girls Inc. creates a pro-girl environment and evidence-based programming, providing girls with opportunities to build positive relationships with both peers and adult role models.

In 2021, with support from the Equality Can't Wait Challenge, Girls, Inc. launched a novel program and initiative: Project Accelerate. Project Accelerate supports young women to successfully transition from high school to post-secondary education, follow a four-year post-secondary completion plan, including placement in a paid internship, and transition into a job or postgraduate education. Simultaneously, Project Accelerate

Supporting the Youth Fields Workforce   127

aims to transform corporate environments to be welcoming, inclusive, and intentionally designed to support leadership opportunities for women, especially women of color. According to Girls Inc., "Project Accelerate will speed the entry of young women, especially women of color into positions of influence and leadership, particularly in sectors where pay equity and gender disparities are far too prevalent" (Girls Inc., 2023, p. 8).

In its third year of implementation, Project Accelerate is actively undertaken by 21 affiliates. The organization is raising funds and building infrastructure to scale to up to 30 affiliates in the near future. Ultimately, their ambition is to eventually scale to all 80 affiliates.

Until recently, Girls Inc. worked exclusively with girls ages 5–18. However, affiliates regularly received requests from girls for ongoing support and services once they finished high school. The participating girls value the network of peers and relationships built with Girls Inc. staff, leading them to want to stay connected after high school. Girls Inc. responded to this need with the launch of Project Accelerate as well as its first Girls Inc. Alumnae Association.

While Girls Inc. staff working on Project Accelerate receive all the same standard professional development as other Girls Inc. staff working with younger youth, this initiative does have a different approach, which requires some unique staff development and resources. For example, Girls Inc. describes Project Accelerate as a "case management model approach rather than a program approach" (Girls Inc., 2023, p. 2). While most affiliates have hired someone new to take on this role, the initiative requires a team approach to recruiting young women, identifying mentors, and working with local companies to place participants in paid internships.

Staff employ a personalized one-on-one case management approach which meets each participant where they are and scaffolds the level of support based on individual need. For example, staff may check in with participants as often as daily or weekly, when needing more support or experiencing challenges, or as infrequently as monthly for those young women who are thriving and need less support. This move to a one-on-one mentoring model is a significant change from Girls Inc.'s traditional program, which focuses more on in-person group mentoring. The one-on-one model focuses on connecting girls to external resources and requires staff to build and maintain close relationships with participating girls who are not in the same place physically and are receiving services virtually. Given this is a new initiative, Girls Inc. is still learning about the types of support this new staff position requires; however, Girls Inc. staff acknowledge that the profile of the youth worker filling this role does not look particularly different from the typical Girls Inc. youth mentor.

Though guiding girls as they enter adulthood and the workplace extends beyond Girls Inc.'s historical programming model, the organization is well positioned to prepare girls for the future of work because they are leveraging and building off the strong relationships, they already have with thousands of girls nationwide. Rather than actively recruiting new young women for Project Accelerate, Girls Inc. offers these continuing services to girls who are already engaged with the organization, who value the positive relationships they have built with Girls Inc. staff and other girls in the program.

This type of network of peers and role models that Girls Inc. intentionally builds out for its young women through Project Accelerate is what enables the organization to support them through college and into their careers. This approach ensures continuity and taps into the support network already established during the participants' formative years. With the potential to scale to all Girls Inc. affiliates, Project Accelerate will "prepare thousands of young women leaders not merely to succeed in workplace environments, but also to affect cultural change from within" (Girls Inc. of Orange County, 2022, p. 1). This holistic strategy positions Girls Inc. as an advocate for sustained progress and advancement, empowering young women to not only succeed within workplace environments but also spearhead meaningful change within the broader societal fabric.

Utah Afterschool Network

The Utah Afterschool Network (UAN) offers a comprehensive approach to professional development for programs throughout Utah. Functioning under contractual agreements with state entities, including Department of Workforce Services Office of Child Care and the Utah State Board of Education, UAN provides professional development and technical assistance to more than two-thirds of programs across the state. The technical assistance includes program observations using the Weikart Center's Youth Program Quality Assessment tool, along with support to complete a quality self-assessment process for programs. UAN staff offer coaching and training directly to programs. Their staff gain valuable feedback from the field, which informs their two statewide conferences.

Within their suite of professional development offerings, UAN has state funding from the Utah State Board of Education to offer training on exposing youth to career pathways within STEM and entrepreneurship. According to UAN, afterschool programs are well positioned to help young people explore careers because of their ability to build relationships, which is key to quality programming. Leveraging partnerships with higher education institutions, industry stakeholders, and mentorship platforms, afterschool programs foster connections which create opportunities for career exploration. UAN noted that staff of afterschool programs for teens

Supporting the Youth Fields Workforce   129

often partner with community organizations and education institutions to bring in speakers that can expose young people to various careers and career readiness. Staff from programs that serve older youth also bring young people out of programs into the community to museums and other experiences where they can be exposed to potential careers.

UAN is seeing a change in who is entering the workforce and the types of supports they need to be successful. For example, programs are hiring young staff for whom this may be their first job ever. Especially coming out of the COVID-19 pandemic, UAN is noticing and hearing from programs that both young staff and youth in programs are equally needing support to adapt back to post-pandemic life and re-establishing regular in-person social interactions. In response, UAN is putting together an "Afterschool 101" track of professional development offerings to equip new staff with the most essential skills they will need to operate a high-quality program. The UAN staff jokingly and lovingly started calling it "Adulting 101," but the name seems to resonate and may stick around. Providers are sharing that they are hiring staff without prior work experience who need to learn the basics like the importance of being punctual and making sure your shift is covered - basic life skills that are also indispensable to being employable. UAN is hoping to offer resources for staff on these basic skills so they can then be role models more effectively for young people.

Another asset UAN has been able to offer the field is the opportunity for financial incentives for professional development completed through a collaborative initiative with the Department of Workforce Services Office of Child Care and Utah State Board of Education. Leveraging this partnership, the Department has made its early childhood financial rewards program available to both licensed and license exempt afterschool programs in the state. UAN takes on the role of reviewing applications from participating professionals, and awards the financial reward based on eligibility and training hours completed. These financial incentives range from $150 to$1,000 per year depending on both eligibility and the years of experience within the field.

Looking ahead, UAN plans to continue gathering feedback from providers to curate their professional development offerings and sharing it back with providers. In collaboration with the Department of Workforce Services—Office of Child Care, UAN is embarking on a statewide needs assessment to better understand what employment in the afterschool field looks like, how employee pay may impact staff retention as well as program quality, and which communities are and are not getting served by afterschool programs. Their professional development offerings will continue to evolve based on changing needs in the field. As more programs aim to prepare young people for work and careers, responsive and high-quality professional development will be needed so that staff, even when young in

130 J. YOUNG and R. GOLDBERG

their career, can serve as effective role models for youth and are prepared
to build young people's work readiness skills.

National Youth Employment Coalition

The National Youth Employment Coalition (NYEC) is a nonprofit membership network focused on ensuring "all young people are supported and prepared to become thriving members of our economy and society, regardless of their race, gender, ability, geography, or means" (Ingram et al., 2023, p. 2). NYEC is committed to providing capacity building and technical assistance, policy and advocacy support, and youth leadership support to community-based organizations, state agencies, and local government organizations focused on supporting youth in transitioning to postsecondary education and employment (Ingram et al., 2023). Specifically, NYEC focuses on opportunity youth, defined as youth who are between the ages of 16 and 24 and out of work and school.

NYEC designs and facilitates project-based work, such as communities of practice focused on increasing collaboration and improving outcomes for opportunity youth. NYEC also conducts research to help provide information on innovative programs, guidance on best practices, and tools that can be used by practitioners. For example, NYEC currently has strategic plans to improve the use of data in the field, shifting the narrative related to opportunity youth, and activating youth leadership and community-based organizations in local, state, and federal policy work.

NYEC offers a wide range of professional development opportunities for members, with content developed and delivered by NYEC, partners, and members. For example, offerings include:

- Monthly office hours with the U.S. Department of Labor, where attendees can ask any question they have about youth apprenticeship and training programs;
- Skills that help youth become leaders in today's workforce;
- Employer partnerships and best practices from the field;
- Financial wellbeing and wealth building for opportunity youth;
- Barriers to and solutions for supporting BIPOC mental health.

Professional development opportunities focus on building skills in youth-serving staff and volunteers to best be equipped to support opportunity youth. First, NYEC focuses on helping adults understand how to identify the barriers young people are facing and know how to navigate community resources to help young people remove those barriers. Second,

NYEC focuses on helping adults identify, understand, and address trauma and mental health issues, such as depression and anxiety. Third, NYEC emphasizes employer engagement, so adults know employers in their community and how to engage them to support youth. Fourth, NYEC ensures that adults have knowledge of apprenticeship programs and other training programs that are available in the community.

NYEC recently conducted a literature review and engaged in focus groups with employers, youth training practitioners, and young people to identify best practices in employer engagement. NYEC released a brief detailing their findings, takeaways, and best practices, which serve as opportunities for both youth service providers and employers to better support young people. This brief offers several practical tips and insights for youth service providers and employers alike to improve employment opportunities and experiences for young people and support their success. Practical recommendations contained in the brief include:

- Training frontline supervisors on institutional segregation and racism, as these issues can hinder the success of a young person.
- Providing flexible scheduling, as young people may have multiple challenges they are facing and commitments they are managing.
- Considering transportation challenges, as many youth reported challenges in getting to work, such as cost, commute time, and exposure to violence.
- Providing and supporting childcare to support the needs of young individuals with familial responsibilities.
- Providing additional support via resource navigators and offering tuition reimbursement.
- Helping youth understand the hidden rules and unspoken guidelines of a workplace, such as the unwritten do's and don'ts that are not typically shared during onboarding, and showing how they fit into the organization and what career pathways exist for them.

NYEC is putting these findings into action by launching a national effort, with seven cities and their mayors, to create a Youth Champion Communities Framework: A Mayors Challenge. NYEC will also use these findings to incorporate additional professional development opportunities for youth service providers and employers so that young people are well prepared, but also so that employers are ready to offer welcoming and supportive work environments for young people.

> *Insights from a Field Leader, Bill Fennessy, Program Specialist, California Afterschool Network; former Director of High School Programs & Director of Work-Based Learning, THINK Together*
>
> Bill Fennessy, with decades-long involvement in leading, implementing, and advising work-based learning programs in OST settings, stands a distinguished figure in the field. He has partnered with Career Technical Education (CTE) programs, and he has developed "grow-your-own" approaches which give high school youth experience working with younger youth within afterschool programs. Bill is now overseeing the development of a youth development apprenticeship program in his role at the California Afterschool Network. When asked about the unique value OST programs offer young people when preparing them for work, Bill shares, "it is the organic mentoring relationship that comes so naturally for folks in youth development." They may have the same goals as CTE programs, for example, helping young people create a resume, but it is the pace that is different and the inclination to go deeper to help young people recognize their own strengths. He explains:
>
>> When I ran programs, we started with an orientation on resume building. If all they walk out with is a good resume, we've moved them a lot. But we also find that young people who have work experience have no clue that they have it. It takes the adults to pull it out. They don't think that babysitting their cousins is work related or that projects at their church or synagogue or other service roles count. They don't associate that with work. So, we added an extra session in which they connect with 5–6 adults and called it 'Resume Reflection'. They needed more foundation work on resumes before moving forward."
>
> Once the resume was in place, they could then scaffold the learning and support the young people to fill out job applications, practice interviews with four to six adults at different stations and have them practice introducing themselves. Bill noted that the hardest thing about placing young people in internships is finding the work placement and maintaining that relationship with the employers:
>
>> Having students really well prepared is key to retaining employer partnerships.... We realized that we could place them in our own afterschool programs, which was the easiest placement, where transportation was not an issue being in their own neighborhood, and we knew to select strong sites to host them and intentionally prepared the site coordinators and program leaders on how to work with the high school youth.

Supporting the Youth Fields Workforce 133

There was intentional training for the site coordinator and program leader who offered these young people a 10-week program that increased the young people's levels of responsibility each week until they were ready to deliver a STEM-based program with kids.

This model was so successful at THINK Together in Santa Ana that they began thinking about intentionally growing their own staff since most of the young people were headed to community college and would likely need a job while in college. In fact, Bill argues that:

> Expanded learning would be an incredible practicum for any role in health and human services (police, nurse, social worker) and that the competencies translate. When preparing young people for work and careers, have them explore and research industries/careers, but start their work experience in your own youth programs. It's a supportive environment in which they can practice the skills they want to develop, and then later, scaffold outside work experiences from other industries, but start in your own program. The peer-to-peer relationship is so strong.

When asked how he thinks about hiring staff and training them to prepare young people for the future of work, Bill approaches hiring in a similar way to other youth development roles. Once he selects candidates for this work, he asks:

> Do they have the competencies to do this type of training with young people? If so, we can take them there. It's really a general hire with training and support. The key is to provide training to the Site Coordinator, because the Site Coordinator provides the rigor in the training and ultimately supports the site leader onsite.

He adds that in addition to basic training, "We often have to help them with lesson planning and ensuring it builds into a linear continuum for learning." In essence, the organization's role is to offer basic training to the site leader as well as good supervision and ongoing support onsite as the youth worker engages young people.

According to Bill, "If professional development is done well, it's cascading leadership, role modeling, showing everyone along the way" from the Site Coordinator to the Program Leader to the young person:

> The things staff need are pretty similar to what the young people they work with need. If I'm not treating my middle management staff with what they need, who are modeling for their staff who are modeling for the young people, I don't know how the young people are supposed to be able to pull it off. It starts from the top down, and it needs to be cascaded learning. It's human development. If you demonstrate that well, they may not realize they're learning, and it's just part of what you do.

CONCLUSION

Youth development organizations serve as a natural place to prepare young people for the workplace and future careers, as their foundation starts with building relationships and helping young people believe in themselves and understand their own strengths. Well-prepared members of the youth fields workforce are key to quality programming and positive youth outcomes. Previous literature on the youth fields workforce and recent findings from the Power of Us Workforce Survey emphasize the importance of supporting the youth fields workforce through professional development opportunities. The Power of Us Workforce Survey findings indicate and underscore that most members of the youth fields workforce have access to professional development opportunities. The findings also illuminate the types of professional opportunities the youth fields workforce participates in or uses. Additional research is needed to learn more about their satisfaction with the professional opportunities available, the topics or content they would like to learn more about, and the approaches or strategies that work best for them. Yet further research is needed to further understand these issues.

Conversations with organizations that support the youth fields workforce to prepare young people to thrive in education and careers offered additional lessons about what is working in the field:

- Professional Development Continuity: Professional development does not necessarily look significantly different for programs preparing young people for work than typical youth-serving organizations, but the key is to provide intentional, ongoing opportunities for professional learning.
- Cascading Leadership and Role Modeling: Role modeling and cascading leadership from the top down is important because young staff often need many of the same supports/skills/experiences that the young people the organization serves need.
- Inherent Strengths of the Workforce: Role modeling, building supportive relationships, and helping young people identify their strengths is a natural strength of the youth fields workforce.
- Site Training: When possible, train the work site—both the individuals who will supervise the young person and their manager—to ensure a successful and supportive placement.

Youth development organizations play a pivotal role in preparing the next generation for the complexities of the workforce and career paths. Empowering the youth fields workforce through targeted professional development, combined with a culture of mentoring and role modeling, fortifies the foundation for young individuals to thrive in their educational and career journeys.

REFERENCES

Afterschool Alliance. (2022). *Where did all the afterschool staff go? A special brief on afterschool staffing challenges from the fall 2021 Afterschool in the Time of Covid-19 Survey.* Washington, D.C. http://afterschoolalliance.org/documents/Afterschool-COVID-19-Wave-6-Brief.pdf

Afterschool Alliance. (2023). *Afterschool programs open, but still recovering post-pandemic: More work remains for full return to normalcy.* https://afterschoolalliance.org/documents/Afterschool-Programs-Open-But-Still-Recovering-Wave-8.pdf

Akiva, T., Li, J., Martin, K. M., Galletta Horner, C., & McNamara, A. R. (2016). Simple interactions: Piloting a strengths-based and interactions-based professional development intervention for out-of-school time programs. *Child Youth Care Forum*, *46*, 285–305. https://doi.org/10.1007/s10566-016-9375-9

Blattner, M. C. C., & Franklin, A. J. (2017). Why are OST workers dedicated—or not? Factors that influence commitment to OST care work. *Afterschool Matters*, *9*, 9–17.

Bodilly, S. J., & Beckett, M. K. (2005). *Making out-of-school-time matter: Evidence for an action agenda.* Rand Corporation. https://www.rand.org/pubs/monographs/MG242.html

Borden, L. M., Conn, M., Mull, C. D., & Wilkens, M. (2020). The youth development workforce: The people, the profession, and the possibilities. *Journal of Youth Development*, *15*(1), 1–8.

Bradshaw, L. D. (2015). Planning considerations for afterschool professional development. *Afterschool Matters*, *21*, 46–54.

Cantor, P., Osher, D., Berg, J., Steyer, L., & Rose, T. (2019) Malleability, plasticity, and individuality: How children learn and develop in context. *Applied Developmental Science*, *23*(4), 307–337. https://doi.org/10.1080/10888691.2017.1398649

Cole, P. (2011). Building an afterschool workforce: Regulations and beyond. *Afterschool Matters*, *13*, 12–21.

Cooper, B. (2013). Teaching the what as well as the how: Content-rich OST professional development. *Afterschool Matters*, *14*, 1–8.

Durlak, J. A., Weissberg, R. P., & Pachan, M. (2010). A meta-analysis of after-school programs that seek to promote personal and social skills in children and adolescents. *American Journal of Community Psychology*, *45*, 294–309.

Garst, B. A., Baughman, S., & Franz, N. (2014). Benchmarking professional development practices across youth-serving organizations: Implications for extension. *Journal of Extension*, *52*(5), Article 11. https://doi.org/10.34068/joe.52.05.11

Girls Inc. (2023). *Project Accelerate adult participant framework.* Internal Girls Inc. Report: Unpublished.

Girls Inc. of Orange County. (2022). *Project Accelerate program overview.* Internal Girls Inc. Report: Unpublished.

Hall, G., DeSouza, L., Starr, E., Wheeler, K., & Schleyer, K. (2020). Sustaining passion: Findings from an exploratory study of the OST program workforce. *Journal of Youth Development, 15*(1), 9–23.

Henig, J. R., Riehl, C. J., Houston, D. M., Rebell, M. A., & Wolff, M. R. (2016). *Collective impact and the new generation of cross-sector collaborations for education.* Teachers College, Columbia University. https://www.wallacefoundation.org/knowledge-center/Documents/Collective-Impact-and-the-New-Generation-of-Cross-Sector-Collaboration-for-Education.pdf

Ingram, E., Haley, M. A., & Hiteshew, C. (2023). *Deeper understanding of employer partnerships: Exploring best practices in the field.* National Youth Employment Coalition. https://x33888.p3cdn1.secureserver.net/wp-content/uploads/2023/04/Deeper-Understanding-Core-Practice-Brief-FINAL-1.pdf

Naftzger, N., Hall, G., Wheeler, K., & Mitrano, S. (2020). *Findings From the Quality to Youth Outcomes Study Connecting Afterschool Program Quality to Social and Emotional and School-Related Outcomes.* American Institutes for Research.

Naftzger, N., Sniegowski, S., Smith, C., & Riley, A. (2018). *Exploring the relationship between afterschool program quality and youth development outcomes: Findings from the Washington quality to youth outcomes study.* American Institutes for Research.

National Commission on Social, Emotional, and Academic Development (2018). *From a nation at risk to a nation at hope: Recommendations from the National Commission on Social, Emotional, & Academic Development.* Aspen Institute. https://www.aspeninstitute.org/wp-content/uploads/2023/02/Nation-at-Hope.pdf

Osher, D., Cantor, P., Berg, J., Steyer, L., & Rose, T. (2019). Drivers of human development: How relationships and context shape learning and development. *Applied Developmental Science, 24*(1), 6–36. https://doi.org/10.1080/10888691.2017.1398650

Osher, D., Pittman, K., Young, J., Smith, H., Moroney, D., & Irby, M. (2020). *Thriving, conceptualization of the contributors to youth success.* American Institutes for Research and Forum for Youth Investment. https://forumfyi.org/wp-content/uploads/2020/07/Thriving_Equity_Learning_Report_July312020.pdf

Peter, N. (2009). Defining our terms: Professional development in out-of-school time. *Afterschool Matters, 9*, 34–41.

Power of Us Survey. (2023). About the survey. https://powerofussurvey.org/about-the-survey/

Robideau, K., & Santl, K. (2020). Youth work matters: Online professional development for youth workers. *Journal of Youth Development, 15*(1), 70–78.

Shanahan, A.. & Sheehan, T. (2020). Creating community through cohort learning: A training model for youth development professionals. *Journal of Youth Development, 15*(1), 79–93.

Vance, F. (2010). A comparative analysis of competency frameworks for youth workers in the out-of-school time field. *Child Youth Care Forum, 39*, 421–441.

Vance, F., Salvaterra, E., Atkins Michaelson, J., & Newhouse, C. (2016). Getting the right fit: Designing a professional learning community for out-of-school time. *Afterschool Matters, 24*, 21–32.

Vandell, D. L., Reisner, E. R., & Pierce, K. M. (2007). *Outcomes linked to high-quality afterschool programs: Longitudinal findings from the study of promising afterschool programs.* Policy Studies Associates.

Vandell, D. L., Simpkins, S. D., Pierce, K. M., Brown, B. B., Bolt, D., & Reisner, E. (2022). Afterschool programs, extracurricular activities, and unsupervised time: Are patterns of participation linked to children's academic and social well-being? *Applied Developmental Science, 26*(3), 426–442.

Wiedow, J. S. (2018). Supporting effective youth work: Job-embedded professional development in OST. *Afterschool Matters, 28*, 19–28.

Woodberry-Shaw, D., Akiva, T., & Lewis, S. (2020). *Youth workers' experience during the covid-19 pandemic survey results report*. University of Pittsburgh. https://www.education.pitt.edu/sites/default/files/COVID-19%20YOUTH%20WORKERS%20STUDY%20(2).pdf

SECTION III

ROLE OF OST IN SPARKING CAREER PATHWAYS

CHAPTER 8

CREATING AUTHENTIC SPACES FOR YOUTH

A Conversation About the Role of Youth Agency and Its Future

Monique Miles, Angelica Portillo, and Byron Sanders

INTRODUCTION

"Creating Authentic Spaces for Youth: A Conversation about the Role of Youth Agency & Its Future" is a thought-provoking dialogue, featuring prominent figures in the field of youth development and advocacy. In this exclusive Q&A session, Monique Miles, the Managing Director of the Aspen Institute Forum for Community Solutions, Angelica Portillo, the Director of Advocacy & Workforce Initiatives at the National Afterschool Association, and Byron Sanders, President and Chief Executive Officer of Big Thought, came together to discuss the pivotal role of youth agency in our society.

The conversation was driven by the recognition that the landscape of youth development and education has been evolving rapidly, with a shifting focus from traditional "soft skills" to what are now referred to as "21st Century Skills," described as critical, durable, and workforce skills. The participants delved into the importance of nurturing these skills in young individuals and the emerging trends in this domain, examining the impact of youth agency in creating spaces that support their holistic development. This dialogue transcended the conventional perspective of education and

---

Built for More: The Role of Out-of-School Time in Preparing Youth for the Future of Work,
pp. 141–152
Copyright © 2024 by Information Age Publishing
www.infoagepub.com
All rights of reproduction in any form reserved.

youth development, touching upon a paradigm shift from the traditional "Carnegie Model" of education, where students were mere recipients of knowledge, to a more contemporary approach that emphasizes the role of young individuals in shaping their own learning experiences. The participants explored the concept of youth agency as a dynamic and transformative force in the education sector, highlighting the need for more inclusive, self-guided, and self-directed learning environments.

As leaders in their perspective areas, they delved into the significance of youth agency for "opportunity youth," emphasizing the necessity of enabling marginalized and underserved youth to have a voice and a role in reshaping the systems that have often failed to serve their needs. This discussion underscored the importance of authentic youth agency in creating equitable opportunities for youth and amplifying their voices in policymaking, program design, and educational transformation. They also considered the role of organizations, policymakers, and funders in fostering youth agency. Focusing on the importance of centering young people's voices and creativity in the decision-making processes, and how to create authentic spaces for youth participation and co-design. The conversation highlighted the mutual benefits of involving young people in shaping their experiences, both for their personal growth and for the organizations that serve them.

Ultimately, this conversation emphasized the critical need for nurturing youth agency, not just as a facet of youth development but as a fundamental element in creating a more inclusive, equitable, and forward-thinking society. It presented a vision of a world where young people are empowered, their voices are heard, and their creativity is celebrated, with an understanding that this transformation can have a ripple effect, impacting not only individual lives but also communities, institutions, and society at large.

CONVERSATION

BS: With all the context, I am grateful that both of you, as leaders in your sectors and as friends, have agreed to have this conversation. In recent years, people have started to name things like 21st Century Skills building as something that is more important than we used to have categorized as. We used to call these things "soft skills" but are now seeing them coined critical skills, durable skills, or workforce skills. From your perspective and the seat you sit in, why is it important and what emerging trends in this area have you seen over the past few years?

AP: The National Afterschool Association (NAA) has the core knowledge, skills, and competencies, which outlines what professionals who work with youth need to know, show, and grow to positively impact young people.

Creating Authentic Spaces for Youth   143

That looks at how you work with young people and how you implement character building. By character building, we see the foundation including, but not limited to, being patient, creating a welcoming environment, being able to be relatable to the students. It is important for young people to learn these soft skills too. Just as our young people need to learn them, so do our out-of-school time professional in order to teach them.

MM: Seeing the rise in the focus on 21st century skills is exactly right. To your point, it is part of the zeitgeist of the moment. In our work at the Aspen Institute, part of what we've been committed to, that feels like it is a perfect complement to the 21st century skill set, is an emphasis on belonging, meaning, wellbeing and purpose. We think about student wellbeing and youth and young adult wellbeing, and how they fit into the 21st century skill sets. As we are thinking about the teaching of those skills, we need to think about what those skills mean for students who need to connect with programming that's meaningful to them and that gets them on a path toward their future. At the same time, we want to create spaces for young people to meaningfully belong, for young people to practice and express agency for 21st century skill building. Additionally, we want workforce development to be tied to a young person's purpose. In the center of all of that would be a deep commitment to supporting a young person's wellbeing. The compliment to the piece to 21st Century skills needs to be about creating spaces of belonging for youth and young adults, spaces of wellbeing that are tied to young people identifying, exploring, and discovering their purpose so that they are able to meaningfully self-determine their futures.

BS: That is so good! It feels as though there is a current or flow toward less of a traditional, maybe industrial, way of thinking about education and youth development. Moving further away from the Carnegie Model of "butts in seats" and how that translates to a better life outcome. It is almost like what I've seen Aspen Institute, for the first time, inserting the soul and the framework of purpose and belonging. They are being equally positioned in importance, and one could argue, a higher importance in the framework of how young people are able to navigate this learning journey.

Angelica, you just talked about how you are doing in the out-of-school professional space. As we are starting to define those skills that we called "soft skills," it is becoming increasingly important to change the design of youth experiences so that, the experience itself, is building those assets as opposed to testing a couple of frameworks and using quizzes to be an artifact that shows youth built a skill. It is almost like you have to embed it in the design itself.

One of those emerging trends is creating more agency for youth in the learning experiences and space. I am contrasting that against our historical models have been through the years, "i.e., where Sage on the stage, give

144　M. MILES, A. PORTILLO, and B. SANDERS

it back to the kids, can you repeat what I just said to you." Talk about this concept of youth agency in a learning experience that is so important, and quite frankly, dynamic or transformational to the education sector?

AP: This past December, I was in Chicago, with Every Hour Counts because they recently released a study, "Powered by Youth Voice: Future Directors for Afterschool." In the study, youth were able to answer the questions, "What does afterschool look like for you in the future? If it could be anything, what would it be?" It was interesting because the study found the activities that would be most meaningful to youth were cooking, physical movement, learning how to manage money, gardening, entrepreneurship, outdoor activities, music (singing and musical instruments), and mental health supports. I see that list of things and that is just the beginning, right? That is just their top things. And you can't have that in your traditional school day. There's just, quite frankly, not enough hours. So many other things teachers are trying to pour into our students and youth. When you think of out-of-school time, it is so important that they have the opportunities to voice what they need and want. Another thing the youth said is that they really do get to explore these areas in afterschool because they can't in the school day. In order to create these environments, as out-of-school time professionals, we have to allow them to speak their mind, explore things that they want to, and get opportunities they wouldn't have otherwise, either at home, school, etc. It is just amazing that the variety of things they want learn and the things they care about, I didn't even think they needed or wanted. We could assume all we want, because we think we know what kids need based on what we may have needed. But these youth are not the same as we were. It is amazing to give them that voice and agency to determine what a program looks like and feels like for them.

To add on to that, you have to have a skilled professional working with them to deliver that programming. You cannot just put somebody in the room and have them create a space where the youth can have a voice because they may not feel safe. Creating this environment where they want to share is important. It takes the right person that knows how to create a safe environment where they can share and recognize the value of youth voice.

BS: It honestly sounds like we are talking about a fundamentally different job from what we have said teachers and educators used to be to what it now can and should be, if youth agency is going to be embedded. Monique, what do you think?

MM: I was thinking about the shifts from a Carnegie Model to a Montessori Model, the focus on self-guided and self-directed learning. Young people have a menu presented to them that they've been able to co-design, and they have been able to articulate because it is meaningful to them. Ideally, from our work and our vision, it's going to touch their culture, their

Creating Authentic Spaces for Youth 145

racial identity, their community, their family, and what is really important to them. In that menu of options, they can then self-determine and select what's most relevant to them, and particularly as they are envisioning their future. So that is truly what I love, and what we are dreaming up at the Aspen Institute is that education is transformative. We can be talking about out-of-school time, and we can be talking about the many different places and spaces that young people occupy.

At the same time, we can still do this work both inside and outside the K–12 school system. It really can transform into what our young people need, and we should see this in all of the different areas that touch the lives of youth and young adults. When we talk about agency, we are talking about young people, self-guiding and self-determining, what is meaningful to them. Because when something speaks to them, when it resonates with them, when they are able to express their choice, we know the evidence-based research supports their agency. The research supports not only an opportunity to transform or transcend, but it is also an opportunity for their peers to transcend, for their cousins to transcend. We have young people say that when they finally connected with this program, a program that meant the world to them, they "had to call my cousin and I had to go get my sister" and others shared that when they "finally got on track to getting a post-secondary education, I encouraged my mom to go back to school." Placing agency at the center of self-determination and of options, it doesn't just benefit that young person but also benefits their families and their communities. That's why it is so important.

BS: That radiating effect of youth being at the center. That's a really powerful thought, and I think even more powerful given the youth you specialize in, Monique. This needs to happen to young people writ large. But I would say even more so for those niche groups or special groups where the systems, as they currently are, have not well served them. Talk about why this is even more important for "opportunity youth" and the systems change where this is the norm.

MM: You are exactly right. I'll take it back to history because that's where it starts. Sometimes, we talk about history like something in the past, but for any person who has experienced harm, trauma, been marginalized, especially for youth and youth adults of color, youth and young adults who are system involved, foster care, justice care, that trauma is with them and all of the ways that experience has reduced their sense of agency and their sense of wellbeing. It becomes important for us, in creating the conditions in the spaces for them to thrive, that we are thinking about how we heal, and how we create a space in an environment that accelerates their healing, that wellbeing and their sense of agency. So much of their lived experience has been about stripping rights and so much of the historical context that it has created the conditions that they face. Again, for youth and young adults of color, who are on a path of transitioning into the workforce and then from workforce to adulthood. What we know is that part of even making meaning of their racial identity has happened in the backdrop of a country and systems that were not designed for them and that do not value their humanity. We already need to be focused on account narrative and need to start thinking about priority populations—young people, foster care system, justice system—it is even more important that we, from an equity perspective, that we can set some universal goals. But then really begin to target the very specific needs of priority populations so that they receive an abundance of the resources that we have and the ways we can meet their needs. From our work at the Aspen Institute, that's why we focus on opportunity youth, youth and young adults of color, and system involved youth, because so much of our work is about the prioritization of resources in ways that are meant to both really hold the history and be a redress for the history. In addition to also planning for a future that is determined by young people and this part of their healing and identity, and to prepare them for the future of their visioning.

BS: It makes so much sense because if you ever follow a 3- or 4-year-old to see if they think they have power, they feel like they have all of the agency, all of the power. And it's almost like our systems are retrying youth, who will eventually become adults, telling them that this isn't the space for your voice, and this isn't the place where you speak up. Add the layer on that you just mentioned of youth who have been extremely impacted by these additional systems that double down on that message. Whether it is justice systems, foster systems, you just highlighted that you can't snap your finger and say "Hey guys! You are free to think, you are free to be" in one day, because maybe the last 20 years of their life told them otherwise.

It brings us back to the conversation I asked Angelica to put a pin in. That's a very different proposition for someone who is coming to work with young people. If now, my job is not just to keep kids safe, engaged, and making sure that they can regurgitate the things that I told them that are important. Now all of a sudden, I am supposed to move from being the instructor to being a facilitator. How in the world do we make sure the adults, who are already in the industry or new ones coming in, whether through formal education or in the out-of-school time space, know that this isn't something they have experienced, and probably their mother or grandmother have experienced before. Same word, but a very different definition of what this job is and means. How do we start to make those shifts and what are some of things you are seeing?

AP: You are right, the job of afterschool and the afterschool workforce is definitely changing. And I see it in three ways. One, there is a public narrative of the afterschool professional that is shifting. You can no longer come in and just do a head count, make sure the kids are there and getting what

Creating Authentic Spaces for Youth   147

they need. I also think it's the person doing this work who is skilled and knowledgeable, and getting training to create environments for the youth to really grow and explore. This job is way beyond what even I or many others did not know that it could be, or what the career could lead me to.

Second, there is the practice piece of the afterschool profession, and specifically I am referring to the job quality. We have to ensure that people are coming into this job, know that this is a career you can be in, and that this is something that you should be paid beyond a liveable wage, and it should go with the skills you have. There should be a shift with this role to that you can have benefits, career development, and all the other things that go into any other job with this career path. Something we look at NAA, is our "quality connection," which means once we prioritize job quality, we have stability in our workforce that will enable afterschool professionals to deliver high-quality programs we know that matter. It starts with ensuring job quality from organizations to the people, who know they can advocate for themselves.

Lastly, the policy piece. Something we are doing at NAA (with our national policy partners) is ensuring that every time that we are advocating for policy, we are also advocating that staff does get professional development, they are getting paid what they need to be paid, and that we are developing career ladders for them. We are ensuring that these are jobs people want to work. One of the biggest problems to the question you asked last time about access to these programs, if there is no staff to work them, then the children won't have access.

BS: Right! It sounds so simple, but it is truly an issue. It cuts across to the note you put up there, Monique, about the professionalization of the sector. People need to stop treating it like the icing when it is actually the cake. Did you have anything you wanted to add to that thought?

MM: I feel like I am going to say no and then say all of these things. But, Angelica, what you shared was just so good and so strong and really comprehensive. I put in the chat that you were describing the professionalization of the field, and I think that sounds exactly right.

AP: Yes, that was my goal.

MM: I loved that you framed it under narrative change because, like in our work around narrative change, it's about what is possible. Being able to articulate that is entirely different from what it is and changing to what you want it to be. So, beginning to identify those things and name those things in order to do the policy, organizing, and policy work around how you get from where the field currently is to where it needs to be. I think it is exactly right that there are lots of structural shifts, organizing and public funding. Then it also is about the stories we tell about who we are hiring and what their stories are, and the young people being served. Just thought your comment was really good and comprehensive.

BS: I love it when we are talking about, you know, real systems change. Often times, especially as we are focusing on this concept of youth agency, when I have brought it up in many settings, and even, kind of opening up the kimono here, even at Big Thought, right? Even in our own work, usually when we think about youth, we are like "How do we make sure that we bring more agency into programs so that the end user experience needs to make sure that it is truly youth centered and youth driven?" We have started to ask ourselves to take it to the next level. Should we be swimming further upstream with regard to youth input and engagement around things that ultimately are going to have a lot to do with their own lives. So, with this concept of "nothing for us without us," are you all seeing what that whether it's organizations, policy or even funding incentives start to require or incentivize having young people as a voice in organizations before they get to the programs. Thinking of the governance level of an organization that is supposed to be serving young people, or actually hiring youth as consultants. And not just in the programs, but even asking them to help shape the professional development for the adults. Do you see this happening or emerging as a trend in your areas?

AP: I have one prime example of basically everything you just said: Youthprise in Minnesota. They have the Minnesota Youth Council, and that's a strategic partnership between Minnesota Alliance with Youth and Youthprise. They are a representative statewide body of 36 youth and their adult mentors. They provide input on their legislative agenda and their education agenda for all policies that are affecting youth. That's incredibly important beyond just OST.

BS: Absolutely!

AP: I am familiar with the group, having done site visits, and the way they incorporate youth voice into every single thing they do is just phenomenal, and I wish I had more concrete examples. But, whenever I think of youth voice and out-of-school time, they are a true champion in that.

MM: Aspen Institute funds Youthprise and we work closely with Marcus and his team. I love that, and that model and example. There are so many like them and we are preparing for our next convening in Aspen, and we will be featuring Youth Speaks, an organization out of California.

BS: Yes—love them!

MM: So yeah, you know Youth Speaks and to the conversation about narrative change a bit ago, these are young people leading on narrative strategies, cultural strategies, and the relationship between narrative and cultural strategy. But you know, that is youth work that is driving all of that. Youth Will is another organization that we work with out in California, very similar to a self-organized public agenda. Another organization we worked closely with for years, Opportunity Youth United. Again, young people, former opportunity youth, coming together to set up policy agendas and

Creating Authentic Spaces for Youth 149

do everything from voter registration to organizing for additional seats for alternative options for their peers. There is just a range of different types of models that we have seen.

The very last thing that I'll say is that they type of work we fund, and this is part of why Youthprise is one of our grantees, the type of way we think about funding community change, is very much youth led, youth at the center. What that means is that we end up working with community-based organizations. Again, this is why Youthprise is such a great example. Where they are very clear about what their community wide agenda may be for youth and young adults around academic attainment and workforce, and not just connecting to jobs but advancement, upskilling careers, beginning to build intergenerational wealth, and financial stability. In doing that work and bringing different sector and system partners together, all of that, there are so many examples across San Francisco, Boston, Philadelphia, Los Angeles. LA is a powerful example, especially because those are foster care involved youth where the agenda is co-design, co-own, and co-led by youth and young adults who are impacted by these systems. And that's our model, we think it is so important. Angelica, you said this earlier. Like adults, we might think that we have solutions but when you create authentic spaces for young people to share not just what's top of mind, but even how they're dreaming about the future and their path to getting there. So much of that is baked into how we think about supporting community change, work, community agency, and community power building, with youth at the center of all of that.

BS: Love it! It is what you both described, I see it as a two-way beneficial road. One, the young people, especially in this world, need to have been able to build the muscles of acting within their own agency. Not waiting necessarily for your assignment, but to look around, make an assessment, use data to decide, and say "Hey, this is what I would like to see happen." Then getting to work on doing it. You can't just expect people to do that without ever having had practice. So, these ways to engage young people in a range of different exercises of agency just seem to be great for them.

Then on the other side, the organization's benefit so much. Youth have amazing ideas! My kids, especially my own son, is probably one of the most creative human beings. He will drop a pun on you that you did not see coming, right? It's just how his brain works, and I think we discount that as a society, generally.

MM: I would add to that—it is exactly right—and this is what I was saying earlier about the ripples. It impacts peers, it impacts families, it impacts communities. But the truth is, it also is an opportunity for us to shift the social sector more broadly. Like when we think about, particularly, the social sector that was designed and now the incentives, I should say, in some ways are really perverse. Especially around philanthropy being so outcomes oriented and maybe not holding place for belonging, culture or racial identity.

BS: Absolutely!

MM: This is an opportunity to help the social sector make the types of shifts that are so necessary because they are community owned and community led. What I would argue is that if it's good at that level for the social sector, then it also ultimately becomes good for our democracy. We need it to be good for our democracy because we need it to be good for our young people who are going to run our democracy. And in many ways, they are already doing it, but it creates space for them to build their muscles and capacity to do that in the future as well.

BS: This isn't just about good programs; this is about the future of humanity.

BS: Absolutely! What you are calling back to me, Monique, is that I am currently going through the new novel, *King: A Life*, and it is a beautiful reminder of just how critical youth are to advance society. Period. You know, as much as, Dr. King was a young professional, by our common vernacular, but was actually within the opportunity youth age range when he stepped out on the scene in a major way. When you listen to him, there were a lot of people who were kids. And it was kind of dangerous out there, right? People were asking themselves; do we really want to put young people in this fight? And he told them that they don't have a choice because they were moving and he wanted them in this. So, keeping with the notion that youth agency, harkening back to the civil rights movement, is a perfect example. Young people literally changed the world because some of the leaders, Martin Luther King Jr. being one of them, saying get these young people involved. Let them do what they are doing, as a matter of fact, let's follow them.

MM: I'll just add that Ella Jo Baker is one of my favorite civil rights leaders because that was her role and that was her work. We named our middle child, Ella, after Baker, and we used to tell her when she was little that Baker's nickname was Fundi, which is Swahili for the teacher of the next generation.

BS: Amazing!

MM: She was very much about we are only doing this with young people! That is why I love Sweet Honey in the Rock because they made a song to dedicate to her called Ella's Song. It is all about the power of young people in leading the movement for the future. I just agree with all my heart and it's one of my favorite stories of the civil rights movement to tell.

BS: You are absolutely right! SNCC would not have been SNCC without Ella's coming. I can nerd out about this stuff all day, but a lot of the old school, old head Southern Christian Leadership Conference leaders, she

Creating Authentic Spaces for Youth   151

would tell them to chill out and these kids are doing what they need to do. Create space and get out of the way.

We are coming to the end of this conversation, and as we look ahead and looking towards how do we start to make some of these shifts in what we have talked about here. How do we move ourselves, as policymakers and funders in this sector, to allow the voice in that creativity and energy of young people to be more central in how we work with them and alongside them. If you had to wave a magic wand and something existed in society, the way you think it would need to be in order for us to have the kind of world manifest where youth agency is a given and youth experiences are valued, what would it be?

AP: Like we said, youth know what they want, and they just need the opportunity to voice it and believe in what they say. But it's going to take the adults to realize that and make that possible. I think my magic wand would be to acknowledge afterschool as a profession and allowing funding, practices, and all the agencies coming together to uplift the profession. How do we ensure that we can create those possibilities for young people. Because as adults and youth development professionals need to balance what you say they want versus what we know they need. It is going to take us acknowledging both of those things.

It is *US* also listening to them, is *US*, youth professionals, being given the time, incentives, opportunity to engage professional development that goes beyond what is already out there. There is so much training on classroom management, behavior, and program development, but there is so much more, and it goes into really developing the person that's working with the youth.

BS: Awesome!

MM: I agree with all of that and the only thing I would add is what Angelica said earlier. I think a lot of what we can do to advance this, and I mean meaningfully advance it so that it becomes both bottoms up and top down, is through narrative change work and especially about the narratives of young people. You know the stories that we tell about what young people are not able to do or what we believe, the biases we hold, about young people. So, if we can begin to create different narratives that really are about the agency, the expression, the wisdom, the joy, the power of young people, and that then become the water we all drink and the air that we all breathe. Truly, the beliefs that we all hold about what young people know, what young people are able to do, and the power that young people hold, I think that we can begin to see this transformation in every space that young people inhabit. Whether it is as young as elementary school, middle school, high school, post-secondary—their trajectory into adulthood. But I would try to focus on specifically changing the narratives and the beliefs that we hold about young people. I think it's one of the most important strategies to get us to how we are all dreaming about youth agency and youth power.

BS: Monique and Angelica, thank y'all. This conversation has been everything we were hoping it would be. Your expertise and your experiences, and quite frankly, your imagination—because I could literally picture the world that each of you were describing. Thank you for your time.

CONCLUSION

This conversation serves as a powerful reminder of the dynamic shifts happening within the field of youth development and education. It is evident that youth agency is not just an abstract concept, but a transformative force that can shape the future of our society. Miles, Portillo, and Sanders illuminated the necessity of adapting to changing times and recognizing the evolution of "soft skills" into essential 21st Century Skills that encompass not only academics but also personal well-being, a sense of belonging, and a purposeful journey towards the future.

These leaders highlighted the need to move away from traditional education models, such as the Carnegie Model, which viewed students as passive recipients of knowledge. Instead, the focus has shifted towards self-guided and self-directed learning, where young individuals play an active role in shaping their education and personal growth. This shift challenges educators and youth professionals to become facilitators of exploration and agency, creating environments that foster creativity and independence.

Moreover, the conversation emphasized that the significance of youth agency extends beyond individual development. It has a profound impact on marginalized and opportunity youth, whose voices and aspirations have often been ignored by systems that were not designed to meet their unique needs. By elevating youth agency, the participants envisioned a future where young people, especially those who have experienced systemic challenges, could redefine the systems that affect their lives and, in doing so, heal their communities and build a more equitable world.

Miles and Portillo underlined that transforming the social sector and ensuring youth agency is not only a benefit for young individuals, but a necessity for the betterment of society as a whole. The importance of narrative change as a vital tool in shifting societal perspectives about the capabilities and potential of young people. In this vision, youth agency is celebrated as the cornerstone of a more inclusive, equitable, and democratic future, where young people are empowered to lead and effect positive change on a global scale. They have illuminated the path forward, one where youth agency is not merely a concept but a dynamic force that holds the promise of a brighter future for us all.

CHAPTER 9

NON-ARTIFICIAL AUTHENTIC INTELLIGENCE

Creating Ecosystems of Development for Young People Outside of School and in the World of Work

Gabrielle Kurlander and Christopher Street

INTRODUCTION

"In order to change an existing paradigm, you do not struggle to try and change the problematic model. You create a new model and make the old one obsolete."

—R. Buckminister Fuller

"As a young Black man, you don't get exposure to people who know how the world works and, in many cases, run it. Unless you are a 'certain person' in America, you don't get access. I found it at 'All Stars.' I met people I thought of as 'just suits,' and you know what? They cared about me."

—Glenroy Wason, Development School for Youth Alum (2023)

Built for More: The Role of Out-of-School Time in Preparing Youth for the Future of Work,
pp. 153–172
Copyright © 2024 by Information Age Publishing
www.infoagepub.com
All rights of reproduction in any form reserved.

> "All Stars reaches far and wide because poverty reaches far and wide, and they teach young people to develop themselves through performance theory by pretending to do things they never imagined possible."
>
> —Khalil Gibran Muhammad, PhD, Ford Foundation Professor of History, Race and Public Policy, Harvard Kennedy School (2019)

Over the last 25 years, All Stars Project, Inc. (ASP) has created a thriving youth development ecosystem that introduces high school students from economically disadvantaged communities to the broader world, including the world of work. Our out-of-school time (OST) programs have brought in corporate professionals and institutional resources as "partners in development." This partnership with the private sector has created new growth pathways for young people who are most in need.

In 1997, we launched our award-winning Development School for Youth (DSY) program. This program comprises of visits to corporations, engagements with corporate professionals and leaders, developmental workshops, and relationship-building activities with staff. The culmination of the program involves a paid, high-quality summer internship. Since DSY's founding, over 5,000 youth have completed the program. Their internship placements have been at hundreds of corporations and institutions, large and small, across seven cities spanning most regions of the nation.

In this chapter, we will share how, through the DSY, we built an effective partnership model with caring adults in the corporate community. Furthermore, we will also offer an emerging vision for a new kind of partnership between education, workforce development, and the nonprofit sectors. The context of the discussion is a rapidly changing world of work, accelerated by the impact of COVID-19-driven societal shifts over the last three years, game-changing technological advances, and the intransigence of poverty in America.

Within this chapter, we include the voices of colleagues who played critical roles in the building of ASP, often as volunteers. Additionally, we spotlight the perspectives of "the partners," DSY alumni and corporate executives, who wholeheartedly embraced "two-way development." Pioneered and promoted by ASP, this philosophy and its corresponding practices underscore the societal significance of mutual growth and enrichment.

PREPARING FOR THE FUTURE OF WORK

> "I think that an America without poverty is a better America, a safer America, a more democratically engaged America, it's a freer America. It's an America that activates its full potential, right? That takes all those kids that, but for poverty, would have been engineers, and scientists, and

diplomats, and poets and priests. And takes those kids and unleashes their potential in a way that we're just not doing now."

—Matthew Desmond, PhD, Maurice P. During Professor of Sociology, Princeton University (2023)

"All Stars got me my first job I ever had of any kind, at the age of 16. It gave me a significant head start in getting out there and just getting more exposed and getting more comfortable in these environments, practice and repetition were really important. We should not downplay the very important implications of race and class and how they play into success because those things are always present and always very important. But thinking of that as performance and as a series of acts and statements makes it for me feel more manageable and learnable."

—Lindsay McKenzie, Development School for Youth Alum (2023)

Jeremy Rifkin's (1995) work delving into the exploration of economic dislocation caused by the technological revolution of the 1980s and 1990s was a stark and sobering analysis. It precedes the current discussion and concerns about artificial intelligence's impact on the workforce over the next decade. Although Rifkin's conclusions of massive unemployment have not materialized (yet), in the context of an America undergoing de-industrialization, job growth has been primarily in service-related industries and sectors. These sectors are traditionally lower wage and offer fewer pathways to economic advancement (Bureau of Labor Statistics, 1999).

In ASP's view, the drivers of the future of work discussions in America today are centered around two principles. The first involves how to prepare the current workforce for today's job openings, which require a higher level of technical skill or specialization than the current workforce possesses. The second principle pertains to how to train a workforce to develop the flexibility, agility and learning capability needed to navigate the fast pace of change in today's world. The focus so far has primarily been on the former. We argue here that much greater emphasis and investment are needed in the latter. This is at the heart of what we mean by youth development.

Founded in 1981, ASP emerged as a response to the mounting shortcomings of America's education system in preparing millions of children from economically disadvantaged communities for mainstream success. The crisis state of education was easy to see at the ground level in the communities we were dedicated to, and hard data signals were and continue to be abundant. Notably, the large college enrollment gap between graduates of high-income high schools and high schools in high-poverty, urban areas is frequently cited (National Student Clearinghouse Research Center, 2019). Today, from grade school to higher education, our education system is straining under the pressures of a rapidly changing world. This struggle is particularly pronounced among young people in secondary education; their performance is impacted and exacerbated by challenges, such as the COVID-19 pandemic and other related challenges (Dorn et al., 2021; Shell, 2018).

In addition to these challenges at the secondary level, many philanthropic and corporate leaders argue that America has a broken model of post-secondary, higher education. This is evidenced by exorbitant costs, which burden students with debt, and outdated modes of teaching and curricula that are not responsive to the needs of most students seeking gainful employment. This includes vocational and skills-based trades that offer pathways into the middle class (Docking, 2022). Furthermore, large numbers of Black and Latino students are starting their college journeys, assuming debt, only to fail to complete their studies. In 2021, the six-year college completion rate for Black students was 44.5%, and for Hispanic students, it was 51.5%, compared to 69.6% for White students (NSC DEI Data Lab, 2023).

It is unclear whether the existing governing framework—beset by conflict and politics—can produce a system that can change the trajectories of underserved young people. This uncertainty is exemplified by research showing that long-established, government-run summer youth employment programs in New York, Boston and Chicago have not improved outcomes in young people's employability (Gelber et al., 2016; Valentin et al., 2017).

Against this backdrop, leaders and organizations like ours are achieving success through new approaches and initiatives. Our effort emerged from an unusual confluence of experimentation in forging partnerships that bridge differences and distances between economically disadvantaged and affluent citizens. Also, our foundation in performance and community organizing have served as critical tools in welding a powerful connection between our diverse stakeholders. This connection has empowered them to thrive in a new, co-created environment that changes the lives of all involved. Currently, we see a strong push from corporate, philanthropic and even some educational leaders to pivot away from college degree requirements for employment. Instead, there's a growing emphasis on skills-based training as either a requirement or a preference (Caminiti, 2022). This shift is important for removing barriers to workforce participation for people who either do not graduate from college or choose not to attend. However, there is another necessary step to be taken.

Collectively, we need to seek out and gather private and public resources that can be invested "upstream"—that is, in early and broad outside-of-school and developmental programming for high school-age and even

Non-Artificial Authentic Intelligence   157

younger students. While this is important for all young people, it is especially critical for those growing up in difficult economic circumstances.

FOUNDATIONS OF ASP'S YOUTH DEVELOPMENT MODEL

"I grew up in a predominantly Black and Brown, lower-income environment. Then, on my Tuesday evenings at DSY, I'm entering a new world where I'm on Wall Street hanging out with business professionals and executives and being exposed to this new world. As a 17-year-old, I knew I needed to do something to position myself closer to this world because this was the type of lifestyle and life that I wanted for myself."

—Wadnes Castelly, Development School for Youth Alum (2023)

"America has not completed its task of integrating the African-American population, and communities of color, into mainstream America."

—Lenora B. Fulani, PhD, Co-founder, All Stars Project (2013)

The breakthroughs achieved by ASP were shaped by, and helped to shape, the work that leading researchers, writers, and educators conducted in the 1990s to create new fields of youth-focused inquiry and study. Central to this evolution was the emergent concept of Supplementary Education with a specific focus on young people of color in America. The idea was popularized by Dr. Edmund Gordon, a founder of Head Start and a professor at Columbia University's Teachers College (Bridglall & Gordon, 2002).

Dr. Gordon's exploration into improving the academic success of African American, Latino American, Native American and economically disadvantaged students led him to focus on the family and community activities and learning experiences that support academic development outside of formal school hours. These include available household resources—such as computers, books and the academic support of siblings and parents—as well as community resources like clubs, private lessons and cultural activities. He underscored that for low-income students, opportunities to participate in these supplementary, enriching activities are either unavailable or underutilized compared to those available to peers in higher socioeconomic backgrounds. Driven by this insight, Dr. Gordon advocated for concentrated efforts to introduce a wide variety of supplementary education opportunities for low-income families and communities—an effort that he and the many scholars and education leaders he influenced have continued to champion.

The turn toward "other than school" solutions to addressing poverty and inequality was a common ingredient in this cauldron of innovation.

158 G. KURLANDER and C. STREET

This shift spanned different generations, intellectual views, and specialties of scholars such as James Comer, MD; Derrick Bell, Esq.; Kwame Anthony Appiah, PhD; Henry Louis Gates, Jr., PhD; Pedro Noguera, PhD; Khalil Gibran Muhammad, PhD; as well as ASP co-founders Fred Newman, PhD; Lenora Fulani, PhD and their close intellectual partner Lois Holzman, PhD.

The works of Bell (2004), Appiah (1997) and Newman and Holzman (1993/2013) illustrate this interconnected evolution. Bell, a towering figure in the civil rights movement, was extensively involved in handling hundreds of desegregation cases in the 1960s. Forty years later, he was in the process of rethinking the assumption that a policy of school integration would improve educational and life prospects for Black children. Concurrently, Appiah, a cultural theorist and philosopher, was exploring the benefits of cultivating broader, more cosmopolitan identities as a means of developing a citizenry. Newman and Holzman were bringing new ideas from Lev Vygotsky and other progressive thinkers in psychology about the fundamental socialness of human development and learning, as well as the close association of performance and development, into both their scholarship and community activism.

Around the same period, the field of psychology was making a comparable shift from a focus on abnormal to positive psychology. This shift, in the case of young people, meant studying and understanding their strengths and the role that outside-of-school programs, particularly those involving the performing arts, could play in enhancing development and learning (Holzman, 2017). Finally, while afterschool programs had historically responded to young people's needs for care, recreation and socialization, some of these programs began to consider how afterschool could itself be advanced to become an arena for the development of youth in the context of a changing world (Halpern, 2003). This confluence of activism and inquiry served as a catalyst for innovative thinking and action aimed at reshaping the landscape of youth-focused endeavors.

ASP's share in and contribution to this "emerging market" was a brand of youth development that encompassed several key elements: (1) recognizing that authentic development environments outside of school were critically important for the success of our country's most disadvantaged youth in school, the workplace and life; (2) placing performance at the center of youth development methodology; and (3) creating an unlikely partnership with some of America's more iconoclastic philanthropists, prominent corporate leaders and their companies, who fund it, volunteer for it, and grow by participating in it. In essence, ASP's imprint within this evolving landscape was characterized by a holistic and performance-driven approach to youth development, underpinned by innovative partnerships that defied traditional boundaries.

PERFORMANCE AS A BREAKTHROUGH
TOOL FOR YOUTH DEVELOPMENT

"Performance was a new concept to me. I saw how corporate leaders and executives presented themselves using the same strategies we learned at the 'All Stars.' Some people are born with it. Others develop it by people with theater backgrounds literally showing them tangible examples. You see it in action, and then you can repeat it."

—Chioma Igwebuike, Development School for Youth Alum (2023)

While the performing arts have long held a special place within youth programming—encouraging young people to explore their emotions, expand their imaginations and develop their voices—ASP has taken it a step further. ASP has harnessed the act of performing in everyday life as a powerful tool for growth and transformation.

The close association between our capacity as human beings to perform and continuously develop is one of the most relevant, cutting-edge discoveries in human science in the 21st century. In the simplest terms, actors do far more than present lines of a play. They create their character—a new version of themselves—that they bring to the stage. Importantly, they do this without giving up any of "who they are." The breakthrough insight is that this capacity to perform, which every human being possesses, can be *intentionally exercised in everyday life*—to create new versions of who we are and try things we have never done before. In choosing to perform, human beings have the power to transform and go beyond where they are and bring along all of who they are, their culture and their life experiences (Heath, 2000; Holzman 1997, 2017; Holzman & Mendez, 2003; Newman & Holzman, 1993/2013).

ASP has emerged as a pioneering and leading community laboratory demonstrating the profound and practical value of this discovery. We have learned that young people in underserved communities, who often have been isolated and left without hope, not only need and deserve resources and opportunities but also need a way to make the journey into the mainstream. Performance gives them a way to take the risk of trying out new roles and doing new things. Since DSY was launched, grassroots educators Lenora Fulani, PhD; Pamela A. Lewis; and Gloria Strickland, MA, led the creation of an extensive body of program structures and practices that constitute our performance-based approach. These include organizing our program participants as "ensembles," teaching them the basics of improvisational performance, training and positioning our program staff as performance directors and educating and training our partners within the business community so that they can adopt and practice performance methods (Lobman, 2017).

AN ENDOWMENT OF FRIENDSHIP:
BUILDING PHILANTHROPIC SUPPORT FOR INNOVATION

"We were selling hopes and dreams. We were willing to put our time and
sweat equity into building something speculative. In our hearts, we felt
we could uniquely contribute to New York City and the country. This
unshakeable belief fueled thousands of hours of grueling grassroots
fundraising. This was our seed capital."

—Richard Sokolow, ASP Board Chair, 2008–2017 (2016)

"The All Stars Talent Show Network brought joy,
creativity and hope into my life and my community in Bed-Stuy, Brooklyn.
We learned from the amazing leaders to build something new that was
ours, something we could be proud of ... and seeing that the early funders,
who were mostly white adults with money, cared enough about who we were
to partner with us by giving their money, time, influence and guidance has
positively shaped my life since."

—Antoine Joyce, Senior Vice President/City Leader, ASP of Dallas (2022)

During the 1980s and '90s, ASP's founding years, the country was undergoing severe cutbacks in government funding for the arts, along with policy
changes that exacerbated and stigmatized poverty, especially affecting Black
and Brown young people in urban neighborhoods. Within the anti-poverty
activist community, ASP's choice to partner with wealthy philanthropists,
prominent corporate leaders and their companies was unusual. For many,
the business community was frequently seen as an enemy, not an ally.

One of ASP's leaders, its first paid staff member and co-author of this
chapter, Gabrielle Kurlander, held a firm conviction that Americans—
including many in the corporate world—would want to be part of creating
an independently funded, innovative effort to engage poverty through
experimental methods like the performance approach to development. As
a working actor, she also had a deep understanding and love for performance. Beginning in 1989, when she became ASP's president, Kurlander
led the creation of a new kind of philanthropy known as "Involvement
Philanthropy." This innovative approach would not rely on elected officials
dispersing government funds, but would be built on and by people from
very different walks of life, coming together to grow.

With that founding philosophy in hand, a group of more than 50 ASP
volunteers spent seven years, from 1990 to 1997, canvassing door to door,
raising money on street corners and conducting cold-call telephone campaigns to generate thousands of small individual donations. These early
funds did not include corporate donations or foundation grants; most
contributions were between $25 and $100. With no formal fundraising

Non-Artificial Authentic Intelligence   161

training but a fair amount of gumption, Kurlander and a small team of skilled volunteers began to engage with some of these donors at a higher level. They started asking for $1,000 donations and sought to meet and get to know those who agreed.

ASP embarked on a daring challenge in the public marketplace by announcing a goal of raising 50 first-time donations of $10,000 in a campaign aptly called "The Founding Fifty." By December 1998, 34 families had stepped forward with one-time gifts of $10,000. This marked the inception of a transformational journey for ASP to bring the organization, its performance-based approach to growing young people from poor communities and its focus on new kinds of partnerships into the mainstream of American life. To this day, some of these Founding Fifty families remain All Stars' most generous champions and steadfast advocates.

As the sphere of contact and engagement grew and deepened, and as increasing numbers of young people joined ASP programs, philanthropic partners were called upon to do more—both financially and in terms of their direct involvement with youth. These early pioneer families, whose personal views spanned the political spectrum, put their differences aside and stepped forward and partnered with Kurlander to lead ASP's expansion across the country. Notably, at this time, very few funding networks were being created specifically to support innovation and experimentation among young people in urban centers.

In the 15 years following the Founding Fifty campaign, Kurlander was able to bring ASP to Newark, NJ, and establish a Center for Afterschool Development on West 42nd Street in Manhattan. With current CEO Chris Street, she expanded the organization to Chicago, the San Francisco Bay Area and Dallas, TX, while also funding new research and training capabilities. This remarkable journey exemplified the power of philanthropy and collaboration in driving meaningful change in the lives of young people from underserved communities.

INVOLVEMENT PHILANTHROPY:
NEW WAYS OF GIVING AND TWO-WAY DEVELOPMENT

"As a corporate leader looking to engage my teams more broadly, the hook was not, 'I'm going to treat these interns like our other college and master's level interns and expect a similar level of work from them.' It was, 'Wow, here are these amazing young people that don't normally have this opportunity, and I have new and emerging supervisors whom I would like to see get some management experience. We'll set them up to develop together and see how they do.' The program was developing both sides of the relationship—youth and supervisors."

—Maria R. Morris, Retired EVP, MetLife,
ASP Board Chair, 2017–2023 (2023)

ASP program leaders and development professionals linked arms to create partnerships with diverse corporations and caring adults. We started small, with a cohort of senior executives, including Joseph A. Forgione at Merrill Lynch, Steve Alesio at Dun & Bradstreet, Maria Morris at MetLife, Nathaniel Christian at Blaylock & Partners and approximately a dozen other early partners who emerged as champions to fund and validate this innovative enterprise. Our explicit goal was to harness the dynamism and resources of the corporate sector for developing youth. Despite encountering skepticism and, in some cases, criticism from both academic and community leadership circles, ASP asked our investors to engage directly and deeply with our young people. For many, this meant willingly stepping out of their own comfort zones to build something new. Overall, our investors responded with enthusiasm and creativity.

Our donors and philanthropic partners directly participated on a weekly basis in creating DSY experiences. They performed side by side with young people during the weekly DSY workshops, which covered topics relevant to their businesses and roles. These workshops, typically held in corporate conference rooms, included sessions on resume writing and public speaking and were meticulously planned and led by the corporate partners. DSY students were directed to perform as question-askers and to get to know these caring professionals and their roles. The DSY students had to extend themselves to respond to professionals who were far advanced in the larger world and learn about corporate activities beyond anything they had been previously exposed to. For their part, the corporate professionals had the challenge, one that was a real stretch for most, of figuring out how to connect with young people who do not automatically "get it." We also added explicit training in our performance approach for the professionals who were supervising interns. Everyone—the young people, the supervisors, the donors and the companies—grew in the process. Everyone had new and developmental experiences that added to and enriched their lives.

Creating these partnerships based on two-way development for the young people involved and the adults who volunteered taught us powerful lessons on relationship- and partnership-building. ASP continued to build the ship as we went along, creating highly intentional experiences for students and training caring adults and corporate professionals as developmentalists. Driven by the enthusiasm and demand from both their partners and young participants, ASP expanded its efforts. Today, more than 100 corporations actively collaborate with DSY. This remarkable achievement underscores the enduring value and impact of ASP's commitment to nurturing these partnerships and fostering two-way development, which has become a cornerstone of its mission.

CO-CREATING BEST PRACTICES

"Inner-city young people really need extra guidance as to how to plan for their lives after high school, whether that's college, vocational training or straight to the workplace. The school systems they are in are doing their best to educate them, but the effort needed to help them plan for the rest of their 'career-oriented' life is lacking and must be enhanced in order to break cycles of poverty."

—Steven W. Alesio, Chairman & CEO,
Dun & Bradstreet, 2001–2010 (2023)

"When the DSY launched the supervisor training, it exposed internship supervisors to the reality and conditions of the lives of the students, the challenges they and their families face and how to create a shared language of growth and expectation together. This equipped our team to create a successful internship experience, a growth experience for all involved."

—Anne Sylvester, Managing Director and
Senior Banker, JP Morgan Private Bank (2020)

Collaborating closely with our partners, we saw that corporate leaders and larger firms were making significant investments in executive and employee development using some of the most advanced methods available, such as performance and improvisation. However, in many instances, these advanced approaches had not "trickled down" to entry-level employees and interns. Fortunately, through the dedication and contributions of the dynamic leaders at Performance of a Lifetime—Cathy Salit, David Nackman, and Maureen Kelly, who were also volunteers and builders of All Stars programs—we were able to create a series of performance experiences for employees and interns that dramatically contributed to the success of the internship program (Salit, 2016). We also came to appreciate and learn how invaluable and important it was to ask our corporate leaders and their employee volunteers to be out front—along with youth participants—in advocating for what they often called the "step function" growth of the internship program.

Figure 9.1 illustrates two essential practices that became part of our DSY playbook as we built the program and partnerships in all of our ASP cities.

From 1998 to the present, ASP's Involvement Philanthropy model has attracted over $206 million in private investment. These funds have played a pivotal role in developing new programs, as well as in advancing research and evidence-based practices that we believe can now be expanded and even scaled. The underlying principle is both straightforward and profound: to bring about transformative outcomes, innovative approaches are imperative. ASP's commitment to pioneering new strategies and actively

Figure 9.1

Key Practices

Two Key Practices from the Development School for Youth Playbook

PRACTICE 1
Provide advanced training to corporate professionals supervising youth interns.

Why:
Corporate professionals who volunteered with DSY or were assigned by their companies to supervise one or more DSY interns by and large had little or no experience communicating or interacting with youth of color and from under-resourced communities. Professionals needed support to be effective coaches and mentors.

What:
All supervisors are asked to attend a **Supervisor Development Training Workshop** focused on:

– Identifying and bridging cultural gaps between underserved youth and corporate America.

– Development-oriented communication and relationship building tools.

How:
Staff introduce performance language and tools, encouraging supervisors to approach the internship as a 4–6 week play where they are the directors.

– Young people help lead the training. They openly share what they are "up against" in their lives and neighborhoods, explain why they want supervisors to be straight with them and give examples of performance directions that are helpful to them.

– Staff share effective work assignments and professional development activities from past internships.

– Supervisors do role plays and scenario work with young people.

PRACTICE 2
Harness the power of corporate networks and peer relationships to scale internships.

Why:
Potential partners need to hear from their peers as to why they sponsor "upstream," full-time, paid summer internships and how these internships work in high-level corporate contexts.

What:
We worked with our closest partners to underwrite, host and lead **DSY Internship Corporate Summits** to which they invite members of their corporate networks.

How:
Summits are typically 90-minute breakfast events held at a corporate conference center. The agenda includes:

– A welcome by a high-profile corporate champion.

– A panel of executives who share proven strategies for winning internal support for internships and best-practice internship structures.

– Peer table discussions led by experienced corporate champions, program alumni (youth) and staff.

ADDING SCIENTIFIC MEASURES

"RBC has been building from a single-city engagement with the All Stars Project, which we launched in 2010, to a multi-city engagement, one that has proved to be leverageable. Our goal is to expand the number of interns we can take on. We are not unlike other companies, who want the measurement of effectiveness. DSY's outcome study validated a number of the points where we were heading. It added some more urgency as to how we're thinking about expanding our partnership and our impact going forward."

—John Thurlow, Managing Director & U.S. COO, RBC Capital Markets (2023)

"One of the things that resonates with me is All Stars' view that schools won't or can't entirely change the calculus for young people without community and individual development. With the outcome study, we now have qualitative and quantitative evidence of how the ASP approach is changing this calculus."

—David Chard, PhD, Dean, Boston University Wheelock School of Education and Human Development (2023)

In the field of youth development, there is often a scarcity of comprehensive measures to assess development. In 2015, an outcome evaluation project led by researchers Annie Wright, PhD and Yetunde Zannou, PhD based at Southern Methodist University's Center on Research and Evaluation (SMU CORE), set out to address this gap. Notably, their objective was not only to fill the measurement void but also to systematically quantify and capture the distinctive concepts and methodologies of the ASP approach, as well as its impact on young individuals. Over five years, the research team created, tested, and validated a construct of development. Bonny Gildin, PhD, a leader within the All Stars team, built the process and the environment for ASP youth, staff, donors as well as experts from the broader youth development field to contribute insights and expertise (Wright et al., 2023).

The validated construct of development—which outlines the strengths and capabilities that ASP has established to empower youth to succeed in educational and workplace settings and to fully participate in all aspects of society—is comprised of eight dimensions. As shown in Figure 9.2, the dimensions pertain to relating to others, engaging with the world and navigating professional or mainstream settings.

Figure 9.2

Validated Measures

By conducting a comprehensive study involving 700 DSY participants across all program sites, both at the beginning and the end of the program cycle, the research team found statistically significant increases in each of the eight dimensions of development.

The eight-dimensional development construct and the positive results added important new evidence on the impact of "All Stars" programs on the young people who participate. Much like how the design and implementation of IQ tests made intelligence a measurable construct, the ability to scientifically measure development makes it equally tangible. This

Non-Artificial Authentic Intelligence   167

provides a new tool for OST time programs and the nonprofit community to demonstrate the value of offering developmentally supportive experiences as we pursue equitable outcomes for historically marginalized youth.

THE NEXT FRONTIER:
EXPERIMENTING TO CREATE SCALABLE SOLUTIONS

"We've discovered at the grassroots level in Newark, New York, and cities across the country how to ignite development for young people who are traumatized and isolated by growing up in poverty. Performance has become a powerful, transformational tool that opens up whole new worlds of possibilities for our young men and women growing up in Black and Brown communities."

—Senior Vice President/Programs and Strategic Initiatives; Director, ASP of New Jersey (2023)

"We need new definitions for student success. America's dysfunctional relationship with college and job training has become a driver of economic and racial inequality. A bachelor's degree is not the promise it has long claimed to be for everyone."

—Roger Low, Founder and CEO, Colorado Equitable Economic Mobility Initiative (2023)

The question confronting leaders in education, nonprofit and workforce development across the country is clear: How can we collectively build new systems at local and regional levels to dramatically increase the capabilities and skills of millions of children growing up in America? The task is both daunting and historic. For ASP and many of our peer organizations, we aim to ensure that this new response addresses the chronic inequality between communities of color, poor and under-resourced communities, and their middle-class and affluent peers.

ASP is taking a proactive stance by leveraging the innovations, teachings, and discoveries of the last 25 years to create thought and action solutions for this profound macro challenge. Well-meaning forces have not always identified the right inputs and processes to scale in the understandable push to create scaled systems. ASP offers a concentrated focus and an ability to build small-scale, high-quality local partnerships and collaborations to bring the performatory-developmental approach into larger institutions and eco-systems. This step cannot be omitted even as we drive toward a goal of broader societal solutions.

As new efforts emerge, key questions for us are:

1. How do we add a developmental component—the program and training models that use the performance-based approach—into more traditional or institutional settings?
2. How do we construct ongoing collaboration among nonprofits and innovators to test how to scale ideas from multiple sources working at the grassroots level?
3. Can we engineer multi-organization partnerships between the nonprofit, education and corporate communities to drive scalable impact?

Building mutually beneficial partnerships, where shared resources and best practices yield much greater results, is possible but not easy. This entails aligning organizational staff leadership, board-level leadership, and funding priorities, as well as front-line staff practitioners. In 2023, the All Stars began a series of pilot partnerships (Figures 9.3 & 9.4) through our Social Development Partners training department, led and shaped by dynamic performance leaders Shadae McDaniel and Antoine Joyce. Even as we are actively managing over 100 corporate and nonprofit partnerships, we are using these pilots to test and learn potentially scalable solutions. We are pairing this activity with very high-level data capture and analysis in conjunction with our partners. As we advance the All Stars' approach to workforce solutions through these pilots, we hope to contribute towards an overall societal push for transformational programs that can be scaled with public–private partnerships. This vision underscores our commitment to driving systemic change and fostering collaboration as a means to achieve impactful and sustainable results.

CONCLUSION

We heartily acknowledge that we are not working in isolation. Many strong and focused efforts across the country are working at local and regional levels to create their version of solutions that work. We wholeheartedly commend these efforts and recognize their importance in driving positive change. Whenever possible, we have begun to work together or uplift each other's efforts through shared recognition.

Some of these fellow travelers include national nonprofit efforts like Year Up!, Genesys Works, Cristo Rey Schools, NAF and Per Scholas. We also align with local or regional initiatives like Big Thought, Newark Youth Career Pathways, Boston WINS and Urban Alliance. Additionally, charter school systems like the KIPP Academies, Success Academy Student, Partner

Figure 9.3

Test and Learn Pilots Education Institutions

Two Key Practices from the Development School for Youth Playbook

PRACTICE 1
Provide advanced training to corporate professionals supervising youth interns.

Why:
Corporate professionals who volunteered with DSY or were assigned by their companies to supervise one or more DSY interns by and large had little or no experience communicating or interacting with youth of color and from under-resourced communities. Professionals needed support to be effective coaches and mentors.

What:
All supervisors are asked to attend a **Supervisor Development Training Workshop** focused on:

- Identifying and bridging cultural gaps between underserved youth and corporate America.

- Development-oriented communication and relationship building tools.

How:
Staff introduce performance language and tools, encouraging supervisors to approach the internship as a 4–6 week play where they are the directors.

- Young people help lead the training. They openly share what they are "up against" in their lives and neighborhoods, explain why they want supervisors to be straight with them and give examples of performance directions that are helpful to them.

- Staff share effective work assignments and professional development activities from past internships.

- Supervisors do role plays and scenario work with young people.

PRACTICE 2
Harness the power of corporate networks and peer relationships to scale internships.

Why:
Potential partners need to hear from their peers as to why they sponsor "upstream," full-time, paid summer internships and how these internships work in high-level corporate contexts.

What:
We worked with our closest partners to underwrite, host and lead **DSY Internship Corporate Summits** to which they invite members of their corporate networks.

How:
Summits are typically 90-minute breakfast events held at a corporate conference center. The agenda includes:

- A welcome by a high-profile corporate champion.

- A panel of executives who share proven strategies for winning internal support for internships and best-practice internship structures.

- Peer table discussions led by experienced corporate champions, program alumni (youth) and staff.

Figure 9.4

Test and Learn Pilots Corporate

Pilot Partners: CORPORATE

KPMG

In 2023, Big Four accounting firm KPMG created a new national internship program, Empower High School Experience, for a diverse group of 200 young people around the country.

Why:

"The KPMG Empower High School was designed to immerse students in our KPMG culture, build a sense of belonging in a professional setting and provide an opportunity for interns to interact with KPMG mentors as they begin to navigate their academic and career journey. When creating this program, we sought out nonprofit collaborators with a mission-based synergy and All Stars was high on that list. We knew they would be a strong collaborator, both in referring students and in using their development through performance approach in the design of the program, which allowed students, coaches and mentors to work more effectively and to grow personally and professionally."

Jennifer Flynn Dear
Managing Director of Community Impact,
KPMG

How:

KPMG hired All Stars Project to:

- Help shape the internship program.

- Deliver in-person and virtual trainings for adults, volunteers and all student participants.

Paramount Global

Paramount Global partnered with the All Stars Project to create an apprenticeship training initiative as part of their efforts to ensure that young people of color who apply to the company will emerge as successful candidates for employment.

Why:

"DSY really puts the young people at the center of everything that they do… They not only provide them with incredible opportunities for growth, but also equip them with the tools to succeed in those opportunities. It's not just development, but development through performance. When you see the impact these young people are making, you can make the business case for further investment. Because of our success working together, I've now launched a new apprenticeship program for All Stars young people. This program is creating real, tangible pathways into full-time jobs."

—Marco Cuoco
Vice President, Strategy and
Business Planning, Paramount Global

How:

Paramount and DSY created a pipeline process:

- Paramount scaled up its summer internship commitment to the DSY.

- Summer interns apply for a follow-up six-month rotational apprenticeship.

- At the end of the rotation, apprentices are considered for full-time employment.

- 50% of the first cohort of apprentices were hired as full-time employees, and we are now planning how to institutionalize and expand this effort.

Alliance, Police Athletic League (NYC), and others are valued partners in our collective mission.

Our aspiration is to help weave together these diverse education, youth development and workforce development initiatives on local, regional and national levels. In doing so, we can create a 21st-century ecosystem for youth and community development where all children have a chance to grow, prosper and pursue their dreams and happiness.

ACKNOWLEDGMENTS

We are grateful to our corporate and education partners—Steve Alesio, Kate Barton (EY), Marco Cuoco, Dr. David Chard, Dr. Karen Kenkel, Dr. Joe May, Maria Morris, Anne Sylvester and John Thurlow—and to the alumni of the DSY who contributed their voices to this chapter. We are especially excited to highlight the success of the latter: Wadnes Castelly (DSY–NJ'11) is a Global Product Marketing Specialist at TikTok; Lindsay McKenzie (DSY–NYC'04) serves as Assistant Attorney General in the Office of the New York State Attorney General's Civil Rights Bureau and also teaches at Columbia University Law School; Chioma Igwebuike (DSY–NJ); Glenroy Wason (DSY–NY'09) is a Senior Accountant at RBC Capital Markets in Jersey City.

We would like to acknowledge other great initiatives across the country, including After School Matters, LINK Unlimited Scholars, Greenwood Project, EAGLE Scholars, C5 Youth Foundation of Texas, Afterschool All-Stars, Economic Mobility Systems, Dr. Emmett J. Conrad Leadership Program, Uplift Education (Charter School), Dallas ISD P-TECH and Early College Programs, Dallas County Promise, Paul Quinn College, UNT Dallas, The Gem Project, Student Partner Alliance, MENTOR Newark, North Star Academy, Thompson Drive and YouthBridge-NY. Special thanks to Jackie Salit and Bonny Gildin for their editorial guidance and support and to Sarah Cotton Nelson and Mary Fridley for their assistance with research.

REFERENCES

Appiah, K. A. (1997). Cosmopolitan patriots. *Critical Inquiry, 23*(3), 617–639.

Bell, D. (2004). *Silent covenants: Brown v. Board of Education and the unfulfilled hopes for racial reform*. Oxford University Press.

Bridglall, B., & Gordon, E. W. (2002). The idea of supplementary education (ED464173). *Pedagogical Inquiry and Praxis, n3*. ERIC. https://eric.ed.gov/?id=ED464173

Bureau of Labor Statistics, U.S. Department of Labor. (1999). *The Economics Daily: Service sector dominant source of new jobs*. https://www.bls.gov/opub/ted/1999/nov/wk5/art05.htm

Caminiti, S. (2022, April 25). *No college degree? No problem. More companies are eliminating requirements to attract the workers they need.* CNBC. https://cnb.cx/37INO3B

Docking, J. R. (2022, March 31). *The higher education model is broken. Together we can fix it.* EdSurge. https://www.edsurge.com/news/2022-03-31-the-higher-education-model-is-broken-together-we-can-fix-it

Dorn, E., Hancock, B., Sarakatsannis, J., & Viruleg, E. (2021, July 27). *COVID-19 and education: The lingering effects of unfinished learning.* McKinsey & Company. https://www.mckinsey.com/industries/education/our-insights/covid-19-and-education-the-lingering-effects-of-unfinished-learning

Gelber, A., Isen, A., & Kessler, J. B. (2016). The effects of youth employment: Evidence from New York City lotteries. *The Quarterly Journal of Economics, 131*(1), 423–460. https://doi.org/10.1093/qje/qjv034

Halpern, R. (2003). *Making play work: The promise of afterschool programs for low-income children.* Teachers College Press.

Heath, S. B. (2000). Making learning work. *Afterschool Matters, 1*(1), 33–45.

Holzman, L. (1997). *Schools for growth: Radical alternatives to current educational models.* Erlbaum.

Holzman, L. (2017). *Vygotsky at work and play* (2nd ed.). Routledge.

Holzman, L., & Mendez, R. (Eds.). (2003). *Psychological investigations.* Brunner-Routledge.

Lobman, C. (2017). Performing on a wider stage: Developing inner-city youth through play and performance. *Mind, Culture, and Activity, 24*(3), 217–231. https://doi.org/10.1080/10749039.2017.1315673

National Student Clearinghouse Research Center. (2019, October 7). *High school benchmarks—2019.* National Student Clearinghouse Research Center. https://nscresearchcenter.org/high-school-benchmarks-2019/

Newman, F., & Holzman, L. (2013). *Lev Vygotsky: Revolutionary scientist.* Psychology Press. (Original work published 1993)

NSC DEI Data Lab. (2023). *Measuring equity gaps in completion.* NSC Dei Data Lab. https://www.studentclearinghouse.org/dei-data-lab/research-data/completion/

Rifkin, J. (1995). *The end of work: The decline of the global labor force and the dawn of the post-market era.* G.P. Putnam's Sons.

Salit, C. (2016). *Performance breakthrough: A radical approach to success at work.* Hachette Books.

Shell, E. R. (2018, May 16). *Opinion: College may not be worth it anymore.* New York Times. https://www.nytimes.com/2018/05/16/opinion/college-useful-cost-jobs.html

Valentine, E. J., Golub, C. A., Hossain, F., & Unterman, R. (2017). *An introduction to the world of work: A study of the implementation and impacts of New York City's summer youth employment program.* MDRC. https://www.mdrc.org/publication/introduction-world-work

Wright, A., Zara, Y., & Gildin, B. (2023, April 13–16). *Co-creation of a youth development scale: Expanding possibilities for development and equity in community education spaces* [Paper presentation]. American Educational Research Association Annual Meeting, Chicago, Illinois, United States.

CHAPTER 10

LEVERAGING THE COMMUNITY AS A CIVIC CLASSROOM

Fernande Raine and Emily Wegner

INTRODUCTION

With the 250th anniversary of the Declaration of Independence on the horizon, there is a growing sense of unease pervading discussions about the health of democracy in the United States. Recent research presents a dismal picture: Only 20% of Americans trust their government. Over a third of Americans believe that people generally cannot be trusted. Another third of Americans report not having a strong sense of belonging beyond their immediate family and friends (Vallone et al. 2021. Moreover, more than 40% of Americans across all ethnic backgrounds are worried about being left behind (Eyoel, 2022). In short, the people that make up our democracy are drained, afraid, and disconnected.

When looking at data specifically on teens, the indicators of democratic health are even more troubling. Nearly two-thirds of teenagers hold more fear than hope for the future of democracy (IOP Harvard, 2023), only 12% trust Congress (Hrynowski & Marken, 2023), and a higher rate experience anxiety regarding the future (approximately 75%) than ever before (Featherstone, 2021). Democracies require citizens who have a sense of agency and hope, who can make informed decisions, are committed to the concept of democratic governance, and can navigate negotiations and problem-solving among varied stakeholders. We, as communities, are not providing this through our current approach to learning.

Built for More: The Role of Out-of-School Time in Preparing Youth for the Future of Work,
pp. 173–189
Copyright © 2024 by Information Age Publishing
www.infoagepub.com
All rights of reproduction in any form reserved.

Conversations about the future of work usually miss this larger picture of the state of democracy. Policymakers and school districts talk about jobs of the future, the impact of AI, the needs for STEM expertise and future-ready skills without referencing whether these jobs exist in a community that is governed by a democratic system—however imperfect--that is safeguarding the rights and interest of all people. The future in which our children and our children's children will live and seek employment will, however, fundamentally be shaped by whether we prepare young people to strengthen, innovate and adapt our democratic systems of governance of, by and for all.

It is for that reason that we make the case in this chapter that out-of-school-time providers (OST) play a central role in preparing young people for their future not only in the employment market, but for their civic roles in a democratic governance system.

The world in which we are living today was described a decade ago as being volatile, uncertain, complex, ambiguous and hyperconnected (VUCAH). In the past few years, the impact of this VUCAH reality on people of all ages has been exacerbated by accelerated innovation in the field of artificial intelligence (AI), the ever-harsher realities of climate change, and the rise of populism and polarization. This sense of uncertainty, anxiety, and fear places a simultaneous strain both on the economy and democracy: people who lose their jobs and feel left behind and powerless tend to lose faith in democracy and place their bets on promises made by populists with little respect for the systems of participatory governance.

In this dynamic situation in which we live, preparing young people for the future of work requires giving young people more than knowledge and competencies to get a specific job. It requires giving them the opportunity to develop durable competencies, a broad understanding of the world in which they live, hope for the future and a commitment to building a robust, inclusive democracy. It requires giving them opportunities to understand how we got here, to imagine a new tomorrow, and to see themselves as pivotal actors in the arc of history, on whom the shaping of the future depends. These are the lessons that can be drawn from engaging with the story of humanity through history.

But history teaching has been experienced by young people as little more than a litany of facts and figures, with proficiency rates hovering around 15% for over 100 years (Wineburg, 2020). Our failure to teach history and civics effectively has failed to make our young people prepared to craft community and cope with complexity. Therefore, this chapter is focused on how to use OST and in-community experiences connected to history to build the civic competencies and dispositions needed to prepare young people not only for the jobs that are presented to them, but to be co-creators of the new jobs that will be needed to solve society's pressing problems.

Leveraging the Community as a Civic Classroom   175

In the following sections, we will explore the interconnection between civic readiness and workforce preparedness, exploring how history-related experiences within OST programs can serve to develop youth agency and interest in career pathways that solve problems and advance well-being and thriving for our community—whether at the local, national, or global scale. Through our illustrative case studies, we will showcase young people who have created award-winning media, contributed to work in museums, and facilitated public discourse.

This chapter does not propose a silver bullet solution. It showcases examples of community-connected learning that is being designed and delivered by creative educators across the country. These activities occur continuously but are not being recognized as the essential experiences that young people—and our communities—need to thrive.

By highlighting the capacity of learning in and with OST providers to develop future-ready skills, we are proposing a path towards civic learning ecosystems that deliver community-connected learning to strengthen democracy. Taking history out of the textbook, out of the classroom and integrating it into a community can prepare young people as peacemakers, democracy-builders, and changemakers. Experiences with the past in new ways can prepare young people to see themselves as ancestors of generations to come, whose mandate is to creatively imagine and work towards a vision for a better future. In our perspective, that is the core mission that "Out of School Time" to truly support youth thriving.

OUR ORIGIN STORY:
LOVE, LEARNING SCIENCE AND THE POWER OF COMMUNITY

In 2019, triggered by the growing health crisis of American democracy, two passionate individuals from disparate backgrounds converged on a shared mission. One, a historian/systems-change entrepreneur from Boston and the other, a community-builder/social studies teacher in Kansas City, began collaborating to find and spread the most effective ways of building civic competencies in young people. Under The History Co:Lab, we connected in a shared love for history as a source of inspiration for the future, and in a shared conviction that the current system of delivering history was broken. The prevalent approach, characterized by an under-resourced, textbook-heavy, content-focused, frontal model of history and social studies education, clearly was calling for redesign. Early on, we agreed that the key to this redesign would be breaking down the barrier between in-school and out-of-school learning.

As we researched how to bring this form of experiential learning to life, we found that the field of learning science had developed rich insights on what it takes to help all young people thrive and what conditions need to be met so that they can absorb content and engage in discovery. The literature emphasized how to leverage play, inquiry, and project-based learning to support young peoples' growth and to activate their eagerness to learn (Vander Ark et al., 2021). Tragically, we also realized that these insights were often being ignored in the practice of traditional learning formats.

We set about working and collaborating with a network of educators in metro Kansas City schools and museums of Kansas City. Our goal was to prove that by leveraging the power of place, play, projects, and people, we could provide young people with the kind of experiences that trigger curiosity and develop a full range of competencies and skills. Over time, this effort has grown to a network of civic museums nationwide, with the goal of becoming a national movement of community institutions acting as hubs for competency-based, community-connected civic learning. We have been privileged to work with colleagues in dozens of states, across all different kinds of institutions.

Drawing upon four years of work at a local and national level, we share examples and a framework for civically impactful OST experiences to promote and open career pathways that advance the thriving of people and the planet. More importantly, we will offer a framework of why this type of learning experience is so critical to the development of any young person's capacity to be prepared for an uncertain future–regardless of what career path they choose. We believe these kinds of OST experiences are essential to giving a young person the opportunity to make an informed choice about their pathway and understand the implications of their choices. We encourage community conversations to engage and align educators, parents and OST program leaders in cultural and youth-serving organizations around a common understanding of how to ensure that young people get what they need to thrive.

THE FUTURE READINESS FRAMEWORK

Over the past years, we have developed a framework for Future Ready Learning based on the Science of Learning and Development. This framework consists of four key components:

1. The foundational biological building blocks of learning
2. The competencies that young people need to thrive
3. The content and concepts that provide context
4. The future-thinking that is needed to reach new horizons

To ensure these components of learning are effectively delivered, educators must apply methods based on the science of how young people

Leveraging the Community as a Civic Classroom 177

learn, leveraging the pedagogies of inquiry, play, place, projects, and human connection.

When we collaborate with community members and educators to co-create inspiring learning experiences, we design around these core components and pedagogies. We establish a clear shared language between educators, transcending institutional and disciplinary boundaries, enabling them to articulate how they are hoping to have the student develop in the course of the unit or project. In the following sections, we will delve into each of these four components of effective learning, highlighting how OST experiences within history contribute to the young people' future readiness.

The Foundation: The Biology of Civic Readiness

Civic readiness is often thought of primarily as a body of knowledge about how democracy works, and—specifically—how *American* democracy works. The citizenship test developed by the Immigration and Naturalization Services, seen as a significant milestone for many on the journey into the body politic of America, sets a basic standard to measure a person's readiness to engage in community affairs. No doubt this knowledge is mechanically important—and yet, knowing those facts does not yet make a citizen feel ready and empowered to influence decisions and systems.

What determines a young person's ability to engage as a caring, curious, critical citizen are precisely the building blocks of learning as established by experts in psychology and neuroscience (Stafford-Brizzard, 2017). While the full set is more complex, the key ones from the perspective of an educator trying to design learning experiences in history are the following five:

- Identity/Being seen
- Belonging
- Relationships/Bridging
- Relevance
- Agency

Each of these components represents a key condition for the ability of a young person to thrive as a learner. Thanks to research across disciplines in the Science of Development and Learning, we know how, when, and why young learners develop, as well as what prevents them from accessing opportunities for growth. We now understand that if they do not feel seen for who they are, they shut down or tend to withdraw (Cantor et al., 2021). If they are not able to build relationships with other human beings, they cannot accumulate the social capital they need to stay informed, be safe, and have access to opportunities (Freeland Fischer, 2021). If they do not have a sense of belonging, it impacts their success and socio-emotional well-being (Boix-Mansilla & Strom, 2023). If they are not given the opportunity to exercise their power, voice, and choice, they may lose the skill (innate to young children) of asking questions and engaging (Dweck & Yeager, 2019). If they are not given the opportunity to envision different versions of their possible selves, they struggle to develop an agentic mindset (Oyserman & Dawson, 2021).

A deep understanding of the biology of learning prescribes a new set of priorities in civic learning. Science-backed teaching for student agency becomes not just about teaching them content or giving them the chance to practice a channel of democratic engagement, like writing a letter to an elected official. It becomes the project of creating opportunities for every young person, no matter their background and dispositions, to experience being seen and invited to contribute as the unique person that they are. Civic education, particularly in an era of rising machine power, becomes a commitment to ensuring that every child can develop their full humanity.

Appreciating the importance of experiences that create this bedrock of self-awareness and agency is essential for the conversation about OST and career pathways. Only if young people receive this foundation will they even see themselves as potential creators and contributors in the field of civil or community service. Learning across the K–12 age range, whether within the confines of school, at home, or in the community, should be designed around these foundational goals of civic growth.

Social studies and history curricula inside of schools are not designed around these objectives. While some states, like California and Maine, have adopted legislation mandating coverage of indigenous and ethnic history in curricula to ensure that all students feel represented, the specifics of what should be covered and how it should be taught remain unclear. In practice, the lived reality of history education in classrooms counteracts what young people need from the topic. Instead of being nurtured in their sense of self and agency, most young people in social studies and history classes do not see themselves in the material they read. They are rarely given the opportunity to connect learning to human beings or to the place in which they live. The connections and relevance to current issues are spurious at best and most young people leave the class feeling disengaged, lacking agency and, as previously noted, disconnected from the American promise.

Community organizations such as libraries, museums, archives, theaters, and even retirement homes offer endless opportunities for young people to have experiences that build up these foundational blocks. In their book *The Power of Place*, Tom Vander Ark and Emily Liebtag (2021) outline how

Leveraging the Community as a Civic Classroom   179

place-based and project-based learning specifically delivers the kind of experiences that foster these essential skills and competencies.

Many museums have been going out of their way in the past years to develop new offerings that allow for the development of these skills. These institutions have recognized the potential to serve as catalysts for experiential and transformative learning. By engaging young people in dynamic, interactive, and immersive exhibits and programs, museums are bridging the gap between history, culture, and contemporary life. They are providing platforms for young people to connect with history and the world around them, enhancing their sense of identity, connection, belonging, relevance, and agency.

Case Studies: Truman Presidential Library and Museum and Rhode Island Latino Arts Center

The Truman Presidential Library and Museum stands as a vital partner in our regional efforts. Collaboratively, we coordinated a project that utilized their newly renovated exhibit in conjunction with a local art teacher. This initiative was to design a piece of art to be showcased in the museum. The art piece was supposed to express how a student related the themes of the Cold War to their own lives and biographies. Each student created a piece of artwork that conveyed a highly personal story of how they were affected by the themes addressed and questions raised by the museum, for example, a colorful image portraying a vision of the future in which LGBTQ+ rights are realized, crafted by a student who questioned the narrative of America the Victorious. Their art was revealed at the grand reopening of the museum, with emotional presentations by the young people who reported being overwhelmed by a sense of gratitude for being seen and heard in such a prominent public institution.

In a similar vein, the Rhode Island Latino Arts Center has invited young people to explore their identity and connect to the community by participating in an oral history project. By offering tools to help young people collect oral histories from their family members that are then archived in the museum, the institution gives young people multiple ways of building relationships and agency. Throughout the project, youth meaningfully engage with a human being from another generation, forge connections with the adults from the museum, and establish bonds with their peers. Participant young people report developing a strong sense of belonging as they explore the rich history of Latin culture in Providence. According to director Marta Martinez, as students gain an understanding of the role their ethnic community plays and has played in shaping their town, they develop a proud sense of heritage and draw on that pride to feel more powerful and connected.

Both instances illustrate simple ways in which community organizations created opportunities for young people to actively engage in the community in ways not available in the traditional educational experience. They were designed to allow for student agency, and to be more than "just an assignment." These opportunities allow young people to see themselves reflected and represented in the spaces around them—spaces they may be able to access, but often overlook.

These cases exemplify the potential of community institutions to become partners in transformative learning experiences. There are countless other institutions with equally powerful learning taking place and opportunities waiting to happen. All that is needed is a shift in thinking from those who are directly involved in the day-to-day interactions, from delivering content to inviting to participate.

OST and Human Competencies

In recent years, there has been a tremendous upsurge in competency-oriented learning, largely driven by global employers' concern that applicants and employees are lacking the skills they would need to succeed in the workforce, or even to thrive in their lives today. School districts nationwide, often in collaboration with their communities, are redefining profiles of a learner or graduate that codify the set of core skills that they expect young people to have so that they are ready for the jobs and for civic needs of the future. Although the variety of models and taxonomies may be head spinning, in the end, they all align on a set of durable skills that employers and community stakeholders value most.

One of the most comprehensive frameworks, along with an accompanying set of cards for experience design, was developed by the XQ Institute and is accessible online at no cost. We have used these tools with in-school and OST educators across six states, leveraging them to energize and engage community members in co-creation of learning. These tools have proven to be potent in placing the whole child at the center of the project of learning design.

While comprehensive frameworks are powerful, efforts to organize them into categories are helpful to support prioritization and enable the implementation of these learning outcomes into practice. One is known as the "6C's" framework, as developed by Kathy Hirsh-Pasek and Roberta Golinkoff at Brookings. In Table 10.1, we have illustrated how history connected OST experiences not only develop these skills directly, but how history can be used to show why these skills are important to succeed and make a difference in the world. Additionally, we have included a seventh dimension—curiosity—as a vital component of this framework.

Leveraging the Community as a Civic Classroom   181

Table 10.1

Developing the 6-Cs in Learning by and From History

Competency Expressed	How We Develop this by "Doing" History	How We Can Learn the Value of This Competency in/From History
Collaboration We take action and collaborate with others on a shared goal or passion. We solve problems with others and are able to work in diverse groups.	We recognize that we need varied expertise and knowledge to build the deepest understanding we can of complex topics and historical phenomena;	We notice that people who collaborate with others make big historic shifts happen. We see what different kinds of collaboration have resulted in change (artistic, intellectual, military, engineering, research)
Communication We can convey information effectively, both verbally and in writing. We can actively listen and understand non-verbal cues.	We practice writing and speaking clearly and effectively about questions that are of relevance to us and to others; we discuss controversial issues and develop and express opinions from multiple perspectives; We learn how to understand and appreciate different cultures, perspectives	We can see how communication is a powerful tool for establishing power and having impact. We recognize the ability of effective writers and speakers to take the knowledge, beliefs and perspectives of their audiences into account and lead with clear vision.
Content We have in-depth knowledge and understanding about various topics. We use and apply our knowledge effectively and correctly; we see connections between things and know how to build on current knowledge.	We acquire a scaffolding of the chronology and multiple interpretations of major historical events; We develop global awareness and the ability to navigate a globalized world and engage in cross-cultural communication	We can see how knowledge of history and an understanding of the complexity of human systems helped people make informed decisions in key moments
Critical Thinking We realize there are multiple points of view and people think differently. We take information from different sources and come to our own conclusion or form an opinion. We question authority and use reasoning to understand the reasoning of others and shape our work.	We learn how to find and evaluate multiple types of sources (diaries, letters, memos, objects, images etc.) on an event or an historical issue; Learn how to identify trustworthiness of a digital or printed source; We learn how to ask questions about perspective and motives of the author; Learn how to recognize patterns of power and authority and how to question them;	We realize how critical thinking is the drive of progress and positive change: from scientific innovation to revolution and reform— they all come from people questioning given assumptions and finding new knowledge; we also realize what can go wrong when people become instruments of propaganda and hate.

(Table continued on next page)

Table 10.1 (Continued)

Developing the 6-Cs in Learning by and From History

Competency Expressed	How We Develop this by "Doing" History	How We Can Learn the Value of This Competency in/From History
Creative Innovation We exercise our creativity with a goal in mind and preparation and knowledge in that area. We are able to generate new ideas, and approach challenges with fresh perspectives. We can adapt to change and are open to new ways of doing things.	We use creativity to tell stories employing different media and techniques; we take the perspective of key players in a historical event to see how they tackled problems; we use creativity to imagine other possible outcomes.	We see the importance of innovation and new ideas in history. Innovations in technology, art, and social structures have propelled societies forward, solving critical problems and opening new possibilities.
Confidence and Character We are confident enough to fail, knowing that the greatest achievements happen when we step out of our comfort zone. We are able to make decisions based on ethical principles and moral values and can consider the broader impact of our actions on society.	We build a sense of identity and belonging by engaging with our own past, by connecting our story to the story others and needs of our community; we develop confidence and self-efficacy as we develop the skills above in an iterative manner, realizing how we learn when moving past our comfort zone.	We see the throughline of failures and unintended consequences in history; Confidence and character must be paired, so that we don't boldly stride off of cliffs of humanity; We realize that human beings can build a better world when develop bold ideas for the future that are grounded in character and ethics; human learning is iterative and non-linear
Curiosity and Life-Long Learning: This involves a commitment to continuous learning and skill development, as the pace of change in the 21st century requires individuals to adapt and acquire new knowledge and skills throughout their lives. This includes adaptability to change.	We foster our mindset of inquiry and critical thinking by practicing historical research, which involves asking questions and uncovering new information; We broaden our understanding and embrace an open-minded approach by exposing ourselves to various historical viewpoints and perspectives. we practice self-directed learning and seek out resources that can help us grow	We realize the impact of curiosity on societal advancements by learning about historical figures who were driven by a continuous quest for knowledge. History teaches us that curiosity-driven exploration can unlock new frontiers and change the course of human progress.

Despite the fact that OST organizations have often been trained to frame their offering through the lens of the core content standards to attract teachers working within the industrial school format, it is evident that museums, libraries, and cultural spaces inherently offer experiences and resources that contribute to building key competencies essential in the 21st century.

- Collaboration: Museums can encourage participants to engage in collaborative projects, discussions, and activities
- Communication: These institutions serve as arenas for encounters with other people, to create a public discussion and share perspectives. They facilitate dialogue and exchange, honing communication skills in the process.
- Content: By creating direct engagement with artifacts, exhibits, and narratives, museums bridge the gap between abstract historical content and personal experience.
- Critical Thinking: Within these spaces, individuals are able to experience the complexity of narrative creation and storytelling from artifacts and pieces of information. This process prompts critical thinking as visitors navigate historical contexts and piece together narratives.
- Creativity: Museums and cultural spaces stimulate the imagination and experimentation with new ideas and visions for the future.
- Character: These spaces serve as environments for reflection, to allow individuals to be in an environment with new stimuli and to connect with their own emotional responses. The possibility museums offer of providing strong emotional responses and then reflecting on what they mean is a critical contribution to developing empathy, emotional regulation, and confidence.
- Curiosity: Museum and cultural spaces offer a space for exploration and discovery of how human society has evolved in relationship with nature, and how diverse perspectives, cultures, and systems have emerged.

Creating a common language and shared understanding of the most valued learning outcomes across institutions—schools, museums, and parents—helps to shift the dynamic of learning towards civic growth. It enables a partnership of players across different institutions to deliver genuine child-centered, community-oriented learning experiences.

In our collaborative efforts with museums and schools, we have created learning experiences that are not solely geared towards delivering content.

184 F. RAINE and E. WEGNER

Instead, these experiences are intentionally designed to foster the development of these core competencies. By leveraging the unique strengths of OST organizations and their inherent capacity to inspire curiosity, critical thinking, and creativity, we contribute to preparing young individuals for a future that demands more than rote knowledge, but a holistic skill set essential for thriving in a rapidly evolving world.

Case Studies: American Public Square at William Jewell and Truman Presidential Library and Museum

American Public Square at William Jewell in Kansas City, MO, offers an inspiring example of an OST initiative focused on developing the skills of communication, collaboration, and character through discourse on divisive topics. American Public Square offers groups of young people the opportunity to learn about how to engage in civil discourse in a world riddled with misinformation, disinformation, bias, and negativity. Participant young people first complete a discrete amount of theoretical course material, after which they work collaboratively across multiple school districts to create a public panel discussion over a topic of their choice.

In this project, young people take on roles of identifying the participants, creating the questions, conducting fact-checking, and managing the event itself. It not only empowers young people to discuss difficult topics, but it allows them to be a part of the solution by providing space where people with different opinions can learn from each other in a safe and respectful environment. For instance, in 2023, at the height of the domestic dispute on the overturning of *Roe v. Wade*, the group of young people chose the topic of access to abortion for their panel discussion. These young people stunned the community with their professional management of a highly sensitive and contentious topic. Not only did these young people build the skills of project management, critical thinking, communication, and self-management, but they also learned that they can lead the way in their community to shift the culture of discourse.

Another compelling example of empowering young people as leaders in the community is allowing young people to lead tours in museums–a model embraced by one of our partners in conjunction with the Truman Presidential Library and Museum. This project invited eighth-grade young people from a school district to tour the museum, following compelling inquiry questions provided by the library. Subsequently, these students were then tasked with researching a specific section of the exhibit related to that question, and with creating and delivering tours to the sixth-grade students from the same district who toured the museum later that year.

An unexpected outcome of this project was on the date of the sixth-grade field trip, public visitors of the museums listened in awe to the student tours. One of the students remarked on the experience, "I don't really like talking in school, but I really enjoy teaching in public." This underscores the ease with which OST experiences can give young people a voice and sense of connection to the community. These case studies exemplify the transformative potential of OST initiatives in shaping young people into leaders and active contributors to their communities, equipping them with essential skills and instilling a sense of agency and connection.

Developing the Content and Context You Need to Thrive

The third vital component of effective future-focused learning is providing young people with the content and context they need to thrive. The world is, indeed, a complex place and one sure characteristic of the future of work is its accelerated pace of change. Employees will constantly have to adapt, so only those who can discern fact from fiction, and who can process complex information, will be able to adjust their course of action. Indeed, among the top skills demanded by employers in 2023 are curiosity and lifelong learning and analytical and critical capacity (Masterson, 2023).

Advanced literacy and curiosity to learn is not only critical for adapting to changing realities, it is also critical to overcoming the polarization in our society. Extensive research underscores the connection between the lack of media literacy and the rise of susceptibility to propaganda and the culture wars of our present (Hobbs, 2021). Building the skill to understand nuance and complexity is a critical step towards rebuilding civic discourse and engaging across differences to solve problems for the community.

However, advanced literacy and the desire to delve deeper are seldom placed at the core of curriculum. Teachers are required to cover vast amounts of content, leading to textbooks offering only brief excerpts of documents, and teachers often select only a paragraph of a novel to cover a work of literature. Consequently, OST becomes a critical space for developing the skills necessary for exploring media consumption and creation of quality content.

OST organizations have the unique capacity to offer young people in-depth, context-rich learning experiences that go beyond mere content coverage. They can provide the time and space for young individuals to engage deeply with complex subjects, fostering critical thinking, media literacy, and the ability to navigate the multifaceted landscape of information and ideas. These experiences empower young learners to become discerning consumers and creators of knowledge, preparing them not only for the future of work, but also for active citizenship and constructive engagement in society.

Case Studies: The History Co:Lab "UnTextbooked" Podcast

One example of an OST project that focuses on media literacy is the "UnTextbooked" history podcast, incubated by The History Co:Lab in collaboration with a team of teens. This innovative project was conceived as a way of showcasing the power of complex history to inspire young people as changemakers. The formula is elegantly simple: teens find a topic about which they are passionate, find a famous historian who has written a book, read the book, and then engage the author in a conversation for the podcast. This intergenerational, passion-driven podcast delivers the thrill of exploring the past to find inspiration for how humans today can engage to bend the arc of history towards justice.

The driving philosophy behind "UnTextbooked" is the belief that history is complicated, and that only when we embrace that complexity can we find a way to contribute meaningfully to shaping a better future. The podcast's topics, spanning multiple seasons, encompass a vast spectrum of historical events and issues, ranging from the tense standoff of the Cold War to the crucible of presidential leadership, and from the annals of the AIDS crisis to the relentless spirit that combated segregation.

The impact of "UnTextbooked" was nothing short of extraordinary. In 2021, Apple, recognizing its transformative influence, bestowed upon it the coveted accolade of "new and noteworthy." Today, it commands a larger audience than a staggering 97% of podcasts across America. It was even nominated for an "Oscar" of Podcasting, an Ambie® in the category of History in 2024. The producers have been speakers at international conferences, sharing the power of youth voice in designing the future of education.

The triumph of "UnTextbooked" was a testament to the powerful synergy between young minds and seasoned historians. It underscored the transformative potential that emerges when generations collaborate, harnessing the force of history to fortify our democracy and shape our collective destiny. This case study illustrates how OST initiatives, such as the "UnTextbooked" podcast, can effectively engage young learners in diving deep into relevant issues of our times, providing them with the tools to navigate complexity and contribute to a more just and informed society.

Imagination and the Arc of History

The final building block of leveraging history-related OST for career-readiness in public service is using time in community as space for imagining the future: a future in which there is more joy, less suffering and greater thriving. Adults are often quick to dismiss the teen brain as one that is impulsive and lacks judgment, but as Dr. Susan Rivers at iThrive Games has written about extensively, it is precisely the underdeveloped stage of a teenager's frontal cortex that drives novelty-seeking behavior that also allows them to imagine endless possibilities. Young people must have access to learning experiences that activate and tap into this power of imagination so that they can avoid the anxiety trap and see a future that is worth working towards, and a future version of themselves that they find desirable.

Engaging with history is always an engagement with the future, for the present we are in is the future that was created by generations past. Both the systems we appreciate and the ones that hurt us were designed and created by humans. Understanding those efforts and drawing lessons for our own role as ancestors is an essential ingredient of building career readiness and opening up career paths for young people.

The questions are substantial and complex: How can we reach a state of being in which we are in harmony with the planet? How can we create a diverse and inclusive democracy of problem solvers? How do we ensure that our communities become more adaptive to the changes that for so many people present a threat to their old way of being? How can we move beyond the culture wars to find civil discourse across differences?

All of these are questions that require time and space to explore–time and space that so rarely is given in the constraints of a day of school. OST is a luxurious offering of this future-casting and exploration–both for young people as they see themselves and for how they see the world around them.

Recent work by Marielle Burt and the Stanford School of Education highlights just how powerful future-focused thinking can be for teens. In "Our Futures Forum" (https://ourfuturesforum.com/educator-resources/), Burt created a learning experience that connects climate justice, community research, and youth creativity. In a series of lessons, the course helps young people recognize their power as both architects of their own learning and architects of the future world. These lessons could be used by any cultural institution or OST provider.

Case Studies: Smithsonian's Anacostia Community Museum

Museums and libraries can also actively engage young people in future-casting. For example, the Smithsonian's Anacostia Community Museum designed a unique experience that ran in 2022, capitalizing on the heightened desire for imaginative thinking following the COVID-19 pandemic. The Utopia Project was a dynamic endeavor aimed at deconstructing the dynamics of social change. Through a series of experiential activities, visitors first learned to connect with the causes that resonated with them.

188 F. RAINE and E. WEGNER

They were then welcomed into an imaginative "Dream Space," a realm where they could envision a world unencumbered by the challenges at hand, reaching for an awe-inspiring end goal. With this vision of success as their guide, they delved into research-informed tactics that had consistently driven measurable social change. The journey culminated in the maker space—a hub where dreams were transformed into tangible actions. Equipped with an array of materials, from cardboard and tape to Legos and whiteboards, visitors were encouraged to prototype their concepts for a better world.

Throughout the gallery, objects, photographs, and narratives drawn from the ACM collection were featured, grounding abstract concepts in tangible examples of community members effecting change across history. These accounts of everyday changemakers served as a powerful reminder that the seeds of change resided within each of us. The Utopia Project demystified and brought within reach a process that turned the seemingly impossible into reality. This kind of experience exemplifies the power of OST opportunities to enable young individuals to see themselves as active participants in shaping the future—an essential aspect of career readiness that extends beyond traditional education.

CONCLUSION

OST experiences connected to history are critical to prepare kids for the future. They provide essential building blocks, competencies, content, and a sense of their role in time. Youth groups, museums, libraries, and many community spaces have a unique opportunity and vital role to play in delivering transformative learning experiences that awaken the potential of young people as changemakers. These experiences offer the foundational elements of learning, critical competencies, rich contextual understanding, and the power of imagination.

Expanding and increasing these opportunities and connecting these into the rhythm of school is paramount to ensuring that kids can thrive. Relying solely on schools to initiate these changes may prove challenging, given the systemic obstacles that hinder swift adaptation within the education system. Bureaucracy, red tape, traditional ways of doing things, personal agendas and conflicts, and disagreements over the business of operations of a school district all get in the way of the changes we need to do better for our young people. However, the OST community can rise to the occasion and can take action immediately to weave a civic learning ecosystem that offers young people the opportunities they desperately need to develop the building blocks of learning, durable competencies, context and the ability to see a different future. In doing so, OST providers, in partnership with schools, can help young people—and, indeed, learners of all ages—be properly equipped to become the leaders of tomorrow. If we do so, democracy will not only survive, it will rise stronger and more resilient from the crisis it is in today. The power of OST experiences in shaping the next generation of civic-minded individuals cannot be underestimated, and the potential for positive change as it continues to is limitless.

REFERENCES

Boix-Mansilla, V., & Strom, A. (2023). *A world on the move: Reimagining how we teach immigrant students and their peers* [Unpublished manuscript].

Cantor, P., Lerner, R. M., Pittman, K. J., Chase, P. A., & Gomperts, N. (2021). *Whole-child development, learning, and thriving: A dynamic systems approach.* Cambridge University Press.

Dweck, C. S., & Yeager, D. S. (2019). Mindsets: A view from two eras. *Perspectives on Psychological science, 14*(3), 481–496.

Eyoel, Y. (2022, April 19). *The role of proximate democracy entrepreneurship in building a multiracial democracy.* Nonprofit Policy Forum, De Gruyter.

Featherstone, L. (2021, September 16). *75 percent of young people are frightened by the future: That's the only sane reaction to climate change.* New Republic.

Freeland Fisher, J., Fisher D., Christensen, C. M. (2018). *(Foreword), Who you know: Unlocking innovations that expand students' networks.* Wiley.

Hrynowski, Z., & Marken, S. (2023, September 14). *Gen Z voices lackluster trust in major U.S. institutions.* Gallup. https://news.gallup.com/opinion/gallup/510395/gen-voices-lackluster-trust-major-institutions.aspx#:~:text=Members%20of%20Generation%20Z%20in,Gallup%20and%20Walton%20Family%20Foundation

IOP Harvard. (2023). *Democracy study.* Harvard. https://iop.harvard.edu/news/nearly-two-thirds-young-americans-fearful-about-future-democracy-america-harvard-youth-poll

Masterson, V. (2023). *Future of jobs.* World Economic Forum. https://www.weforum.org/agenda/2023/05/future-of-jobs-2023-skills/

Oyserman, D., & Dawson, A. (2021). Successful learning environments support and harness students' identity-based motivation: A primer. *The Journal of Experimental Education, 89*(3), 508–522.

Stafford-Brizard, K. B. (2016). Building blocks for learning: A framework for comprehensive student development. *Turnaround for Children,* 1–16.

Vallone, D., Hawkins, S., Malvar, N., Oshinski, P., Raghuram, T., & Yudkin, D. (2021). (rep.). *Two stories of distrust in America.* More in Common.

Vander Ark, T., Liebtag, E., & McClennen, N. (2020). *The power of place: Authentic learning through place-based education.* ASCD.

Wineburg, S. (2020). *Why learn history (when it's already on your phone).* University of Chicago.

CHAPTER 11

PATHWAYS TO COLLEGE AND CAREER READINESS IN SOUTH LOS ANGELES

A Case Study of the Al Wooten Jr. Youth Center

Naomi McSwain

INTRODUCTION

We had limited knowledge about college and career preparation when we established the Al Wooten Jr. Youth Center in South Los Angeles in 1990. The youth center bears the name of my cousin, killed in a drive-by shooting at the age of 35 in Los Angeles, a victim of a gang initiation. Wooten's mom, my aunt Myrtle Faye Rumph, was a businesswoman without a high school diploma. At the time, I was studying journalism at California State University, Northridge (CSUN) and would later become the second individual in my very large African American family to obtain a college degree.

My aunt, along with our founding family and friends, chose me to serve as executive director given my experience as a teen gang member turned college student, thanks to an afterschool program in the 1970s. Fueled by a strong desire and passion for helping students overcome the same conditions I faced as a youth, I assumed the role of executive director at the Wooten Center for our initial four years. I left the position after graduating from college with a Bachelor of Art in Journalism and embarking on a career as a newspaper reporter. I returned to the center 16 years later after covering too many stories about gang violence. In March 2023, I retired from my position as executive director after a total of 17 years of service.

Built for More: The Role of Out-of-School Time in Preparing Youth for the Future of Work,
pp. 191–210
Copyright © 2024 by Information Age Publishing
www.infoagepub.com
All rights of reproduction in any form reserved.

192 N. McSWAIN

Upon my return to the center in 2010, there was very little in my credentials that had prepared me for what became a model free afterschool program, dedicated to providing college and career readiness for more than 500 students annually, ranging from Grades 3–12, in the South Los Angeles area. Workshops including board development, strategic planning, and proposal writing at capacity buildings agencies like the Center for Nonprofit Management, and a certificate in nonprofit management from USC proved immensely critical to my professional development. More important was taking time to understand the challenges of youth, families, and community members, primarily through surveys.

Defining the Problems

Returning to the Wooten Center more mature and committed to a career in youth development, I started researching on the internet to understand the historical problems that had existed in my community, the same challenges that I faced as an underserved student at Thomas Jefferson High School where things are looking up today with 61% of graduates meeting UC/CSU course requirements in 2021–22, compared to 38% in 2019–20 (Ed-Data, 2021–22). The following excerpt is drawn from the needs statement in the theory of change in our current proposals in our current theory of change:

- Children and youth residing in South Los Angeles face multiple barriers and obstacles that challenge their ability to thrive and survive. In the 2021–22 academic year, approximately 98% of students in two local elementary schools (Manhattan Place and LaSalle) were eligible for free/reduced lunch, serving as a proxy measure for low-income status (Ed-Data, 2021–22). The poverty rate in South LA, also known as Los Angeles County Service Planning Area (SPA) 6, stands at 33.3%, twice that of the county average (Children's Hospital Los Angeles, 2022).
- Over half of South LA residents have grappled with food insecurity, and the area experienced a greater impact from job loss due to the COVID-19 pandemic, more so than other areas of Los Angeles County (Children's Hospital Los Angeles, 2022).
- Gramercy Park, the community where the Wooten Center is located, and adjacent neighborhoods represent seven out of the top 10 areas with the highest rates of violent crime in Los Angeles County (Los Angeles Times Mapping Project, 2023a). We have witnessed it first-hand at and near our youth center. Returning in June 2021 to reopen our six storefront buildings after

Pathways to College and Career Readiness in South Los Angeles   193

15 months of closure, we found a bullet hole in a front window. This was the third time in three years that stray bullets hit our buildings. Within weeks of our reopening, police found the dead body of a gang intervention worker shot in a car two buildings down from our entrance on Western Avenue. Shortly thereafter, they found another young adult male murdered in gun violence around the corner on a residential block. In response, I joined the steering committee of a Public Health violence prevention collaborative and raised about $30,000 in foundation and corporate gifts to install Kevlar on walls and bullet-resistant glass in windows to help shield our building occupants from the crossfire.

- The pandemic exacerbated and deepened existing student achievement gaps, particularly across racial and economic lines. For instance, at nearby Manhattan Place Elementary, only 5% of students performed at grade level in English, and 4% in mathematics in the 2021–22 academic year, a decline from the already low figures of 12% on grade level in English and 6% in math prior to the pandemic (Ed-Data, 2021–22). In comparison, within the Los Angeles Unified School District as a whole, approximately 42% of students met grade-level proficiency in English, and 28% in mathematics in the 2021–22 academic year.

- In South Los Angeles, only 8% of residents aged 25 years and older hold a four-year college degree, in stark contrast to the more affluent Westside, where 53% of residents possess such credentials. (Los Angeles Times Mapping Project, 2023b).

Despite decades of statistics like these in urban communities, California ended affirmative action in college admissions in 1996. Consequently, students at the Wooten Center no longer have access to support and benefits that allowed thousands of promising students, me included, to attend a university. It is highly probable that without affirmative action and the guidance and assistance I received from a no-cost afterschool program called Anti-Self Destruction (ASD), I would not have been able to enroll in a university in 1977.

At ASD, I found new friends and opportunities, including homework assistance and college and career advisement. The youth center played a pivotal role in helping me complete admissions and financial aid applications and in making the decision to major in journalism due to my passion for writing. They supported my application to CSUN's Educational Opportunity Program and assisted me in crafting a personal essay that secured me an admissions interview. During the interview, when the lone Black female reviewer inquired about my plans if I were not admitted, I responded earnestly, "I guess I'll have a baby and get on welfare." This was a realistic

194   N. McSWAIN

consideration for many families I was acquainted with at the time. Approximately two weeks later, I received an acceptance letter.

In addition to offering academic enrichment and college advisement, ASD provided students with field trips and other fun alternatives to the allure of the gangs and drugs that led to the truancy and belligerence that significantly impacted my academic experience before my transformation in the 12th grade. Unfortunately, my previous two years of indifference and rebellion, having what I considered fun with friends, had left me with a GPA below 2.0, which was the prerequisite to attend a California State University campus. Despite the extensive assistance provided by my youth center, aiding dozens of students like me to overcome such challenges, the nonprofit agency faced closure, along with over 100 Teen Posts in Los Angeles during the 1980s due to state budget cuts.

This was one of the key reasons and motivations behind the founding of the Wooten Center in 1990. Initially, we started out wanting to volunteer at a program like ASD. Our thought was that if the African American teenager with an AK-47 had access to a constructive afterschool program, he would not have been out at 4 P.M. resorting to violence. Unfortunately, by 1989, when my cousin was killed, we found that only four of the original Teen Posts remained operational. This realization underscored why gang violence escalated and surged in the 1980s. The decrease in prevention and intervention services, coupled with the increase in drugs and weapons in our community, was like a bomb dropping on our front porch. We took this crisis very personally and decided to take matters into our own hands. Our mission statement created three years after our opening with guidance from a United Way facilitator perfectly relays our frame of mind, "The Al Wooten Jr. Youth Center is a neighborhood approach to the revitalization and empowerment of a community in crisis. We provide a safe and nurturing environment committed to good citizenship and academic excellence." The following is an excerpt from my aunt's vision statement, created at the same time:

> If anyone could catch the vision of my pain and turn it into something positive for our community, we would be able to save the next generation of kids. We as leaders must change our community's focus by offering our kids education, jobs, love, understanding, and compassion. I see my son in the eyes of every child I meet.

Using sentiments and a phrase from the vision statement, we crafted the slogan, "Making a difference for life. Catch the vision!

I consider myself exceptionally fortunate to have received the support necessary for today holding both a bachelor and master's degrees (the latter in intercultural studies with an emphasis in children at risk from Fuller Theological Seminary, which I earned in 2009, a year before returning to the Wooten Center in my desire to return to youth development work—I did not know it would be the center!). Nevertheless, my journey to improve my life was far from straightforward and easy. Standing on the corner waiting to cross the street to return to the dorms where I lived as a freshman at CSUN, I was shocked by a truckload of young white men yelling, "N—r go home!"—my first experience with the racial epithet directed at me. Unwelcoming behavior like this on a college campus was disturbing for me but was by no means my worst struggle. The worst was dedicating two semesters to remedial math before I could successfully pass the math placement test. Second to this was developing a sense of inadequacy listening to my peers discuss subjects such as sociology, psychology, calculus, urban studies, and other college preparatory coursework that they had encountered in high school. I had never even heard of the classes before seeing them on the general education list at CSUN.

The scarcity of college preparatory courses in my high school was not solely a result of my truancy; rather, it was primarily due to the "disadvantaged" school's emphasis on vocational training over college preparation in the 1970s. Our school offered a wealth of shop and homemaking classes geared towards equipping students to hold careers such as printmaking, horticulture, and auto mechanics for boys, and cooking, hair styling, and sewing for girls. One of my high school teachers even told me, "The best you can do is Trade Tech," where they guided people to so-called non-professional careers like these. I believed her, taking her words to heart and planning to attend the technical school to be a seamstress before my mother, with the support of ASD, offered me the option to pursue my dream of becoming a writer. It is important to note that I do not hold vocational education in disdain. As I always tell students who say they do not want to go to college, "All good work is good work. No problem if you don't want to go to college, but if you change your mind, you'll be ready." I don't have issues with any career students choose, as long as it is an integral one. My grievance with vocational education is not with the opportunity but with a Jefferson High teacher almost laughing and thinking I could never become the journalist I wanted to become. When I shared this experience with my youth center counselor, he expressed considerable frustration on my behalf.

My mother frequently came to mind when we conducted surveys among parents at the Wooten Center, especially when a significant number of them came seeking assistance for students who had fallen behind in their studies during the COVID-19 pandemic. In my personal journey to recovery, my mother had several conversations with the Dean of Girls after truancy officers brought me back to our school campus from a local park where kids ditching class usually congregated. In one discussion, the Dean of Girls referred my mother to ASD. It was not until I had reached adulthood before my mother revealed the extent of her interactions with my ASD counselor. He told her about my involvement with a gang, while she told him I loved to write. They collaborated on a plan of action for my recovery, including my ASD counselor referring me to my first internship at a weekly African American community newspaper where I was thrilled to write photo captions. This more than anything helped me believe that I could become a reporter like the other writers who looked like me.

At the same time, as a senior, I served as an editor and columnist for our high school newspaper. At my graduation ceremony, I received our coveted journalism award and our Dean of Girls award for being one of the two most improved female students (I went from multiple Fs in grades 10 and 11 to a senior with all As and one B (the latter in physical education because we could not afford my uniform on time). I am very grateful for my turnaround and have often shown Wooten students my two framed award certificates, my three diplomas, and pictures of myself as a gang member as proof that they can overcome their challenges as well. I will forever be indebted to ASD and the church my mom also shepherded me to, both helping build my character and resolve, and change my environments.

Likewise, parents at the Wooten Center actively participate in sharing their children's needs and interests through our registration forms and consultations with staff. In addition, at the center, we conduct youth and parent surveys to help further develop and enhance our programming. For instance, tutoring consistently ranks high on the needs list expressed by our community. As we prepared to reopen our center in June 2021, following 15 months of online programming only due to the COVID-19 pandemic, we reached out to parents to ask about their preferences regarding tutoring options. We anticipated an overwhelmingly positive response, favoring in-person tutoring at the center. Surprisingly, the results indicated that 43% of parents responded with "no" they did not want it, while 57% responded with "maybe." Notably, none of the parents responded with a definitive "yes."

Interestingly, our survey results revealed a higher number of students (60%) expressing a preference for virtual tutoring, compared to 40% who said they were unsure about returning to tutoring at the center. The students were like their parents, with none saying "yes" they definitely wanted in-person tutoring. These survey results indicated that both parents and students were still leery about potential COVID-19 exposure. Consequently, this led us to adopt a hybrid model for our afterschool and summer programs, offering activities such as private tutoring, STEM and music classes both online and onsite. We kept our weekly Teen Talk discussion group in the virtual format due to a notable increase in students expressing thoughts of self-harm and suicide during the quarantine. Today, our hybrid model for afterschool and summer programming continues, with most students and parents now comfortable attending activities and events in person.

Embracing College and Career Pathways

Academic and personal enrichment like the support services the Wooten Center offers are critical to increasing college and career attainment in areas where parents might not have the financial means to access them independently. Manual Arts High School provides another example of the challenging conditions we have encountered. In one academic year, hundreds of Manual Arts High School seniors did not graduate because the school had not provided them with the A-G courses they required to graduate. We should have seen this the year before, when 30 out of less than 40 seniors from the same school who went on to four-year universities were participants in our afterschool program's college advisement initiative. A Wooten Center advisor had traveled weekly to the school to help a maximum of 30 students in selecting schools, majors, and career paths, as well as completing college admissions and financial aid applications. Our procedure is to advise seniors to apply to a minimum of 10 colleges and universities. As a result, students typically receive acceptance letters from multiple schools with different offers in grants, scholarships, housing, and more.

Some 20 years after our youth center's founding, as our returning executive director in 2010, I found that my neighborhood still faced significant limitations in access to support services of this nature. A Crenshaw High School college advisor revealed a major part of the problem in stating that it was impossible for her to provide support for all the school's 400-plus seniors. As their sole college advisor, she focused her efforts on the most promising students and sought assistance from our youth center and other partners, like College Bound, to help engage the rest. Once again, we worked with 30 students on a weekly basis, guiding them in identifying potential majors and career paths, and submitting admissions, scholarship, and other financial aid applications.

Cases like these helped me realize how much South LA students continued to face the same challenges that I did, with a very limited supply of the college preparation and advisement needed to gain admittance to top schools. Despite these challenges, our position is to avoid denigrating the schools that are often overwhelmed and under-resourced. In our view, the Wooten Center partners (and never competes) with schools to provide academic and personal enrichment—the nurturing that all children and teens need to thrive and survive. We know that conditions are troubling at schools, exacerbated by the pandemic. As education committee co-chair for the Community Response System of South Los Angeles, a local collaborative founded in 2020 to address pandemic impacts like learning loss and food insecurity, I participated in meetings with LAUSD reps, successfully advocating for services such as private tutoring at schools. But while changing systems is important, our children cannot wait for another school to undergo receivership or "takeover" before current students get the support services they need.

LA County Office of Education (LACOE) administrator, Dr. Erika F. Torres, quoted on progress made toward Inglewood Unified School District's (IUSD) 10 years and continuing in receivership (Spectrum, 2022):

> The city of Inglewood is adjacent to South Los Angeles and considered by many as part of the area. We have made tremendous gains and are far better off today. We balanced our budget, maximized resources for student achievement, improved facilities, built stronger internal and external relationships, and presented new professional development opportunities for our staff. Although we have been making excellent progress, there are still challenging decisions in front of us, such as school closures and consolidations that will be necessary in order for us to maintain stability. In the *Spectrum News 1* article, parent Jazmin Gonzalez said of the receivership, "It makes me feel disheartened because I want to keep my son here in Inglewood. You know, we were all born and raised here. We have to go to outside resources when we should be having them within the city." (p. 1)

Ms. Gonzalez's concerns about inadequate support for her child raises the question of what happens to youth who "fall through the crack" at schools and agencies before we engage in maximizing resources for student achievement. The reality is such improvements should be ongoing endeavors to give our best at all times so that many more students do not have to have potentially lifelong suffering for our neglect. In my experiences working with public and private entities charged with youth development, I find that a lack of equitable and sufficient resources is only half the problem. You can have the best facilities and yet have staff who lack the commitment and care all children need to grow up happy and hopeful. As I always say, a caring heart is the No. 1 qualification to work at the Wooten Center. In my senior year at Thomas Jefferson High, I had a history teacher named Steven Toda, who was said to be the toughest instructor on campus. He was the only teacher I recall who had students take copious notes and write thesis papers like they do in college. It was said that no one received an A in his class. I was the only one who did that semester. Mr. Toda's next class was economics. He pulled me aside after our last history class and asked why I had not enrolled. I said I had gotten my first job after school and would not be joining him. He begged me to reconsider, trying to explain the benefits of an economics class to college and life. I still remember the look of disappointment on his face and his dropped head when I explained that I needed the job and had chosen work experience for my sixth period. I still regret that I did not understand the value of the economics class and how it could help me see why workers like myself earned a low \$3.25/hour taking orders at a furniture manufacturer. I am going to go out on a limb and say we could potentially see some significant improvements at youth-serving agencies if employers hiring new staff could access past performance ratings from students and parents to find more Mr. Todas exhibiting high standards for college and career readiness.

Having people who believe in our students' potential and who strive to give them quality opportunities is critical from the schoolhouse to the boardroom and legislative office. As a newspaper reporter, I asked the campaign manager for a California gubernatorial candidate what their solution was for youth at risk of gang activity in South Los Angeles. He said, "Prenatal care." I asked, "What about the children who are already here?" He surprisingly said (I'm paraphrasing), that is why we have law enforcement! That candidate went on to win and support some very troubling suppression initiatives that filled our juvenile halls. Impacts from external influences like this make it even more difficult for schools and the Wooten Center to achieve 100% success in our outcomes. Furthermore, it is very hard to do the best we can when people do not contribute, whether through volunteerism, donations, or advocacy. For this reason, schools are particularly great partners to help out-of-school time providers offer costly wraparound services such as case management, counseling, healthcare, diagnostics, and more. Schools should be used and appreciated for such contributions.

We hold the same partnership position concerning parents who in my view more often than not fail to provide their children with the support needed at home, not because they do not care, but because they do not have the skills, knowledge, or resources to fully address the needs at hand. I saw my mother sobbing while talking on the telephone about my troubles. Likewise, I have seen Wooten Center parents literally crying for help for their children to improve their skills and/or behavior. As I always say, "Parents love their kids more than we ever will. Respect them for that." Thankfully, seeing my mother sobbing about me for the first time caused me to break up with my gang leader boyfriend and to start listening to my ASD counselors.

Striving to fulfill our mission for the "empowerment of a community in crisis," the Wooten Center started weekly virtual Parent Power Group workshops in 2020 to help parents and grandparents address their families' needs during the pandemic. Discussion topics led by experts in the areas presented have included "Monitoring Your Child's Educational Progress," "Teaching Kids Responsibility and Discipline," "Helping Your Child Master Homework and Studies," "Coping with Grief and Depression," "Finding a Job or Starting a Business During the Pandemic," and

"Budgeting and Managing Your Income." Zoom videos are available at www.youtube.com/wootencenter.

To further enhance our support services for students, in 2013, the Wooten Center established new goals and objectives aimed at providing the academic and personal enrichment necessary for our students to become college-ready, capable of completing post-secondary studies. We outlined those goals in our "STEP Tutorial Model," now known as the "STEP Model for College and Career Readiness."

Developing the Solutions: The STEP Model

STEP is an acronym for Self-directed, Team-oriented, Experiential, and Project-based. We developed the model after reading articles at www.pbl-online.org and www.edutopia.org, both promoting project-based learning (PBL). PBL was at the time among the latest methods to engage students in what many experts agree are the four college readiness skills: critical thinking, collaboration, communications, and creative expression. Gone at our youth center are the days of traditional math and English classes characterized by lectures, worksheets, and rote memory alone. In our approach, the emphasis is placed largely on hands-on, experiential learning, like the college-level science labs. Wooten teachers function as facilitators, guiding and steering students toward harnessing and discovering their inherent talents.

As outlined in Figure 11.1, the STEP Model includes the following tenets and methods:

Figure 11.1

STEP Model

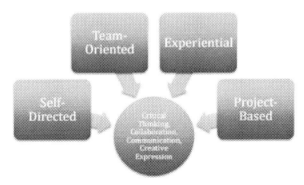

Pathways to College and Career Readiness in South Los Angeles   201

Table 11.1

STEP Model Tenets

Tenet Type	Description
Self-Directed	Teachers serve as facilitators, guiding, instructing, and engaging students. Teachers encourage the use of computers and other technology to promote 21st-century learning and independent study. Students take initiative in completing their work within deadlines, working individually or in groups.
Team-Oriented	Students work in teams to complete and communicate or present their projects.
Experiential	Students observe or demonstrate material learned, gaining direct, hands-on experience. Teachers encourage students to use college and career readiness skills (critical thinking, collaboration, communication, and creative expression) to complete assignments at or beyond their grade levels.
Project-Based	Students complete projects that are rigorous and challenging, relevant to their needs and interests, and based on state content standards (though, at or beyond grade level is preferred). Questions are open-ended, allowing students some choice in deciding how to approach and solve a problem. Projects drive students to think critically and to investigate and analyze results. Results are presented through creative expression such as posters, videos, books, drama, maps, puzzles, illustrations, charts, etc.

Table 11.2

STEP Model Methods

Method Type	Description
Diagnostics and Private Tutoring	Triannual i-Ready.com and Khan Academy assessments in math and reading assigning lessons completed by students one-on-one with tutors.
Homework and Studies	Homework assistance, i-Ready.com study plans, independent study to address challenges and pursue interests.
Drills	Times tables, grammar, and other basic academic skills practice.
Incentives	"Smart Rally" setting monthly goals for students to complete their i-Ready and Khan Academy diagnostics and lessons, a monthly "Fun Friday" event earned with game trucks and more to celebrate the lesson completions, Wooten Dollars earned daily for overall participation and performance and spent at semester-end at our Wooten Dollar Store (extra dollars are earned by students who achieve high-dosage tutoring with at least three 30-minute tutoring sessions per week, per subject), a parent bulletin board with the names of students completing homework and reading and math lessons.

(Table continued on next page)

Table 11.2 (Continued)

STEP Model Methods

Method Type	Description
Project-Based Learning (PBL)	STEM classes, labs (reading, writing, math, arts and sciences, etc.)
Social-Emotional Learning (SEL)	Game Day, Family Day, parent reports, youth and family counseling.
College/Career-Prep and Extracurricular Activities	World languages and culture with cooking, performing and visual arts, SAT-prep workshops, college tours and advisement, College and Career Day, college and career plans, leadership and life skills development (Youth and Junior Councils, Teen Talk, Teen Job Shop, Teen Helper internships, financial literacy), sports and recreation (basketball, soccer, surfing, cooking, gardening, swimming, field trips).
LAUSD A-G Requirements	A. History/Social Science, B. English, C. Math, D. Laboratory Science, E. Language Other Than English, F. Visual & Performing Arts, G. College Preparatory Elective, and others.

In specialized classes like computer animation, music production, and world languages and culture with cooking, Wooten Center youth collaborate in groups to tackle questions while concurrently producing deliverables and sharing results at our triannual showcases. These showcases serve as platforms for students to demonstrate their skills and innovations. Additionally, our students have the opportunity to interact with guest mentors, from aerospace engineers to veterinarians, attorneys, architects, and investment bankers. These professionals actively engage as guest mentors at our monthly College and Career Day, giving students a taste of their work through hands-on activities. As a result, students have undertaken projects such as building robots and solar ovens, preparing Thai and French dishes, creating beats and murals, reading stock sheets and design plans, participating as judges, attorneys, and jurors in mock trials, and much more.

For academic enrichment, we realized we needed a comprehensive approach that was more than homework assistance to bring kids to grade level. Based on a recommendation of a Los Angeles United School District teacher who worked part-time as our education director, the Wooten Center adopted the i-Ready program. i-Ready is an online adaptive learning tool equipped with reading and math diagnostics providing personalized lessons tailored to each student's needs. Since 2015, this addition to our curriculum has yielded significant positive outcomes (see below). Furthermore, in the past year, we started implementing Khan Academy's SAT-prep diagnostics and lessons for high school students in response to colleges eliminating the SAT admission requirement, thereby reducing interest in our workshops. Both virtual platforms give us the ability to assign customized study plans with individual and small-group lessons based on actual student needs and state content standards. We utilize the data generated by these platforms to assess and improve our services, presenting the results to our donors and board members. Notably, both i-Ready and Khan Academy are employed in both online and onsite settings to cater to the diverse learning needs of our students.

To ensure the efficacy of our educational programming in facilitating high school graduation and college admissions, the Wooten Center undertook a comprehensive curriculum overhaul, aligning it with LAUSD's A-G subject requirements. These requirements serve as the foundation for students to earn a high school diploma and are frequently required by both public and private universities for admission.

LAUSD's A–G subject requirements are as follows:

A. History/Social Science (1 year of world history and 1 year of U.S. history)
B. English (4 years)
C. Mathematics (3 years)
D. Laboratory Science (2 years)
E. Language Other Than English (2 years)
F. Visual and Performing Arts (1 year)
G. College Preparatory Elective (1 year)

Remarkably, I never encountered the A–G requirements during my own secondary experience, even though the standards can be traced back to the 1960s when the University of California started requiring students to complete a certain number of high school courses to be eligible for admissions. As detailed in an *Education Advanced* article (Education, 2023), their primary goal and objective was to ensure students were prepared for college-level coursework and to promote equity in higher education.

Our goals to assist the Wooten Center students in achieving high school graduation and gaining admission to a university necessitated that we would have to help prepare them to complete their A–G requirements. This objective was pursued by fostering students' awareness of these requirements through activities like College and Career Day, coupled with the provision of weekly classes, exposing them to the required subjects.

During College and Career Day, in addition to the engaging presentations and activities featuring guest mentors from diverse professional backgrounds, Wooten staff and college interns work one-on-one or in small groups with students ranging from Grades 3–12. Together, they create college and career plans outlining their desired majors, preferred schools, and prospective careers, as well as the extracurriculars, internships, and financing they need to achieve it all. Initially, our approach was centered on engaging teenagers only in completing the plans; however, we soon recognized it was critical to engage all ages in college and career planning long before they reach high school, where each decision counts. Reflecting upon my own experience, I recognize the potential impact of early and continuous support, beginning as early as Grade 3. My mother, who attained only an eighth-grade education and worked as a domestic due to her years of limited schooling in the South, thankfully recognized the value of education and enrolled me in ASD. Today, we are seeing similar from parents, particularly English language learners who desire a brighter future for their children but may lack the skills and resources to provide the necessary guidance.

Furthermore, another improvement the Wooten Center made was in using the term "college and career readiness" instead of solely "college readiness." This change was brought to our attention by a program officer, Celia Brugman, from our funder Kaiser Permanente. She wanted to know what we specifically do to help students prepare for careers, especially those who might not pursue college. This inquiry led to transformative adjustments, including changing our "college plan" to a "college and career plan" and leveraging resources like the College Board's Big Future portal to help students explore diverse career choices. Moreover, we changed "College Day" to "College and Career Day" and started inviting guest mentors who found success without a traditional college degree.

The Wooten Center made the decision to keep the name CollegeTrek Afterschool Program, assuring students who say they don't want to go to college that they'll be well prepared if they change their minds. One memorable instance involved a student swearing, "I'm not going to college no matter what you say, Ms. Naomi!" However, upon her return from a tour of UCLA, I joked with her about all the fun I saw her having. "Do you want to go to college now?" I asked, with a little tease in my voice. To my delight, her response was a resounding, "Well … yes!!" Today, she attends a technical college studying to be a nurse.

This student brings us to another improvement we adopted to help students prepare for college and careers. I served as our de facto college advisor for several years after we were unable to replace our full-time education director due to impacts from the 2009 recession. But by the time students typically made it to me as high school seniors, it was too late to advise them on the AP and other classes and extracurriculars they could have taken to boost their GPA and be more competitive in their college applications. Though we introduced them to these activities in their college and career plans, clearly we needed a next step to engage students in implementing the goals outlined.

With the pandemic further heightening our sensitivity to the need to help students meet the requirements for college access, in 2021 we started

Pathways to College and Career Readiness in South Los Angeles 205

a new activity that we call Teen Scholars. The activity features an advisor from our partner, Educate California, meeting monthly with students from Grades 8 to 12 to guide them in completing what we call "high school success plans." Using our partner's virtual LifePrep Academy portal developed with LACOE, students can save and update their plans and search for new resources to set goals for their life before and after high school graduation. The monthly meetings serve as check-ins to see how students are progressing and to introduce new strategies for success. Parent Alberta Moore credits Teen Scholars and our assistance completing admissions and financial aid applications with helping her son Andy secure a full ride to pursue a bachelor's degree in film and television production with a minor in computer science from Loyola Marymount University. "We lived by the LifePrep website and app we got free through the Wooten Center," Moore said.

To introduce our students to the A-G requirements, we have implemented various activities across the spectrum of subjects:

A. History/Social Science: Utilizing discussion groups, guest mentors, and special events
B. English: Offering resources such as the Writing Lab, Quiet Reading, i-Ready private tutoring and small group sessions
C. Math: Providing access to Math Lab and i-Ready private tutoring and small group sessions
D. Laboratory Science: Engaging students in disciplines like Computer Animation, Robotics, and Aerospace Engineering
E. Language Other Than English: Offering courses like World Languages and Culture with Cooking and commemorating Hispanic Heritage Month and other cultural celebrations as an opportunity to learn and speak words in languages other than English
F. Visual and Performing Arts: Encouraging participation in percussions, piano, dance, painting and drawing
G. College Preparatory: Facilitating initiatives such as Teen Scholars, College Applications Night, SAT-prep, and college tours and scholarships

An invaluable piece of advice: Do not try to do it all yourself. Instead, actively seek out partners with the expertise needed to provide and deliver the quality instruction and materials your program needs. At present, the Wooten Center collaborates with at least a dozen partners each year. These partners contribute to providing STEM, music, art, financial literacy, paid teen helper internships, college tours, and other activities. It is imperative that all these partnerships align closely with your mission, ensuring a focused approach that enhances your qualifications for securing grants and

206 N. McSWAIN

other forms of contributions. We successfully raised $1.7 million in funding in 2022, my last year as executive director before my retirement, a testament to donors' interest in supporting "college and career readiness afterschool."

Additionally, the LA County Department of Public Health Office of Violence Prevention has recognized the Wooten Center as a model afterschool program, noting its contributions not only to academic enrichment but also in providing gang prevention. This recognition holds particular significance in an area where the need for such programs remains high, emphasizing the importance of their expansion rather than reduction.

Reporting the Results

It is not enough to merely provide the kind of targeted and engaging activities that the Wooten Center offers. It is imperative to develop and meticulously track program outcomes to ensure success. Moreover, it is worth noting that virtually all foundations require the establishment of clear goals and objectives to measure performance. It took me about two years after my return to the Wooten Center to really get a handle on collecting and providing the results donors wanted. I doubt we would have gained our current level of impact measurement and funding without support such as the Service Learning Project program at Pepperdine University, which continues to annually provide volunteer interns to work on projects such as community asset mapping, records management, social media marketing, and database development. Graduate accounting students from my alma mater CSUN updated our accounting manual with guidance from their professor. Students pursuing a master's in social work at USC conducted assessments for our afterschool and summer programs. LA County Public Health Trauma Prevention Initiative coaches helped us revamp our employee manual and organization chart. All at no cost!

Professional development became a high priority after a Wooten Center board member, Laurie Inman EdD, attended our staff retreat and advised that better teachers make better learners. We took this to heart and engaged staff in classes at the Center for Nonprofit Management, Grantmanship Center, CompassPoint, Annenberg Alchemy, California School-Age Consortium (CalSAC), and more. Last year, we signed up for a CypherWorx e-Learning account at CalSAC, which solely provides training for out-of-school time professionals. We gave staff paid time to take classes monthly. Some workshops taken by our administration and program staff came through full or partial scholarships provided by Rose Hill, Crail-Johnson, Ralph M. Parsons, Annenberg, and other foundations. The latter awarded a $10,000 grant that is currently funding a two-year strategic planning consultation with our executive team and Bridgespan Group

Pathways to College and Career Readiness in South Los Angeles   207

coaches. At funder forums presented in some workshops, we learned that donors highly value success stories that demonstrate the tangible impact of their investments.

For example, consider Diron, who formerly used to struggle with math and English Language Arts. At Wooten Center's Christmas party in December 2022, Diron's mom, Tracy Thomas, hugged me tightly, sharing how proud she is of her son's improvements and progress. She attributed Diron's success, A+ grades in both subjects, in 2021–2022, to our private tutoring. Mrs. Thomas explained that Diron faithfully met with our lead teachers three times/week, as recommended for high-dosage tutoring. Notably, Diron's diagnostic scores had also shown significant improvements. In 2022, as a sixth grader, Diron went from three grade levels behind in math to on grade level in math and early geometry. Furthermore, he scored mid to above grade level in phonics and vocabulary. Such noteworthy achievements, exemplified by Diron, would remain unquantifiable without the use of diagnostics and the systematic collection of report cards.

Diron represents just one of the successful students included in our 2022–23 outcomes and result metrics, detailed as follows:

1. Math and Reading Score Improvement: By June, 87% of students who took two or more diagnostics assessments demonstrated increased scores in math, while 81% increased their scores in reading, exceeding our set goal of 80%.
2. Grade-Level Proficiency: By June, 39% of students tested attained grade-level proficiency in math, and 25% reached grade-level proficiency in reading, surpassing our goal of 20%.
3. Academic Advancement: By June, 100% of students actively engaged in our afterschool program were promoted to their next grade level.
4. High School Graduation: By June, 100% of high school seniors actively engaged in our afterschool program graduated, surpassing our 80% goal.
5. College Enrollment: Impressively, 100% of high school seniors actively engaged in our afterschool program enrolled in college, surpassing our target of 80%. This has been the case every year since we started tracking this outcome, except for the first year of the pandemic in 2020 when one young man chose to work instead of go to college to help his parents earn income after his dad lost his job.

To effectively track our program results, we utilize an array of tools and systems:

1. KidTrax/VolunteerTrax Databases: These databases enable us to meticulously record registration information, monitor attendance, facilitate communications, and more.
2. i-Ready and Khan Academy SAT-Prep Reports: We rely on these reports for diagnostic assessments and lessons, particularly in reading and mathematics.
3. Chat Check-Ins: Attendance tracking for Zoom meetings, which have become an essential aspect of our program delivery.
4. Zoom Usage Reports: These reports allow us to monitor attendance at Zoom meetings, a key component of our virtual engagement.
5. Wix Booking Calendar: This tool facilitates the booking and successful execution of private tutoring sessions.
6. Weekly Outcomes Reports: These reports provide a weekly overview encompassing demographic data, attendance records, test scores, and more.
7. Annual Outcomes Summary: An annual comprehensive report encompassing demographic data, attendance records, test scores, and other relevant metrics.
8. Surveys: We leverage both quantitative and qualitative data collected from surveys administered to youth, parents, and the broader community.

The ultimate outcome of these efforts is a growing number of students who are well-prepared to embark on their journeys toward higher education and careers, even in the face of formidable obstacles.

CONCLUSION

While we started the Al Wooten Jr. Youth Center with goals to provide caring and quality services for South LA-area students, we never imagined the time, effort, and resources that it would ultimately take to achieve what we envisioned. Even now, we are not satisfied. There is much more we can do to reach and serve many more students. We are in the process of learning how to "scale" our operations. For example, we are removing walls to open spaces and adding more restrooms to increase our facilities' capacity by 30 students. Meanwhile, we are conducting teen workshops at USC Credit Union and Loyola Marymount University where the room capacities are higher. Last year, we held two summer camps concurrently for the first time. One camp was held at the Wooten Center. We directed the second program at a local church that provided the space, furnishings,

Pathways to College and Career Readiness in South Los Angeles   209

and audio equipment at no cost. The Wooten Center provided the curriculum, materials, staff, and field trip buses. We are considering doing the same at schools and exploring a strategic partnership with a similar youth center in nearby Inglewood to provide college and career readiness for more students.

We developed our first capital campaign budget last year to raise funds for the new staff and facilities envisioned. As part of a strategic adaptive planning process in 2022 with Bridgespan Group consultants, we identified three priorities, including increasing major and multi-year funding. The result is $1.7 million in private and public grants and individual donations—our largest fundraising effort in our 33 years. The increased finances helped us achieve our other two priorities: more full-time staff to provide more personalized instruction. Our two new full-time program directors and one full-time program manager and lead math teacher are recruiting, training, and supervising more interns and volunteers than ever before—at least 30 serving as private tutors. In addition to our two full-time interns acquired annually from Public Allies and AmeriCorps at no cost, our executive and associate directors were the only full-time personnel we had for more than 10 years.

Our unprecedented growth starting in 2022 is one of the many silver linings of the COVID-19 pandemic. The global event pushed us to be inventive with private tutoring and music, STEM, and other activities on Zoom and now hybrid. It provided more opportunities for donors to support our work through the personalized instruction and social-emotional learning we developed in response to the learning loss and mental health impacts. The quarantine helped us rally support from college students and corporate professionals who empathized with our youth struggling in at-home learning with less teacher and friend contacts. Many of our volunteers have continued with us after our reopening in June 2021. Our position as one of a few nonprofit youth agencies that remained open in our community during 15 months of closures, although virtually, helped marshal support from public and private leaders looking for solutions. Our city council office has been very supportive in helping us navigate the system for acquiring the permits needed to renovate our buildings to help more students in their recovery.

The takeaway is that out-of-school time providers, especially those facing closure as we were in 2020, need to have as much initiative and persistence as we expect from our students to overcome our own challenges from within and without. When we lost our education director due to the 2009 recession and, therefore, the ability to provide weekly SAT-prep at select schools, we transformed the curriculum into a biannual workshop open to all schools. After canceling our awards dinner and golf tournament the first year of the pandemic and losing some renewable grant support when foundations focused more on emergency services and less on education, we made the tough decisions to either lay off or reassign staff who had provided services like transportation that were nonessential in a virtual world.

My recommendation as the CEO and executive director who experienced our hardest time is to make the adjustments, improvements, and hard decisions needed for your sustainability and growth. Take time to research and register for the information and resources needed for your advancement. Look for professional development and qualified mentors who can serve as models for your ambitions. Set high expectations for yourself, your partners, and your participants. Be the champion and the example our students need to believe in their highest potential and to progress in achieving their college and career aspirations, despite the myriad of challenges in South Los Angeles and beyond.

REFERENCES

Catalina Villegas, (2022). *10 years after state takeover, are Inglewood students better off*. Spectrum News 1. https://spectrumnews1.com/ca/la-west/education/2022/04/17/10-years-since-state-takeover-inglewood-schools

Children's Hospital Los Angeles. (2022). *Community health needs assessment*.

Ed-Data. (2021). http://www.ed-data.org/school/Los-Angeles/Los-Angeles-Unified/La-Salle-Avenue-Elementary

Education Advanced. (2023). *California's A-G Requirements—Where Do We Start?* https://educationadvanced.com/resources/blog/californias-a-g-requirements-where-do-we-start/

Los Angeles Times Mapping Project. (2023a). *Gramercy Park*. https://maps.latimes.com/neighborhoods/neighborhood/gramercy-park/index.html

Los Angeles Times Mapping Project. (2023b). *South LA*. https://maps.latimes.com/neighborhoods/region/south-la/

CHAPTER 12

CREATING CREATORS

How an Out-Of-School Time Ecosystem Is Redefining Creativity and Building Learning Pathways to Future Success

Greg MacPherson, Evan Cleveland, and Armando Banchs

INTRODUCTION

The term "Creativity" has all too often been thought of as a label representing only, or primarily, one's ability to create and perform various artistic endeavors. However, Creativity encompasses a much broader spectrum; it is not confined to a specific set of disciplines. Rather, it represents a critical and in demand set of skills and is an empowering tool for finding future success in both one's career and personal life. We believe Creativity is arguably the most essential skill set needed to address many of the challenges society currently faces and those we will face in the future. According to the Gallup report *Creativity in Learning* (2019), Creativity is defined as "The ability to imagine new ways of solving problems, approaching challenges, making connections or creating products. Creativity is not based on a formula, but on thinking that relates to discovery and inquiry."

The World Economic Forum's *Future of Jobs Report* (2016) outlines the top ten skills in demand, comparing the data from 2015 to the projections for 2020. Remarkably, Creativity ranked 10th in 2015 and rose all the way to number three in 2020. Fast forward a few years and again, in the *Future of Jobs Report 2020*, the World Economic Forum listed Creativity fifth in the top 15 skills of 2025 (World Economic Forum, 2020, p. 36),

---

Built for More: The Role of Out-of-School Time in Preparing Youth for the Future of Work,
pp. 211–236
Copyright © 2024 by Information Age Publishing
www.infoagepub.com
All rights of reproduction in any form reserved.

marking the durability of this skill for the future. Among the skills ranked higher than Creativity are, "Analytical thinking and innovation, Complex problem solving, and Critical thinking and analysis" (p. 36). Referring to Gallup's definition of Creativity, we would assert these are, in fact, not separate skills to Creativity but are the practical activation of Creativity. The World Economic Forum's valuation of Creativity is not an isolated perspective, as numerous other sources make similar endorsements. These sources encompass Indeed's compilation of "20 In-demand Skills for Today's Work Environment" (Birt, 2023), Fast Company's exposition on "Why Creativity is the Top Skill You Need for Guaranteed Career Success" (Stephens, 2022), and the Society for Human Resource Management's *The Global Skills Shortage* (2019, pp. 4) where they assert Creativity is a top three missing soft skill.

The entirety of the education ecosystem, encompassing both in-school and out-of-school (OST) learning environments, should be focused on this guiding principle. If we successfully "Create Creators," then we are successfully equipping youth with one of the most agile and powerful skill sets, imperative for navigating a future work landscape where jobs will look drastically different from what they do today. We do not find it surprising then that Creativity is also the very skill we in the out-of-school time field need to ourselves employ to achieve this objective. Creating individuals who are themselves capable of generating novel ideas and solutions equips them to confront the challenges of an evolving professional milieu. In this regard, the OST sector plays a crucial role. We must lay the groundwork— shaping the environments and crafting experiences—that provide young individuals with the freedom and opportunity to nurture and enhance their own creative faculties.

In Dallas, the nonprofit organization Big Thought has designed and built the "Creator Archetype" (Big Thought, n.d.), a framework to redefine Creativity as a future-focused and forward-looking job skill. Through its Dallas City of Learning ecosystem, which unites a consortium of OST partners and programs, we are deploying this framework through our Learning Pathways initiative. In this initiative, we envision the development of these skills being formally recognized and recorded through micro-credentials, which can become valuable assets for youth we serve.

Credentialing, in its various forms, including micro-credentials, digital badges, and digital credentials, is becoming more common and growing in value and use. This trend is observable within higher education institutions and is gaining traction within corporations for upskilling purposes. The influence of credentials extends beyond these domains as well. Credentials are more frequently noted on resumes and regularly shared through social media sites, such as LinkedIn. Often, these forms of credentials are tied to learning that occurs virtually, either synchronously or asynchronously.

Creating Creators 213

However, it is imperative to acknowledge that the acquisition of skills is not confined to the virtual realm alone. The skill development that occurs during in-person and virtual OST spaces encompassing programs, clubs, and workshops can be just as valuable and impactful to youth, especially those in middle and high school. The efficacy of these learning experiences is comparable in value and impact to their online counterparts.

Creating an OST learning ecosystem that systematically codifies this learning and skill development for youth is of paramount importance. This entails a process that requires rigor in the development and issuance of the credential. The resulting credentials should be presented in a format that is not only easily shareable and widely transferrable, enhancing the prospects for youth as they transition into other learning environments.

In essence, such a comprehensive credentialing system equips youth with a competitive edge when they navigate from OST settings to various other educational and professional spheres. This seamless integration of skill recognition not only acknowledges the value of diverse learning experiences but also enhances the potential for youth to flourish as they engage with a wide spectrum of learning opportunities.

THE CREATOR ARCHETYPE

In order to foster the conditions for an intentional exploration of Creativity, designers and deliverers of OST programs must understand the various elements required to build that muscle. By expanding our perception of Creativity outside of its traditional artistic context, aligning it with the critical thinking and analytical skills mentioned in the introduction, then Creativity arises not from a singular skill set but from a multi-dimensional construct. This perspective prompts us to explore commonalities between, for instance, the poet as they face the empty page, questioning their experiences and their context, and a designer who envisions an artificial intelligence model that can both uncover connections within a dataset and communicate those with clarity and personality. The process a Creator follows to generate the final product—an artifact embodying mastery of content, synthesis, application, and creativity—will necessarily weave throughout multiple dimensions of Creativity. This journey involves the application of distinct skill sets in different proportions, depending on the need.

At Big Thought, our objective was to identify and understand those separate components that cultivate and foster 21st century Creators, pinpointing what skills led to their demonstration and determining how to articulate their acquisition. We undertook an intensive 18-month design process, engaging stakeholders from a spectrum of sectors encompassing

K–12 and higher education, diverse industries, various community organizations, and the youth demographic itself. This collaborative process led to over 200 unique and local insights that were coupled with a contemporary literature review of more than a dozen sources. The culmination of this effort materialized in the "Creator Archetype," a comprehensive framework that repositions Creativity as a future-focused set of skills that can be acquired across any learning endeavor at any age.

Figure 12.1

Creator Archetype Domains

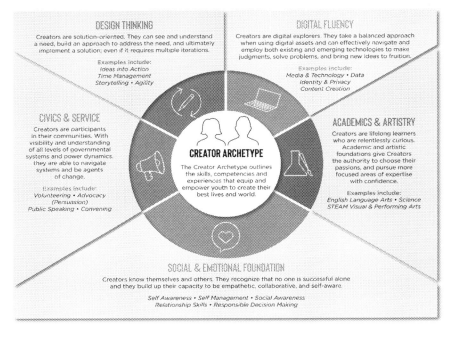

The Creator Archetype is built upon five core domains: Social-Emotional Learning (SEL) Foundation, Academics & Artistry, Digital Fluency, Design Thinking, and Civics & Service. Within these domains are various sub-categories, each comprising a distinct array of skills. In collaboration with CoSpero Consulting, a Dallas-based consulting firm specializing in social impact, we identified how those sub-skills might appear within a specific learning experience and progress along a range of complexity, spanning from beginner to intermediate and advanced levels (Figure 12.2). This extensive undertaking culminated in the formulation of the Creator Archetype Learning Standards (Big Thought, 2023).

Figure 12.2

Creator Archetype Domain 1 Social & Emotional Foundation

2023 Learning Pathways Strategy — 10

DOMAIN 1: SOCIAL & EMOTIONAL FOUNDATION

	I. BEGINNER	II. INTERMEDIATE	III. ADVANCED
A. Self Awareness & Management	a. Identify personal skills, values, and interests and what drives them b. Explain how failure can be seen as a positive experience c. Communicate frustrations and anger appropriately, and practice self advocacy when support is needed d. Stay focused on tasks even in distracting environments e. Describe how positive and negative feedback can be helpful	a. Identify personal weaknesses and apply tools or strategies to strengthen them b. Describe personal lessons from past mistakes c. Practice strategies for coping with and overcoming feelings of rejection, social isolation, and other forms of stress d. Juggle multiple demands without losing focus or energy e. Distinguish between positive and negative criticism and manage emotions around each	a. Evaluate personal biases and describe ways to challenge them b. Demonstrate resilience and optimism by looking at a problem from a different perspective c. Analyze what triggers a strong emotion and identify appropriate coping strategies for various situations d. Select tools and strategies to help manage time and tasks effectively e. Demonstrate a growth mindset by proactively seeking and applying constructive feedback
B. Social Awareness	a. Demonstrate empathy by identifying verbal, physical, cultural and situational cues that indicate how others feel b. Respectfully disagree with others without starting an argument c. Describe the differences between a culturally homogeneous vs. diverse community	a. Demonstrate empathy by considering multiple perspectives b. Show respect for differing opinions in a disagreement c. Promote an inclusive community by inviting others in to your groups and spaces	a. Demonstrate empathy by validating the opinions of others and engaging with diverse cultural and generational perspectives b. Demonstrate flexibility by adapting opinions after considering diverse cultural and generational viewpoints c. Create a safe and participatory environment where each member of a team can contribute as their true selves, regardless of background, age, or lived experiences
C. Relationship Skills	a. Build positive relationships with peers and adults and show appreciation for diversity and intersectionality b. Openly acknowledge and compliment others' accomplishments c. Recognize others' needs and values and work to ensure that others feel heard d. Describe what makes an effective team vs. an ineffective team e. Listen to most perspectives during disagreements	a. Engage with diverse groups of people while showing genuine interest and curiosity in their lived experiences and the perspectives they have to offer b. Encourage others to overcome challenges c. Practice active listening to understand the needs of others and take action to meet those needs d. Contribute constructively to project teams, assuming various roles and responsibilities, to work effectively toward a common goal e. Engage all parties involved in conflict by asking questions and repeating back what you heard to help all members feel heard	a. Celebrate diversity and intersectionality while recognizing that intersectionality of different social categories can impact how a person shows up in a space b. Empower, inspire, and affirm self and others through words and actions c. Engage in healthy dialogue to reach respect and understanding of one another's differing viewpoints d. Galvanize a group towards action by assigning effective roles and navigating conflict together e. Listen to all perspectives during conflict and guide members to reach a common solution and shared understanding
D. Responsible Decision Making	a. Make decisions based mostly on external motivators like rewards, positive validation, etc. b. Explain how decisions and behaviors impact the well-being of others c. Identify sources of unhealthy peer pressures and remain aware of them d. Name possible unwanted or negative consequences that may result from your decisions	a. Recognize personal values/motivators and make choices based on what feels right to you and your relationships with others b. Take initiative and responsibility for what needs to be done c. Apply strategies to resist unhealthy peer pressure d. Consider multiple options, based on input from peers or trusted mentors, before making a decision	a. Explore multiple choice points and make decisions based on internal value systems even when it is difficult to go against popular opinion b. Evaluate your personal role in making decisions that influence your future and your community c. Analyze how one's peers and the media influence the choices we make and apply healthy personal boundaries in these areas d. Analyze the risk or reward of different choices and make a decision that has the highest probability to achieve the desired result

BIG THOUGHT | learning pathways

The levels of complexity should be adaptable to both the program and learner progression. This necessitates consideration of whether an experience is intended for exploration or expertise. Furthermore, within a particular program, the work products could reflect different stages. Within this continuum, the pathway to mastery can be understood and made evident, both for the learner but also for anyone seeking to assess the learner's skill level.

Crucially, the domains that comprise the Creator Archetype do not exist in isolation. Learning experiences will involve interactions between multiple domains simultaneously. To recognize and showcase skill acquisition, programs must consider which domain might be primarily for a particular experience, and educators can confer digital credentials based upon the assessment of a particular artifact. Within the Dallas City of Learning ecosystem, this credential is represented by the digital badge.

Most importantly, this recognition of skill development cannot exist solely on the backend. It is imperative that youth comprehend their acquired knowledge and skill, as well as its position within the skill continuum. Youth must be able to communicate their learning pathway and, ideally, its transferability, enabling the language of skill development to transcend the immediate experience and extend into other contexts, thereby creating other opportunities. The particular skill acquisition we highlight depends on the program and its learning focus. Our exploration will delve into the Creator Archetype's five domains, accompanied by instances illustrating their application, both within Big Thought programs and their potential beyond that immediate learning experience.

Creators are adept at understanding themselves and others. The SEL Foundation domain posits its importance in the necessity for creators to recognize that no one is successful alone, and that collaboration requires both self-awareness and empathy for teammates, end users, and society at large. Central to this domain are the five competencies articulated by the Collaborative for Academic, Social, and Emotional Learning (CASEL): self-awareness, self-management, social awareness, relationship skills, and responsible decision-making (CASEL, n.d.). Although these skills form the foundation of all Big Thought's youth experiences, they most vividly appear in The Fellowship Initiative (TFI), a leadership program for young men of color, supported by JP Morgan Chase. Participating youth, entering as sophomores, engages in a three-year cohort focused on college access. However, TFI equally emphasizes the skills of self-awareness, self-management, and social awareness. In collaboration with a counseling consultant, participants learn to "analyze what triggers a strong emotion" and "demonstrate resilience and optimism by looking at a problem from a different perspective," to reference specific subskills within the domain (Big Thought, 2023).

The TFI program leaders intentionally build each cohort with students from varied ethnicities, socioeconomic backgrounds, and geographic locations throughout the Dallas area. Subsequently, by placing these students in new experiences, such as week-long hiking trips and local cultural events, they cultivate a demonstration of empathy within "a safe and participatory environment where each member ... can contribute as their true selves" (Big Thought, 2023). During the Creator Archetype design process, these skills—often noted by other names, such as 21st century or soft skills—emerged as central themes across stakeholder groups when describing the skills they are either seeking or believe crucial to future success in our ever-evolving global economy.

Creators are lifelong learners who are relentlessly curious and constantly building their knowledge base. Within the Academics and Artistry domain, the Creator Archetype references the authority Creators have to choose their passions and pursue more focused areas of expertise with confidence. This domain can intersect with more traditional standards-based curricula, serving as an essential reinforcement. However, viewed through the lens of OST programming, it represents not only the content itself but the experiential manner through which the knowledge is shared, absorbed, and practically applied. OST experiences assist with bringing relevance to this content in ways that often do not occur in a traditional class setting.

Illustrative of this, Big Thought's Creative Solutions program, a 30-year collaborative partnership with the Dallas County Juvenile Department, offers an arts-as-workforce intervention program for youth who have encountered the justice system. In recent iterations of the program, learners have worked alongside professional artists across diverse disciplines such as photography, ceramics, spoken word, music production, improv, and acting. Positioned within the Academics & Artistry domain of the Creator Archetype Learning Standards, the skills explored in Creative Solutions land within the beginner and intermediate stages of complexity. In these stages, youth create original art pieces "using the technical elements of the artistic disciplines" and communicate "thoughts, feelings, ideas ... through original creative expression" (Big Thought, 2023).

Crucially, throughout this exploration, the focus is on the creative process, raising an awareness of the skills required to plan, design, problem-solve, and collaborate. As one teaching artist stated, these process-based skills can be taken "anywhere to do anything." This awareness of transferability allows participants to articulate how the skills employed in creating a group mural for a local elementary school can also translate into a professional workforce environment.

Creators are digital explorers, and the Digital Fluency domain encompasses the broad skills required to traverse a world increasingly shaped by technology. This domain investigates how Creators navigate existing and emerging technologies to make judgements, solve problems, and bring new ideas to fruition. Concurrently, it underscores the impact of our digital footprint—its influence on both our future selves and the current and continued lives of our connections. Notably, this domain can have the most immediate workforce application, as exemplified in a recent pilot project

Big Thought launched with D Custom, a Dallas publishing company and division of *D Magazine*.

During this project, Big Thought closely supported seven youth between the ages of 16 to 24 through an apprenticeship program. The focus was the creation of a magazine focused on youth voices. Before even considering the magazine's content, the apprentices first learned to "analyze data trends to forecast possibilities," "complete data analysis and calculations using spreadsheets and other programming," and "present information in a variety of ways using graphs, charts and other visuals" (Big Thought, 2023), while learning from and working alongside marketing executives and professionals. They dissected the local, youth-focused publishing landscape and the diverse interests of potential customers. Moreover, they learned how to digest and present their findings through technology, and they created their own tools for a deeper brand and customer analysis. By remixing the skills D Custom professionals taught them, they adeptly tailored these abilities to their unique objectives and showed evidence of the domain subskill "to achieve the desired impact in mind" (Big Thought, 2023).

Creators epitomize a solution-focused approach. The Design Thinking domain encompasses the skills required to imagine and iterate ideas, emphasizing the tenet that failure is not an endpoint, but the next beginning. While design thinking typically calls to mind sticky notes and chart paper, this iterative process is more than that and can be taught to young learners. A compelling example of the Design Thinking domain appears in our Thriving Minds After School Program.

Within this program, an elementary school created an entrepreneur shop, where the children first designed products they then created and sold to raise money for a chosen charity. During the implementation phase, first graders encountered real-world business challenges around supply chains and materials. These youth planned to sell original mosaics within wooden frames. However, they encountered an obstacle; the materials they intended to use were unavailable. In response, they collectively considered other options that would involve the materials they did have while remaining true to their original vision of mosaics. They chose to create smaller mosaics in different frames and then used leftover materials to create jewelry, an entirely new and popular product.

An account from the mother of one of the participating youth further highlights the impact of this pivot. She reported that her daughter was so excited about the new process she and her fellow classmates had developed that she would talk about nothing else, to the point of causing the family dinner to be postponed while she eagerly continued the jewelry-making she'd brought home. This narrative underscores the essence of the Design Thinking domain: the ability to adapt, innovate, and thrive even in the face of unexpected setbacks, translating these experiences into transformative learning opportunities.

Lastly, Creators actively engage within their communities. They must understand present power dynamics and historical marginalization to navigate systems as agents of change. They harness the ability to convene, speak publicly, and advocate for a new vision. This facet of skill development appears most clearly within Artivism, a Big Thought program that thrives at the intersection of art and activism. Here, youth learn about social justice, both on local and broader scales, and they dig into unique issues pertinent to their own experiences. The first step to exploring such vast topics is the basic skill of language acquisition, focused here on the terminology of advocacy. From that beginning, participants then "examine systemic causes for social issues" and uncover their own areas of concern (Big Thought, 2023). They explore these issues through various art forms alongside professional artists. This dual process of examining both society-level problems and personal causes builds the context for future-focused action and advocacy.

It is important to note again that learning experiences encompass multiple domains. However, a program defines and assesses its skills should be understood within the context of that program's individual learning focus. To illustrate this concept, while Artivism operates heavily within the Academics & Artistry domain, its intended learning outcomes are better situated within Civics & Service. Program designers can also consider the positioning of a particular skill within the scope of time, directing the emphasis for that skill development toward the content or toward the future.

For instance, Big Thought operates a program called (A)LIVE, which engages participants in written and performance poetry, using that medium for self-exploration. In this case, skill recognition here could focus on the performance of a poem, which might be conferred as a digital credential - the "Performance Poet Badge," for instance. Alternatively, the very same skill could be positioned for the future as a "Public Presenter Badge". In either example, the assessment would shift along articulated lines to match the intended outcome. This adaptability underscores the dynamic nature of skill development and its malleability to accommodate diverse learning aims.

UNDERSTANDING THE POWER OF ECOSYSTEM

With the Creator Archetype framework in place, Big Thought systematically collects and aligns data on the types of programmatic experiences available within the Dallas City of Learning ecosystem. This analysis garners an understanding of where in the Dallas community certain domains of the archetype are available, for which age youth, as well as identifying gaps where specific types of experiences are not available. This examination is enabled by the programs listed by each individual partner through the Dallas City of Learning online catalogue.

When listing a program, each partner selects up to two sub-categories that characterize that given experience. These sub-categories are framed for front-end users of the catalogue, youth and parents, to facilitate user-friendly searches for experiences they are interested in. Importantly, each sub-category also maps to one or more of the Creator Archetype domains. For instance, a partner may choose to select the sub-category "Spoken Word" for their program, which falls into the searchable category "Performing Arts" for youth, and which is also mapped, on the backend, to the Academics and Artistry domain of the Creator Archetype.

Leveraging this program data, Big Thought conducted an internal Landscape Analysis (Big Thought Institute, 2023) of the program offerings within Dallas City of Learning. This analysis unveiled a total of 1,150 program opportunities distributed across 442 site locations, collectively provided by 61 organizations throughout calendar year 2022. Among these, the Academics and Artistry domain had the highest count of programs, accounting for 693 (60%). This was followed by Design Thinking with 226 programs (20%), Social and Emotional Foundations with 223 programs (19%), Civics and Service with 114 programs (10%), and Digital Fluency with 46 programs (4%).

Additionally, we see 542 programs (47%) were intended for youth ages 0 to 12, while 608 programs (53%) were intended for ages 13+. Analyzing the listed site locations for each program revealed a dispersed distribution throughout the City of Dallas. Programs targeting youth 0 to12 had higher concentrations in southern Dallas, whereas those providing programs for youth ages 13 and over had higher concentrations in southern Dallas, central Dallas, and northeast Dallas. This spatial distribution sheds light on the accessibility and reach of the diverse program offerings. An example of the landscape analysis, highlighting the Academics and Artistry domain of the Creator Archetype, is shown in Figure 12.3.

Armed with this information and fortified by a common language built from the Creator Archetype, the ecosystem is poised to identify gaps in services through any combination of domains, sub-category, geographical areas, and age groups. By developing prioritization and strategies to address visible gaps and provide more equitable access to these types of experiences, the ecosystem can respond.

Through this lens, it becomes feasible to scrutinize which partners are operating in which geographic areas, ask whether new partners need to be

Figure 12.3

Landscape Analysis Graphic 2022

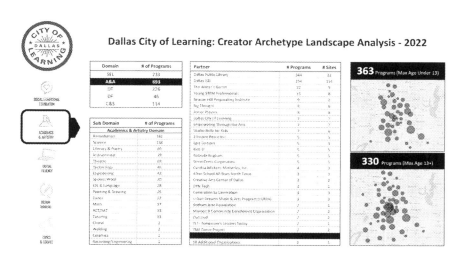

brought into the ecosystem, or whether existing partners have the capacity to provide services in other areas or for additional ages. The landscape analysis is emblematic of accessibility to specific programs, delineating exposure to particular skills. It is crucial to underscore that this analysis doesn't portray utilization figures. However, complementary data points within the Dallas City of Learning dataset provide insights into utilization trends.

It's essential to discern that this analysis primarily underscores access and exposure rather than quantifying skill acquisition or development. To delve into that dimension, an alternate response—the Learning Pathways initiative—was crafted and integrated into the ecosystem's infrastructure. This initiative provides a comprehensive means of assessing and monitoring the actual progression and growth of acquired skills.

LEARNING PATHWAYS

The Learning Pathways initiative, spearheaded by Big Thought, aims to create a world in which the skills developed by youth in out-of-school time are more visible and leveraged by youth as valuable assets in pursuit of a future of their choosing. To this end, the tool and mechanism utilized to define, measure, and fulfill Learning Pathways are digital badges, commonly referred to as micro-credentials.

The Creator Archetype framework is used as the taxonomy for Learning Pathways. It unifies partners across the ecosystem in a common language they can use to build and articulate youth skill development through digital badges. This framework also enables Big Thought, as an intermediary of the ecosystem, to frame communications, conduct analysis of the initiative's progress, and aggregate information and lessons from the ongoing learning experiences.

Among the priorities of Learning Pathways is to ensure that the digital badges youth receive are transferable and extend beyond the confines of the Dallas City of Learning platform, allowing them to be shared through other means, such as social media, and collected in other badging-related digital backpacks or wallets designed for micro-credentials. The key belief underpinning this approach is that the badge represents learning that is personal for youth, and they should have ownership and control over their achievements. For this to be true, digital badges must be flexible to travel with youth should they move from Dallas, or should they want to combine them with other credentialed learnings. This adaptability ensures that these digital badges become long-term assets for the youth as they pursue post-secondary opportunities, encompassing pursuits like college, trade, or employment.

From a youth perspective, digital badges fulfill a dual role. First, they can help communicate their interests and passions. Second, they serve as verifiable validation of the skills they have developed during OST, supplementing their more traditional school transcripts and providing a more holistic view of their learning journey. The Learning Pathways initiative not only empowers youth to craft their narratives, but also accentuates the value and significance of experiential learning in shaping their future trajectories.

While the Creator Archetype landscape analysis outlined provides insight into the skill development opportunities across the ecosystem, it is Learning Pathways that represents the skill acquisition and development that has occurred. In this way, digital badges are an innovative tool and possess the capacity to encapsulate and signify these acquired skills in a profound manner.

Each digital badge issued incorporates detailed meta-data representing the nuance for that respective learning accomplishment. This meta-data not only serves as a way for youth to have a lasting record of the specific skills they acquired during their OST program experience, but it also outlines the context of that learning experience and signifies the tangible results of their efforts. Youth are equipped with verifiable evidence that their work product or artifact met the designated criteria of the program and they have successfully acquired and applied the given skill.

In essence, digital badges within the Learning Pathways initiative extend beyond mere symbolic representation. They assume the role of substantiated records that validate the actualization of acquired skills, granting youth a powerful repository of their growth and accomplishments.

Learning Pathways: How It Works

As the out-of-school intermediary for Dallas City of Learning, Big Thought facilitates the technological infrastructure, referred to as the DCoL platform. This platform allows OST providers throughout the ecosystem to list their program offerings on a public-facing digital catalogue for youth and families. Providers utilize this platform to roster the youth that enroll and attend their programs and to build the digital badges that represent the distinct learning objectives of their respective program offering(s). Throughout this process, Big Thought provides ongoing training and technical assistance to providers.

As providers go through training and build their digital badges, they develop specialized rubrics to guide and determine their review of the youth's work product. These rubrics aid to determine if those artifacts produced by the youth demonstrate their attainment of the stipulated learning objectives. When that is determined, the provider can then award the earned digital badges to youth through the platform. Subsequently, youth can also claim that badge by logging into their account profile in the platform. Once claimed, the badge is the property of the youth, and they begin to utilize it to their advantage by sharing it through social media channels, such as LinkedIn, and referencing them on resumes, college, or job applications.

An early insight of digital badging within Dallas City of Learning is that a badge in isolation has very little value and does not represent a pathway. A critical key to the long-term success of Learning Pathways will be volume over time. The ecosystem must reach a critical mass of badged opportunities being both offered and utilized. The accessibility of a wide array of badged experiences allows youth to accumulate, based on their own interests, various experiences across a range of programs and Creator Archetype domains.

Learning Pathways distinguishes two primary types of pathways or ways that youth may accumulate digital badges over time. The first, termed "organic pathway," denotes a cumulative journey of experiences and learning that a youth opts-in to based on their interests and passions. In organic pathways, you might say the youth are blazing their own trail. For instance, an interest in storytelling could start with a creative writing course, followed by a workshop on playwriting. This youth's organic pathway may also include other experiences, such as participation in a basketball camp, photography course, and debate camp. The options and sequence are limitless; however, each stop along that organic path includes meaningful learning and skill development.

The second type of pathway, "curated pathways," represents a more formal and structured set of experiences and credentials. These often follow a sequential arrangement, occurring within one provider or across multiple providers. These two types of pathways can, and should, co-exist for each participating youth. The points of connection and divergence between each type will vary for each individual youth, representing the uniqueness of their learning journey and that the road to future success does not look the same from one youth to the next.

Learning Pathways in Action

In the fall of 2022, building upon the groundwork laid out in the Creator Archetype section of this chapter, Big Thought joined forces with both an industry partner, D Custom, and a local nonprofit, Brass Tacks Foundry. The primary objective was to create a curated, sequenced, and credentialed learning experience for youth, ages 16 through 24, already participating in one or more of Big Thought's programs. The collaboration put Big Thought's vision "to equip all youth in marginalized communities to imagine and create their best lives and world" to the test. This collaborative initiative combined social and emotional foundations with immersive experiential learning opportunities, and a focus on the development of what Decker (2019) refers to as "middle-skills" (p. 2), equipping our youth with the necessary tools for workforce development.

> The middles-skills pathway is still growing with 16 million workers or 26% of the labor market. Middle-skills pathways include some of our most needed sectors including STEM, healthcare, and business. This training may occur at the post-secondary level (associate degree, diploma, or certificate credential) or through work-based learning (WBL) programs such as an apprenticeship. (p. 2)

The program was born from a conversation between Big Thought President and CEO, Byron Sanders, and D Custom's Vice President and Head of Business Development, Chris Phelps. While discussing the idea of having youth develop an inaugural "Create Great—Youth Voice" magazine, the conversation swiftly transitioned into a broader exploration of what a youth apprenticeship program would look like if it harnessed the philosophy of the Creator Archetype. The human-centered design thinking question posed was "how might we" engage youth to be *ideators*, designers, marketers, researchers, interviewers, and co-creators in a youth-focused, youth voice and agency magazine.

With the vision cast, the three collaborative partner organizations came together to identify the workforce skills each partner would focus on providing, designing the phases of experiential learning experiences to be offered, and which we would collectively designate as the "Big Thought Apprenticeship." Participants in the program would have the opportunity to earn three distinct digital badges, each aligning with a phase of the program design: "Professionalism 101," awarded by BT Foundry, and the "D Custom—Content Academy" and "Big Thought Apprenticeship Badge," awarded by Big Thought. The three-phased approach was intentionally set to allow youth ample time to learn and put to practice a range of skills through work-based learning experiences delivered by each partner and to complete their final work products as evidence of mastery of those skills.

The digital badges were crafted in alignment with the Creator Archetype framework, Creator Archetype Learning Standards, and with all nine categories of Employability Skills from the U.S. Department of Education Office of Career, Technical, and Adult Education Division of Academic and Technical Education (2023). These categories encompass Applied Academic Skills, Critical Thinking Skills, Interpersonal Skills, Personal Qualities, Resource Management, Information Use, Technology Use, Communication Skills, and Systems Thinking (U.S. Department of Education, 2023). This intentionality offers the apprentices the opportunity to earn three distinct digital badges to allow what Shields and Chugh (2017) argue are most valuable about digital credentialing, that "not only the … microskill obtained … [but also] what the participant had to do in order to receive the badge" (p. 1818).

The first phase of the program, provided by Brass Tacks Foundry, was focused on introductory workforce skills and the opportunity to earn the Professionalism 101 badge. In this phase, any Big Thought program youth ages 16 to 24 that were interested were able to participate. This permitted more youth access to the introductory workforce skill development and allowed them to gain more information about the Phase 2 and Phase 3 apprenticeship opportunity with D Custom. Phase 2 and 3 of the program were limited to seven openings, and this approach gave youth the agency and decision-making power to choose whether or not to pursue.

Phase 1 spanned five weekly sessions, each lasting four hours, with an additional two to three hours of research and independent work taking place outside of the classroom environment. This structure gently immersed the youth into the cadence of learning that the future phases, and the paid apprenticeship, would follow. Brass Tacks Foundry facilitated learning in 21st century workplace skills, including:

- code switching—actively deciding on your language and style of communication between formal and informal, and only utilizing colloquialisms in informal communication with peers and mentors;
- knowing your brand—how to be your authentic intersections of identity in the workplace;
- work personality and adaptation—how to work with various work personalities, how to show up differently in work mode versus after hours;
- professional dress and presentation—attitude as well as modality of speech;
- different email and electronic communication styles;
- resume building and interviewing skills via one mock interview with feedback/critique and group question and answer sessions.

Youth who determined they were interested in one of the seven available spots in the next phases of the program created a resume, applied online to Big Thought as paid part-time employees, and participated in a final interview round. As the sponsoring agency, Big Thought provided a program manager, Armando Banchs, throughout all phases to provide a sense of continuity for the youth, project oversight, ensure safety, and mentorship throughout their journey.

Phase 2 of the program began with the apprentices receiving an authentic new hire experience that supported their career development. Apprentices received an official offer letter, reviewed their proposed job descriptions, and completed requisite paperwork. Next, they attended a formal orientation, where they reviewed the employee handbook, learned about Big Thought's history and work culture, were trained on how to track and manage timesheets, enrolled in healthcare benefits, and received their work laptops and an IT orientation. Lastly, they had their first meeting with their supervisor (and mentor) to go over work schedules and to field clarifying questions.

Under the aegis of D Custom, in Phase 2, Content Academy, the apprentices delved into a comprehensive learning journey comprised of five stages: Content Strategy, Situation Analysis, Brand Positioning, Content Plan, and Magazine Brief. Throughout these stages, the apprentices assimilated and applied D Custom's industry-leading best practices for ideating, marketing, and pitching a magazine.

Reflecting on their experiences with Content Academy, the apprentices each spoke about various aspects that left an impact on them. For apprentice Brooke, the content and facilitation were meaningful, "So, I think the whole process, well I feel like at times could be very informative.... So, it was a lot of information to take but it wasn't overwhelming." Apprentices Ty, Ania, and Nalenie highlighted that the D Custom staff provided a safe space for learning and were consistently patient and responsive to the apprentice's learning needs. Ty remarked "I have a hard time getting things on the first take, it was just very open, and I didn't feel threatened to get it the first try…. And I'm, I'm, I'm [expressed emotionally] glad for that." Nalenie felt similarly, stating "D Custom's whole team, they were very patient, and you know, just kind of stuck with us. Even if we had fifty million questions to ask … they were still with us, and they're answering those questions." Ania observed that the safe and supportive experience really helped her, and her peers gain confidence throughout the process:

> And I think the Content Academy was really good. It was really distinguishable. I understood every part of it, and if I didn't, I could ask questions, so I really understood the process, which then helps me better inform my work. So now I'm … I'm really, I feel, a lot more confident with what I'm doing because I know the whole system…. Even though it felt daunting at the end of the day, we had a lot of support and a lot of guidance, so it went really well. And you know, we really gained confidence in that aspect too.

Apprentice Angelica's reflections speak further to the respect the group felt they received from the D Custom staff and the recognition that even in a workplace, they were building personal relationships:

> Yeah, a large part of it was like how the staff were…. They were very like understanding and patient, but they also didn't undermine our ability, just because we were youth. They treated us and respected us as if we were [peers] … and I really appreciated how informative Paul [D Custom President] was, not just from a business standpoint, but also, he gave personal side of it, which I think made like us connect a little more, was not just like, OK, this is the president and that y'all are just the apprentices. No, it was a more, there was a more connection built there and relationship. So, I think that played a big part.

The confidence that Paul Buckley, President of D Custom, and Annie Wiles, Editorial Director at D Custom, held in the apprentices' capabilities was palpable, leading them to assign a meaningful task to the apprentices—presenting the resultant creative brief to key stakeholders at Big Thought. Due to the intentionality of D Custom's curriculum and their rapport building, the apprentices pitched each section of the magazine's table of contents, delivering a cohesive message and compelling vision for the Create Great Magazine. The presentation seamlessly communicated the magazine's essence, the target market, the competitive landscape, and how to frame the magazine to truly be youth-facing and featuring youth voice and agency. The presentation showed the apprentices' mastery of the content and applied learning of the industry skills imparted to them.

The apprentice's capacity to take ownership of the creative brief they had crafted and present it left indelible impressions. This moment served as a catalyst, catapulting them into the next sessions of the Content Academy and into the production of the magazine itself. Angelica remarked:

> Just for me personally, that day was just so ... changing. In the way I present myself, the way, the way I speak, the way, I don't know, like I was, like, "Oh, my gosh! We just did this really hard thing, presenting in front of these really, really important people. An idea that we were trying to convey to them, and after that, answering questions that they had for us on the spot, the fact that we were able to do that. And it was real life, yes. You can't get more real in that. So, I don't know, like, that day I will be forever grateful. Forever ingrained in me, and it's impacted who I am now.

At the conclusion of Content Academy, the apprentices were now two-thirds of their way through their Learning Pathway. Regarding this stage of the program, Ania remarked it "was the best because it showed how far we have come." With their second digital badge now earned, the apprentices transitioned into phase three of the program and the task of transforming their conceptual creative brief into a full-fledged magazine. This pivotal juncture saw the apprentices collaborate to allocate responsibilities for various sections of the magazine, with each apprentice taking on the mantle of lead writer and contributor for their designated segment.

Each apprentice individually met with D Custom mentor Annie to pitch their ideas for the section of the magazine, and she then finalized the role assignments for each apprentice. Apprentices took on responsibility for the angle, tone, and images to accompany their article. They each delved into background research, ideation, interview formulation, conducting interviews, drafting compelling narratives, and meticulously refining and enhancing their content based on D Custom's invaluable feedback.

Phase 3 not only challenged the apprentices to innovate and infuse authenticity into their contributions, but also required them to imbue their agency with a profound sense of purpose. Their work demanded sensitivity to create an inclusive space for their interview subjects to articulate their unique perspectives, with the apprentices skillfully ensuring that these perspectives occupied the focal point of each article. This project stands as a testament to the apprentices' accomplishments, evoking a sense of pride in their achievements. Published in September 2023, the culmination of this endeavor earned the apprentices their third and final digital badge, cementing their journey of skill acquisition and personal growth.

The rich learning that occurred during the Big Thought Apprenticeship program was not limited to the youth. Organizationally, Big Thought acquired learning of its own through informal and formal data collected throughout the eight-month experience. Armando Banch, Big Thought's project manager and apprentice mentor checked in with each apprentice weekly during their face-to-face sessions and tracked any challenges or ideas that they also shared via email or text communication. This approach ensured that the program's design remained responsive and adaptable to the apprentice's feedback.

An important revelation emerged early on as the apprentices shared that they valued the multiple modes of communication and appreciated that our electronic communications required at least two supervising adults on every thread to protect both youth and adult members of the team. The apprentices also shared that they appreciated our willingness to embrace text as a secondary mode of communication, as Big Thought utilizes emails, Teams' chats, and Outlook calendar invites for primary modes of communication, and that youth saw text as a more immediate modality for communicating.

Big Thought utilized three focus group interviews, and each apprentice took part in a one-on-one exit interview with Mr. Banchs. Through these conversations, we gained insights into what the apprentices felt went well and areas they would improve for the next cohort. The apprentices shared they appreciated having the project manager present at each level of engagement to model to other adults the best practices of working with youth, supporting their social and emotional needs and growth, encouraging team development and cohesion, and ultimately modeling to the industry-partner how to create a space of true collaboration with the apprentices.

A notable observation from the apprenticeship program was the Generation Z youth's enjoyment of working in concert with and supporting each other. Whenever given the opportunity to lead, our youth would step forward in partnership with each other and communicate their ideas in a collegial and cooperative fashion. They actively engaged all their fellow apprentices to hear their perspectives, communicate their vision, and worked synergistically to come to consensus on the direction and execution of each specific deliverable.

One noteworthy aspect, a natural peer mentorship developed between the high school age apprentices and those in their early 20s. The older supported their younger project partners in and out of meetings and on deliverables. The apprentices set up a text chat thread to communicate with each other as they worked on key deliverables for each phase of the project, reaching out to each other when needs arose, encouraging each other as they encountered challenges, and communicating support throughout. When an apprentice was unsure of how to proceed or needed a second pair of eyes on copy, their peers would encourage and remind each other to reach out to the project manager and mentors at D Custom. This peer mentorship model was reported by the apprentices during the focus groups as beneficial and that it helped the youth become more comfortable with admitting challenges, learning how to effectively communicate their needs, and reinforced teamwork as a positive model for professional workspaces.

An important lesson learned was cadence and hours of engagement for the project. The apprenticeship was conceived by adults and originally believed to only need 10 to 15 hours of the youth's attention weekly. However, as the project took place over eight months, it became evident that this schedule presented challenges for the youth participants, particularly those still navigating their high school environment. Balancing the demands of navigating their senior year workload, college applications, prom, part-time work elsewhere, and project requirements led to stress and risked project fatigue among the apprentices.

Recognizing these challenges, the project team took a proactive and collaborative approach to address the issue. Continuous communication and positive reinforcement from both the industry-partner mentor and project manager helped to alleviate these stressors and remind the youth their struggles and stressors were valid, and each adult worked with youth in partnership to ideate solutions to each issue. The approach demonstrated to the youth that their concerns were valued and that the adults were committed to working in partnership to find solutions that worked for everyone.

This model of collaborative problem solving, coupled with a strong emphasis on social and emotional practices, has had several positive outcomes. The apprentices reported this allowed them to take ownership of the challenge, develop solutions to navigate challenges, and allowed them to see adults and mentors as partners in their struggles, but ultimately, they had agency to make decisions on how they would move forward. The apprentices added that this model helped them see why collaboration and generational mentorship models had merit and that they would apply this strategy to their education, workplace, and personal development in the future.

The digital credentialing of each phase allowed the youth and adult mentors to talk through the intended and bonus skills developed. Throughout each phase, youth had the opportunity to reflect on their experiences, contributions, challenges, learnings, and how they could apply their new skills to their futures. This intentional process allowed each youth to process their skills development internally, through one-on-one sessions with their adult mentors, and finally as a group where they provided feedback to their peers. In this peer-to-peer setting, they shared how they valued each other and saw each other meet challenges, ask for help, express leadership qualities, and grow. This program feature was pivotal as it helped to validate

Creating Creators   231

each youth's skills development and helped to grow the group's sense of team as they showed vulnerability and accountability to each other. The apprentices also used this time to apologize to each other and appreciate each other's leaning in to support one another during specific times of challenge during the program. This collaborative unpacking reinforced the significance of their digital credentials as representations of real skills development, rather than mere completion badges.

Finally, the apprentices highlighted that they appreciated the project manager, Mr. Banchs, guiding them through the process to create their digital portfolio for college and job applications. This step-by-step guidance helped them create profiles on Big Thought's Dallas City of Learning platform and on LinkedIn. The process of going into their emails to accept the digital credential for each phase reinforced their sense of accomplishment, reminding them of their capabilities, and providing a digital means to showcase their newfound assets. The apprentices also took the initiative to update their professional and student resumes to reflect the skills development for each badge and linked their digital credentials to their resumes.

THE FUTURE OF LEARNING PATHWAYS AND OPPORTUNITIES FOR SYSTEMIC CHANGE

As the Learning Pathways initiative progresses, we are considering the long-term trajectory of the initiative and how best to build downstream currency that will add value for the youth and strengthen the system overall. Downstream currency speaks to the benefit the micro-credentials earned will have post-issuance for a range of stakeholder groups, including the youth themselves, institutes of higher education, and future employers. Four strategic priorities have been identified and are at the time of this writing in various stages of pursuit. These strategies address key aspects of the initiative to ensure credibility, trustworthiness, and alignment of the badges, while also exploring ways to integrate them more closely with traditional education systems. The strategies outlined are to:

1. continually improve the rigor and clarity by which badges are designed, issued, and articulate skill development and complexity,
2. build name recognition for the digital badges that elicits familiarity and trust with downstream stakeholders,
3. increase the alignment with industry skills frameworks, and
4. elevate the visibility of OST digital badges alongside a youth's traditional school transcripts, finding ways for these badges to be recognized through course credit in Texas' K–12 education system.

Rigor and Clarity

For digital badges issued in the OST space to have maximum value, downstream entities such as higher education institutions and employers need to trust the badges awarded accurately reflect the skill development they purport to represent. In the context of the Learning Pathways initiative, a high level of rigor speaks to both the thoroughness of the training, resources, and structures Big Thought provides participating program providers, as well as the accuracy by which these providers design badges, review youth work product, and award the badges to youth.

Clarity denotes the specificity and consistency of the skills addressed within the meta-data of each badge. To enhance rigor and clarity across the initiative, the next phase of work will focus on the piloting and subsequent launching of the Creator Archetype Learning Standards. The standards will serve as a mechanism to explicitly outline key skills and competencies within each domain of the Creator Archetype. This tool benefits OST providers by offering a clear map they can align to with their program offerings and digital badges. For each skill included in the learning standards, there is a corresponding definition of evidence at three levels of youth skill development and complexity: beginner, intermediate, and advanced.

Name Recognition

Name recognition is a crucial factor in establishing trust and credibility for digital badges within the broader landscape of education and credentialing. As the field of digital credentials expands, we can see the value of name recognition already emerging, as courses from entities like Google and Coursera gain recognition and popularity. This begs the question for how digital badges earned in OST settings from community-based organizations can also be valued and not discarded as less than.

Our premise is that name recognition, while not a silver bullet, can aid in accomplishing this. In this next phase of Learning Pathways work, there is a strategic focus on leveraging the regional recognition and reputation of Dallas City of Learning and setting up structures so badges that align with the Creator Archetype Learning Standards will also be eligible to be endorsed by Big Thought. The endorsement will be contingent on a technical review of the badge's design and on a secondary artifact review that looks at whether badges issued were done so with fidelity, meaning the youth's work product meets the criteria outlined by the provider as displayed in the badge design. The endorsement process adds an extra layer of credibility to the badges, akin to a "Good Housekeeping Seal of Approval." It signifies an additional verification to the rigor of the badge development and issuance and adds to the badges meta-data a familiar and trusted name.

Industry-Alignment

The Creator Archetype framework and Creator Archetype Learning Standards were both developed with a lens on the skills various industry employers are seeking in their current and future workforce. There is, however, an opportunity to align with industry more deeply and explicitly. The case study with *D Magazine* is a prime example of how OST providers and industry partners can collaborate to offer rich learning experiences that are credentialed. Building on the learning from this experience, we envision a future phase of work where Dallas City of Learning supports the engagement of industry partners to work alongside OST providers to design programs and accompanying digital badges. These programs and badges would continue to align to the Creator Archetype Learning Standards in addition to industry-specific skills and would be endorsed by both Big Thought and the industry partner. This combination would be a nexus of rigor, name recognition and industry-alignment. The approach not only enhances the value of the digital badges for youth but also strengthens the overall ecosystem by creating a connection point between OST and the workforce.

Connection and Credit

The concept of connecting digital badges earned through OST programs with formal education transcripts and exploring credit-for-learning mechanisms holds significant potential to enhance the recognition, transferability, and value of these credentials. Our prevailing design question is "What if the digital badges earned by youth in OST can be viewed alongside a youth's formal K–12 or college transcripts?" Our exploration of this question has led us to a potential partnership: GreenLight Credentials. As discussed in "Dallas-Based GreenLight's Blockchain Platform is Powering College Readiness for Texas High School Students," GreenLight is using blockchain technology to provide students with lifelong access to their learning records (Edwards, 2020). GreenLight is already partnering with local education agencies, such as Dallas ISD; institutions of higher education, including Dallas College, UNT Dallas, and others; and employers (Edwards, 2020). Big Thought believes there are opportunities for out-of-school-time-issued digital badges to live alongside these transcripts. Imagine a scenario where youth applying for college, or a job, can not only present their verifiable transcript but also include select digital badges that reflect learning and skill acquisition relevant to the opportunity they are pursuing. Big Thought and GreenLight are exploring possibilities around this idea and are currently investigating what a future pilot may entail.

Big Thought has begun exploring credit-for-learning public policy examples and legislation, wherein structures exist where the learning that youth engage in OST can carry credit and be applied to a student's K–12 graduation requirements. In *Credit for Learning: Making Learning Outside of School Count* (Afterschool Alliance, 2021), the need and value for this construct is outlined, emphasizing by "allowing students to pursue experiences that speak to their interests and delve deeper into subject matter outside of the classroom. These programs are a resource to help promote student engagement, prepare students for life after graduation, and provide a broad range of learning experiences for young people, particularly underserved youth" (Afterschool Alliance, 2021). Afterschool Alliance further articulates how credit-for-learning is a student-centered tool to increase motivation and engagement, while simultaneously attending opportunity gaps for historically marginalized youth (2021). Learning from communities already engaged in this work, such as the All Course Network in Rhode Island (State of Rhode Island Department of Education, n.d.) and the Extended Learning Opportunities program in New Hampshire (New Hampshire Department of Education, n.d.), can inform a potential path forward for the Learning Pathways work underway in Dallas.

CONCLUSION

However nascent or advanced one sees the efforts and accomplishments coming from the development and deployment of the Creator Archetype and the Learning Pathways initiative, what is evident is the interconnected and layered nature of ideas that must work in concert with each other, and within the broader educational and employment ecosystems, in order to deliver maximum value for all the youth in our communities. Digital badging could be accomplished on a small scale and in isolation, but what long-term benefits does that truly bring to our youth? Additionally, how is that pushing the education sector to think and do more in service to our young people and their capacity to contribute to society, while also realizing and capitalizing on their assets, interests, and abilities?

It is also imperative to continue to pursue this work through an equity lens so that the systemic barriers which have all too often limited opportunity for those youth and families of color or in low-income households are not repeated or perpetuated. For Big Thought and the Dallas community, this means we must push to expand the pipelines of available badged experiences and outlets for those badges to carry currency, both locally and beyond. A future where this codified OST learning acts as an equalizer in the pursuit of post-secondary opportunities, whether that be in applying for higher education or jobs, is possible. The success of projects like the collaboration with D Custom is evidence of this very fact and of the need. By implementing intentional structures that can be replicated at various levels of scale, we have the ability to institutionalize access for communities that may otherwise not have the same open door to these types of experiences.

Ultimately, the success of initiatives like the Creator Archetype and Learning Pathways lies in their ability to create a paradigm shift in how education is approached. By embracing diverse learning experiences, integrating digital badges with traditional transcripts, and advocating for credit-for-learning mechanisms, we can create a more inclusive, adaptable, and effective educational landscape. This approach not only equips youth with essential skills but also empowers them to navigate their educational and professional journeys with confidence, agency, and a broader perspective on their potential contributions to society.

REFERENCES

Afterschool Alliance. (2021, November). *Credit for learning: making learning outside of school count.* Afterschool Alliance Issue Brief No.79. https://files.eric.ed.gov/fulltext/ED616512.pdf

Big Thought. (n.d.). *What makes a great creator?* https://www.bigthought.org/insights-reports/blog/what-makes-a-great-creator/

Big Thought. (2023). *Creator Archetype Standards.* https://www.bigthought.org/ca-standards/

Big Thought Institute. (2023). *Dallas City of Learning Creator Archetype Landscape Analysis 2022.* Internal Big Thought Institute report: Unpublished.

Birt, J. (2023). *20 in-demand skills for today's work environment.* Indeed. https://www.indeed.com/career-advice/finding-a-job/in-demand-skills

CASEL – Collaborative for Academic Social and Emotional Learning. (n.d.). *What is the CASEL Framework.* https://casel.org/fundamentals-of-sel/what-is-the-casel-framework/

Decker, D. (2019). Student perceptions of higher education and apprenticeship alignment. *Education Sciences, 9*(2), 86.

Edwards, A. (2020, September 17). *Dallas-Based GreenLight's Blockchain Platform is powering college readiness for Texas high school students.* Dallas Innovates. https://dallasinnovates.com/dallas-based-greenlights-blockchain-platform-is-powering-college-readiness-for-texas-high-school-students/

Gallup. (2019). *Creativity in learning.* https://www.gallup.com/education/267449/creativity-learning-transformative-technology-gallup-report-2019.aspx

New Hampshire Department of Education. (n.d.). *Extended Learning Opportunities.* New Hampshire Department of Education. https://www.education.nh.gov/partners/education-outside-classroom/extended-learning-opportunities

Shields, R., & Chugh, R. (2016, July 19). *Digital Badges—rewards for learning—education and information technologies.* SpringerLink. https://link.springer.com/article/10.1007/s10639-016-9521-x

SHRM—Society for Human Resource Management. (2019). *The global skills shortage.* https://www.shrm.org/hr-today/trends-and-forecasting/research-and-surveys/Pages/Skills-Gap-2019.aspx

State of Rhode Island Department of Education. (n.d.). *All course network.* https://ride.ri.gov/students-families/education-programs/all-course-network

Stephens, E. (2022). *Why creativity is the top skill you need for guaranteed career success.* Fast Company. https://www.fastcompany.com/90818131/creativity-soft-skills-career-success-ai

U.S. Department of Education, Office of Career, Technical, and Adult Education Division of Academic and Technical Education. (2023, July 23). *Employability skills.* https://cte.ed.gov/initiatives/employability-skills-framework

World Economic Forum. (2016). *The future of jobs.* https://www.weforum.org/reports/the-future-of-jobs/

World Economic Forum. (2020). *The Future of Jobs Report 2020.* https://www.weforum.org/reports/the-future-of-jobs-report-2020/

CHAPTER 13

A CONVERSATION WITH ANIA HODGES

A Youth Changemaker's Story and Call to Action

Ania Hodges and Byron Sanders

INTRODUCTION

In the evolving landscape of education, Out-of-School Time (OST) programs have often been relegated to the sidelines. Yet, their transformative potential is immense, especially in the context of future workforce building. A key element to unleashing this potential lies in amplifying youth agency, giving those closest to the issue a voice in shaping solutions. Ania Hodges, a young alumna of Big Thought's OST programs, sits down with Byron Sanders, the President and CEO of Big Thought, to discuss her transformative journey. From joining during the pandemic year of 2020 to working in the same organization, Ania has come full circle.

Through their conversation, they set the stage by highlighting the often-underestimated potential of OST programs in shaping the future workforce. It emphasizes the importance of youth agency and sheds light on how OST programs can help young people discover their unique talents and skills, preparing them for the evolving job market and providing valuable transferable skills. It's a reminder that young people are not just passive recipients of knowledge but active contributors to the future workforce.

Built for More: The Role of Out-of-School Time in Preparing Youth for the Future of Work,
pp. 237–244
Copyright © 2024 by Information Age Publishing
www.infoagepub.com
All rights of reproduction in any form reserved.

238   A. HODGES and B. SANDERS

The discussion also touches on the importance of involving youth in the design process and giving them agency in decision-making. Young people have a unique perspective on the digital age, making their insights invaluable in shaping future programs and policies. Keeping in mind the barriers that often hinder effective engagement between adults and youth, such as misconceptions about youth naivety and ego-driven resistance. Ania's evolving career trajectory and her aspirations to create programs for young women and continue storytelling demonstrate the versatility of skills gained through OST programs. Her journey showcases how youth can build diverse skills and apply them in various ways.

In essence, this conversation is a powerful narrative that illustrates the transformative potential of OST programs, the value of youth agency, and the necessity of equipping young people with skills that prepare them for a rapidly changing world. Ania's story serves as both an inspiration and a call to action, encouraging us to rethink how we educate and empower youth of today.

INTERVIEW

BS: Thank you for joining us, Ania. We're here to talk about the essential role of Out-of-School Time (OST) programs in shaping the workforce of tomorrow. The people closest to the issues we aim to address often don't get a say in the solution, which is why we're keen to hear from you today. You joined Big Thought around 2020, correct?

AH: Yes, it was during 2020–2021.

BS: Excellent. Let's dive right in. Can you introduce yourself and share your experiences with OST and non-traditional learning?

AH: Of course. I'm a 21-year-old recent college graduate with a degree in communications and a minor in political science. Initially, I aspired to be a broadcast journalist. But I transitioned to focusing on writing and politics during college. I joined Big Thought's Artivism program during COVID, first drawn by a stipend as a broke college student. It turned out to be a really eye-opening experience.

BS: Artivism does encourage a lot of self-discovery. Elaborate for us.

AH: Certainly. The program was held virtually due to COVID. Our theme was 'Renaissance,' and it provided a space for us to think about the concept of rebirth while in the middle of the pandemic. It was an unexpected outlet for my creative side, which I hadn't realized I had. It opened new avenues for me, making me question, "What else can I do?"

BS: You've continued to be engaged with Big Thought after Artivism. Can you talk about your involvement with the Community Action Team (CAT)?

A Conversation With Ania Hodges   239

AH: CAT is a group of young people between the ages of 14 and 24, aiming to better our community through Big Thought as a platform. It's been an enriching experience for me, and it eventually led me to work at Big Thought. My current role involves program building and workforce development, fields I never thought I'd venture into but are proving to be enlightening every day.

BS: You've covered a lot of ground, and there's more to explore. Often, people participate in out-of-school programs, and it ends up being a small note on a resume or scholarship essay. But you've emphasized that these experiences build crucial skills. Can you talk about how this has played out in your life?

AH: In fields like freelance writing, you have to build your own portfolio. Most people don't have formal training; they train themselves. So, from early on, I focused on documenting what I learned in each experience. It's really important to capture those skills in a tangible form, an 'artifact,' if you will. Being in Big Thought programs helped me identify skills like leadership and digital fluency, which I then proudly display on my LinkedIn and other platforms.

The freelance and gig economy are becoming prevalent among young people. It's essential to know how to market the skills you've acquired through various experiences, like out-of-school programs.

BS: Absolutely, and what's interesting is that these skills can be transferable to entirely different careers, like nursing or finance. How can we in the out-of-school time sector better highlight this?

AH: The Creator Archetype we use is a good conduit. It's a planning framework that outlines five domains of 21st-century skills that are beneficial. These are Academics and Artistry, Civics and Service, Digital Fluency, Design Thinking, and Social Emotional Learning. Once you start sorting what you've learned into these categories, you realize how rich your skill set actually is.

The Creator Archetype helped me understand how to articulate these skills when I go for my next opportunity.

BS: Young people have a wealth of unrefined skills. It's our responsibility in this sector to help them realize and refine these skills and understand their value.

AH: When young people discover their talents and skills themselves, it's much more meaningful than someone else just telling them they're gifted. The power of out-of-school programs and non-traditional experiences is that they provide a context for young people to see their gifts in action.

Can I just say—this reminds me of my own journey with the *D Magazine* (D Mag) program. As you know, I'm a talker. I can talk for days, and I'm also deeply emotional.

BS: Absolutely. The *D Magazine* project was the out-of-school experience where you and a group of youth not only learned about different aspects of publishing, but you collaborated with the real *D Magazine* professionals to produce an entirely youth-led publication, Create Great Magazine. I believe it hits the streets in October or November, right?

AH: I've always been very sensitive. I cry when I'm happy, sad, you name it. I used to think this was a weakness, especially when combined with my extroverted personality. But D Mag taught me that being emotional and communicative are actually skills. Fast-forward to now, working with Generation Liberation at Big Thought, and these skills have been invaluable. I may not have experienced some of the struggles our participants have—like coming out of the foster system or having encounters with the juvenile system. But my ability to empathize and communicate allows me to understand their needs deeply. What I've learned is that the "'soft skills" like empathy are just as crucial as any hard skills. Because I take the time to put myself in others' shoes, I can effectively advocate for what they need. That has proven to be a beautiful and valuable thing.

BS: You've really hit the nail on the head. Often, young folks feel like they don't know anything just because they're 17 or 18. But what you're talking about—emotional intelligence—is invaluable. I sit on the Board of Trustees at my alma mater, the University of Tulsa. We recently discussed how the skills required in today's world are evolving. Traditional jobs are being redefined or disappearing, while entirely new roles are emerging. How could anyone have predicted something like "prompt engineering" as a lucrative career a few years ago? What we can do is foster skills like problem-solving and critical thinking.

Now, shifting gears a bit—how do you see the role of youth voice fitting into this evolving landscape?

AH: Exactly. Our generation is unique because we've grown up during the digital age. Even lawmakers struggle to grasp concepts like Facebook, which is second nature to us. This gives us a sort of foresight. The key is involving young people from the ideation stage, not just the execution. If we can identify what's going to be important in the near future, we can develop programs that truly matter.

The trick is to trust us. Older generations may find some of our insights strange but look at how much has changed. For example, who could have explained the role of "influencers" to someone from a decade ago? These are people who can now sway political opinions, having started with just posting outfits online. So, it's crucial to believe that we know what we're talking about. We're the ones who will be consumers and leaders in the near future. It's essential to trust us when we say what we need and where we see the world going. It's about believing in the youth to shape the future they'll be a part of.

A Conversation With Ania Hodges   241

BS: I have a good friend who says that aging is like leaving Neverland. You can't go back unless you have a guide, someone who's currently a resident there. This rings true for us adults, especially those of us in youth work. We may think we're in touch with young people, but the reality can be different. I just turned 40, and while I enjoy being this age, I'm aware I'm not a young person anymore. What are the barriers that prevent us adults from effectively engaging with youth?

AH: I think it's two-fold. First, there's this idea that being young equates to being naive. Sure, our brains aren't fully developed until around 25, but experiences don't have an IQ. You don't have to be exceptionally academically intelligent to understand your own life and what you aspire to be.

Just because someone doesn't know precalculus doesn't mean they can't understand or envision their future or the skills they need to develop.

The second barrier is sometimes ego, or maybe even fear. Let's say a young person with fresh ideas enters a workplace. The older colleagues might see this as a threat to their job or status. It's as if acknowledging the value in young people diminishes their own worth, which I don't think is the case. Everyone has unique experiences and knowledge to contribute. In my job, I work with Denesha, who has years of experience in youth work. While I might not have her specific experience, I contribute what I know about the skills young people will need in the future. When we combine our expertise, we can create something impactful.

BS: That's a really balanced way to look at it. It seems like the solution lies in collaboration rather than competition.

AH: Exactly. We're not trying to push anyone out; we're working together to create something really special.

BS: Business professionals constantly conduct market research before launching a new product. They want to understand their audience, the people who will use their product. It's the same in youth work. We can't assume we understand young people's needs without involving them in the design process. There's also this fear among adults about giving too much agency to youth. It's like we're scared it could be too dangerous for them to be in decision-making roles. What's your take on that?

AH: It's definitely a big ask to bring young people into these high-stakes conversations. Even I have my own reservations about being 21 and trying to solve complex issues like workforce development. The fear of not doing the best thing for the vulnerable groups we serve is very real. However, my parents have always put me in situations where I learned to handle more than I thought I could.

BS: That's really interesting, and it speaks to the role of guidance in youth development, doesn't it?

AH: Absolutely. For instance, my dad had me participate in cross country to improve my basketball endurance and even made me the pacesetter.

242   A. HODGES and B. SANDERS

I learned that I was faster and had more endurance than I thought. I've also been in leadership camps where I gained useful skills. My parents taught me that we all have something inside us that someone else is going to need. It's about trusting yourself and having a supportive community around you.

BS: And even in your current role, you're not alone, right?

AH: Exactly. I have mentors like Armando, who I can turn to for advice and reassurance. It's this network of role models that helps unlock the 'gold' we young people hold. We have the potential, but sometimes we need that external push or validation to really bring it out.

BS: You know what's interesting? A lot of people who work in youth development, including myself, have always believed that youth need to be involved and have agency in their lives. But doing that is not as simple as we might think. I've often found that if you ask young people what they want to see in the world, the room can go quiet. This isn't because they lack ideas; it's because they've rarely been asked to contribute them. You have to show them through actions and consistency that their thoughts and experiences are valuable. Would you say that's true?

AH: Absolutely. You need to convince young people that they know themselves best. Their opinions and perspectives are important, not just for them, but for their entire generation.

BS: That's a really insightful point. I'm wondering how having that kind of agency—within the Community Action Team and through other programs like the D Magazine project—has affected you. Did these experiences shape your journey in ways you didn't expect?

AH: Every program surprises me. I start with the idea that it's going to be a challenging experience, and when I come out on the other side, I'm amazed at what I've accomplished. Each successful program boosts my confidence and makes me want to tackle even bigger challenges.

BS: It sounds like this approach isn't just about giving you agency; it's about empowering you to be a lifelong learner, right?

AH: Exactly. In traditional school settings, learning can become a very tense and competitive space. The pressure of deadlines, tests, and benchmarks can make you afraid to be curious or admit you don't know something. That's why these out-of-school experiences are so valuable. They offer a more supportive learning environment where it's okay to ask questions and not know the answers right away.

BS: I couldn't agree more. When education becomes about memorizing facts just to pass a test, we miss the point. The goal should be to cultivate an openness to learning and a willingness to explore. That's when true growth happens. Would you say these experiences have contributed to your overall confidence?

A Conversation With Ania Hodges 243

AH: Absolutely. The space to be curious and the freedom to ask questions without fear of judgment has built my confidence tremendously. I've learned how to be comfortable with not knowing everything, which I think is an essential step in personal growth.

BS: That's good. Let's switch gears a bit and talk about your future. Given where you are today, how have your past experiences contributed to your aspirations? What are we looking at in terms of your next steps?

AH: Absolutely, my career trajectory has been constantly evolving. Every three years or so, I find myself stepping into a new role. I've wanted to do so many things—I mean, when I was 5 it was wedding planning. I've done things in broadcasting, then to article writing, and even podcasting. The beauty of these varied experiences is that they've equipped me with a skill set that's versatile. Whatever I decide to do next, I know I can.

And through programs like Big Thought, I've found a love for nonprofit work and community-building. So my long-term aspiration is to create a sisterhood program for young women, one that offers camaraderie and self-discovery while helping them achieve their goals.

But I also haven't given up on my love for writing. I love stories; I love giving people a platform to share their stories. So, whatever I do will incorporate storytelling as well.

BS: And the good news is your experiences have led to real-life outcomes, right? You transitioned from Artivism to an apprenticeship with D Magazine, and now there's a dope opportunity with them on the horizon even while you're still in school, correct?

AH: Well, correction, I actually just graduated in December. And yes! My apprenticeship with D Magazine has led to a freelance assignment with them. They're like the biggest publication in my city, won national awards. And I'm now going to be a contributed author with them. This opportunity is exciting, and I think it's opening up new avenues for me.

BS: That's fantastic, congratulations! It's like you're living proof that young people can build diverse skills and apply them in unique ways. Your journey is a testament to what can be achieved when someone has both the confidence and the opportunities to exercise their agency. You've gone from one experience to the next, building essential 21st-century skills along the way. And now you're leveraging them in both your work at Big Thought and in your burgeoning journalism career. I love it!

AH: Exactly! And three years from now, who knows? I might be doing something entirely different. The skills are transferable, so the sky's the limit.

BS: Absolutely, it's a good day. Last question to close us out: If you had a magic wand to make the world more accessible for young people, what would change? What societal shift would make the world more relevant to youth?

AH: I would focus on reimagining the education system. We need an approach that emphasizes skills over just how many facts we can retain. Kids are smart, but they often don't realize their potential because they haven't had the chance to apply knowledge in meaningful ways. So, my magic wand would create an education system that puts the emphasis on skill application rather than just rote learning. I would create an education system that focus more on using skills than learning them.

BS: Ooh, that's it right there. That's the benediction. That's the exclamation point. Just once again, you're showing your brilliance here. Ania, thank you so much for this time.

CONCLUSION

Ania Hodges' story is a compelling example of how a diverse skill set, combined with confidence and opportunities, can pave the way for a dynamic future. Through her journey, we see the transformative power of 21st-century skills and the crucial role they play in shaping not just individual trajectories, but also the future of our communities.

The conversation with Ania Hodges makes it clear that youth agency *is* skill-building for the future of work. In a world that often views young people through a deterministic lens—imposing predefined paths and limiting their agency—Ania's journey showcases the power of self-directed growth. Her story is an example of how a combination of opportunities, mentorship, and most importantly, personal agency, can create a rich mix of experiences and skills.

The focus on 21st-century skills—adaptability, creativity, and discovery—takes center stage in the dialogue. Ania's range of interests and ventures, from wedding planning to broadcasting and article writing, isn't a fluke but a function of her agency, facilitated by platforms that empower youth.

We have to heed her call to action. Ania's challenge to move to a skills-based educational system highlights the need for institutions to catch up with what young people like her already know: that the world is not only changing but has already changed. Traditional educational models, both in schools and out of schools, that concentrate solely on knowledge accumulation, are out of sync with the times. Instead, curricula must focus on equipping young people to apply knowledge in real-world contexts, thereby harnessing their innate agency.

In essence, Ania's journey and aspirations serve as both a model and a mandate. They show that when young people are given the tools and the agency to craft their own paths; they do not just meet the future; they shape it.

CONCLUSION

During my time in banking, I served as Vice President at Bank of America's private bank, specializing in investment management for high-net-worth individuals. Eventually, I transitioned to the same work with institutions, such as museums and university endowments, and even helped a few corporations establish their foundations. My role involved a unique blend of investment management and nonprofit advisory, which I found deeply meaningful. It allowed me to engage multiple facets of my intellect and was truly fulfilling.

During this time, I came upon a study that had a profound impact on my perspective. This study focused on socially impactful investing, often referred to as conscious capitalism. It became evident that the market was undergoing a significant transformation, redefining the concept of valuable assets. Over the past five decades, there had been a remarkable shift. The study, conducted by the firm Ocean Tomo, which specializes in this area, revealed some compelling insights (Ocean Tomo, 2022, p. 1).

The study delved into the valuation of the S&P 500, specifically examining the division between soft assets and hard assets. Soft assets encompass intangible elements like patents, intellectual property, brand equity, and the emotional connection a company has with its employees and customers. In contrast, hard assets are tangible, including physical assets like fleets of trucks, real estate, and commodities.

What made this study particularly intriguing was the breakdown of valuation. It highlighted the changing dynamics between hard and soft assets, providing a fresh perspective on the market's evolution.

The findings of the study were truly remarkable. Starting in 1975, an astonishing 83% of the market value of the S&P 500 was attributed to tangible hard assets, with only 17% attributed to soft assets. Fast forward

---

Built for More: The Role of Out-of-School Time in Preparing Youth for the Future of Work,
pp. 245–249
Copyright © 2024 by Information Age Publishing
www.infoagepub.com
All rights of reproduction in any form reserved.

246 CONCLUSION

a decade to 1985, and a significant transformation had already occurred. Hard assets had declined to 68%, while soft assets had risen to 32%. However, it was in 1995 that a pivotal shift became evident. For the first time, soft assets overtook hard assets, accounting for 68% of the valuation of the S&P 500, while hard assets represented only 32%.

This trend continued unabated, reaching its zenith by 2020. In that year, an astonishing 90% of the S&P 500's valuation was determined by soft assets, leaving just 10% attributed to hard assets. This seismic shift signifies a fundamental change in the United States economy at a macroeconomic level, transitioning from a manufacturing and production-driven economy to an ideas-driven, creative, and service-based economy—a concept we've coined in our organization the "CreatEconomy."

While this macroeconomic shift is significant, its micro implications are equally profound. Economies are composed of companies and corporations, and these entities are ultimately driven by people. The success, productivity, and market relevance of these companies and corporations hinge on the quality, quantity, and development of their workforce. In the past, physical prowess, and the ability to perform repetitive, physically demanding tasks were prized attributes in a hard asset-driven economy.

However, in the emerging ideas economy, the requirements have shifted. Individuals now need to excel at synthesizing disparate concepts into meaningful solutions. Their role is no longer solely about crunching numbers but using their analytical skills to address complex challenges uniquely, whether in society or for customers who may not even be aware of their needs.

This transition signifies a shift from a workforce focused on physical endurance to one requiring emotional intelligence. It is about understanding how ideas will impact human behavior, society, and the future. Remarkably, amid this transformative shift, society has often been unaware of just how fundamentally different the value of human beings in the world of work has become.

This realization raises questions about the need for a reimagined educational system that aligns with this evolving economic landscape. The book outlines a compelling case for why this change is imperative.

Another critical revelation is the primary arena for our recalibration—toward the establishment of a skills-building ecosystem for young people that is guided by their choices. This personalization is of paramount importance. In this era, we require individuals who possess creativity, critical thinking abilities, and problem-solving skills. They must not only understand the digital world but also have a mindset that can adapt to the rapidly changing future. The out-of-school time space plays a vital role in nurturing this ecosystem.

Conclusion   247

The silver lining Is that while we await policy changes and adjustments in our K–12 education systems and higher education institutions, which often involve bureaucracy and red tape, we can leverage the out-of-school time space as a pioneering force to demonstrate how it is done.

What's truly remarkable is that this aligns with what we have been doing all along. An out-of-school time experience, be it in theater or any other domain, contributes to the development of essential workforce skills, such as public speaking, communication, and empathy. These skills have been identified in various reports and publications as crucial for corporations and companies to thrive.

However, it is imperative that we recognize and channel these efforts in an official and structured manner. This publication provides several examples of how practitioners in the field are already doing this. I do not speak of this as a theoretical concept but as someone who has experienced it in my own journey.

I recently had the privilege of delivering a keynote address in front of thousands of people, passionately advocating for juvenile justice reform as a key lever for creating a more just society. Afterward, a gentleman approached me and inquired about my public speaking ability, assuming I had undergone formal training like Toastmasters. I smiled and reflected on my journey, realizing that I hadn't paid for professional public speaking training. Instead, I benefited from my mother's decision to enroll me and my brother in a free summer theater camp led by Selmore Haines at St. John's Missionary Baptist Church in Oak Cliff, Texas, a part of Dallas on the southern side. Little did I know that those three consecutive summers of theater were actually building a workforce skill that has served me exceptionally well in all my professional and civic endeavors throughout my life.

In every measurable way—materially, economically, and in terms of physical health and life fulfillment—I have experienced significant improvement due to that foundational experience.

When my mother enrolled me in this program, I highly doubt she thought, "Byron, I'm doing this because I want you to develop a 21st-century skill that will serve you exceptionally well 30 years from now." Similarly, did Selmore Hanes, our program leader, envision that he was imparting a valuable, enduring skill that would prove indispensable across multiple sectors of my professional journey? Probably not. And as for little Byron at the time, did I consciously think, "I'm doing this to prepare for a future where I need to transform concepts into accessible opportunities due to shifts in the economy?" Almost certainly not.

But here's what I'm truly grateful for—there existed an out-of-school time experience that provided me with an opportunity to develop a skill rarely nurtured within the confines of a traditional classroom.

248 CONCLUSION

Imagine if Selmore Haines had been aware of the full scope of the skills he was imparting, if he had known that he was essentially providing job training for a 21st-century economy focused on creativity, problem-solving, and emotional intelligence. Imagine if my mother had known just how critical the skills were that I was accessing in that church during the hot Texas summers. Imagine how confident young Byron would have been had he known he was cultivating an asset that was transferable across multiple careers and portable through every phase of his life. What choices would have been made for each of us were we aware of the fullness of these experiences' centrality to a person's journey through life? What chances did I opt out of because I did not think I had relevant skills or experiences? Would I have taken a different educational journey? Perhaps I had have stepped into the room without the at times crippling imposter syndrome that dogged me as a young Black boy from modest means attending a wealthy high school on the other side of town. Could I have reached for something different, more audacious, bolder if I knew I was walking around with figurative gold in my hands from these experiences. It adds an additional layer of gravity to the already important work of Out-of-School Time.

And lucky for me, to have had the right mother, who lived near the right church, at the right time and at the right price for me to happen across such a life-changing program. Yet I was just one child, and serendipity is not a system.

This is why it matters. It's not just my story; it is the story of thousands of individuals who may not even realize that their journeys share this common thread. What we cannot accept is the continuation of a narrative where young people possess untapped potential, unaware of the skills they are already beginning to build through their out-of-school time experiences.

We have a responsibility to become more cohesive, purposeful, and to grant legitimacy to the recognition of these skills developed outside the conventional school hours—beyond the 8 A.M. to 3 P.M., Monday through Friday, winter, spring, and fall.

We are genuinely excited about the future and the collective efforts of our industry and sector. We are poised to build alongside our traditional learning institutions, both K–12 and post-secondary. It is an opportunity for us to see ourselves in a new light, recognizing our vital role in workforce development because, fundamentally, we are central to human development. *Built for More* has made a strong case from the people in the fight that the strategy matters and demands our investment. A future-ready workforce is a durable skills-equipped workforce. And there is no better positioned sector than out-of-school time to help deliver it.

It is a fascinating twist of fate that in a world increasingly defined by advancements in artificial intelligence, machine learning, and technology, we are beginning to understand that the most valuable contributions we bring to the table are deeply tied to our humanity.

REFERENCE

Ocean Tomo, A Part of JS Held. (2022). *Intangible asset market value study*. http://www.oceantomo.com/INTANGIBLE-ASSET-MARKET-VALUE-STUDY

AUTHOR BIOGRAPHIES

EDITORS

Byron Sanders, CEO and President, Big Thought

Byron Sanders is a relentless advocate for education, economic development, and equitable communities. As the President and CEO of Big Thought, his primary mission is to narrow the opportunity gap, ensuring young people have the chance to fulfill their innate potential. He firmly believes that each of us plays a role in creating a society where youth can thrive.

Byron's impactful leadership has earned him accolades, including the 2022 Dallas Business Journal Most Admired CEO and the 2023 NCAA Legends and Legacy Community Award. In 2017, he was named a Presidential Leadership Scholar, a program led by the presidential centers of George W. Bush, William J. Clinton, George H.W. Bush, and Lyndon B. Johnson. His dedication was further recognized by the CASEL O'Brien Award for Excellence in Expanding the Evidence-Based Practice of Social and Emotional Learning in 2020.

With expertise in banking, finance, education, philanthropy, and entrepreneurship, Byron's journey includes vital roles at U.S. Trust, the Dallas Education Foundation, and leadership in Group Excellence. Beyond his accomplishments, Byron actively engages with various boards, contributing to organizations like the Dallas College Foundation, For Oak Cliff, Young Leaders Strong City, Dallas Symphony Orchestra, and the Dallas Mavericks Advisory Council. Byron is an alumnus of The University of Tulsa and now serves on its Board of Trustees, but his deepest fulfillment comes from spending time with his best friend and wife, Celeste, and their two galactically amazing children.

252   AUTHOR BIOGRAPHIES

Shannon Epner, Director of Impact and Advocacy, Big Thought

Shannon Epner serves as the Director of Impact & Advocacy with Big Thought. She specializes in policy development, civic engagement, and data driven decision making for non-profits and community organizations. She has over 10 years' experience working with communities and youth organizations in Dallas, Texas and Cleveland, Ohio. She has worked with Big Thought in multiple capacities and was thrilled to see the organization grow to new heights.

Shannon has a Bachelor of Science in Education from Kent State University and a Master of Public Administration and Public Policy from American University. Shannon is passionate about promoting social emotional wellbeing, working in the intersection of environmental action and youth, and improving educational resources in communities. In addition to her primary job functions, Shannon serves on Children's Health Beyond ABC Advisory Board, Dallas Arboretum Advisory Board, Dallas Area Cultural Advocacy Coalition, America Forward Coalition, and a Public Affairs Council member. She is happiest traveling with her husband, Anthony, and rescue dog, Rosie.

AUTHORS

Chike Aguh, Senior Advisor at Harvard University's Project on Workforce, Senior Fellow on Workforce at Northeastern University's Burnes Center for Social Change, and Senior Advisor at the McChrystal Group

Chike Aguh (Chee-Kay Ah-Goo) is the first person in his entire family born in America, a Fulbright Scholar, educator, business leader, award-winning non-profit CEO, and Biden presidential appointee. A recognized authority on the future of work, economic opportunity, and innovation, Chike is committed to an economy that creates opportunity for every family just like America did for his. Chike currently serves as Senior Advisor at Harvard University's Project on Workforce, Senior Fellow on Workforce at Northeastern University's Burnes Center for Social Change, and Senior Advisor at the McChrystal Group.

Previously, Chike was appointed by President Biden on day one of his administration to serve as Chief Innovation Officer at the U.S. Department of Labor, the first black person to do so. Reporting to Deputy Secretary and later Acting Secretary Julie Su, he led efforts to use data, emerging technologies (AI, quantum computing, etc.), and innovative practice to advance and protect American workers. These efforts included creating the department's first enterprise data strategy, serving a pivotal role in the $2B modernization of the nation's unemployment insurance system, piloting the nation's first workforce scorecard, and serving as the DOL's designee to the National Space Council.

Chike holds degrees from Tufts University (BA), Harvard Graduate School of Education (EdM), Harvard Kennedy School (MPA), and the University of Pennsylvania's Wharton School (MBA). He is a lifetime member of the Council on Foreign Relations, Presidential Leadership Scholar; and a 40 under 40 honoree from Wharton and *Washington Business Journal*.

Chike, his wife, and their two kids are proud Marylanders and Prince Georgians. Appointed by MD Gov. Wes Moore, Chike serves on the Maryland Higher Education Commission. He is founder of the Aguh Workforce Scholarship at Prince George's Community College and advisor to Prince George's County focused philanthropy Pull-Up Fund. Chike and his family are members of Zion Church in Greenbelt, MD.

Armando Banchs MEd, Sr. Manager—Creative Archetype, Big Thought

As Sr. Manager-Creative Archetype, Armando supports, manages, and creates curriculum in service of Big Thought's Creator Archetype Pathways. This intentional skills development supports our youth as they step into the 21st Century Global Workplace with experiential learning, asset building, and exploration of opportunities where their skill sets would be vital. Armando manages and supports credentialing programs within the College & Career Division, fosters relationships with external stakeholders for the digital credentialing of these pathways, supervises, supports, and manages credentialing pilot programs, and works with pathways partners to raise Big Thought's Creator Archetype skills development and badging to industry standards.

Armando has worked as an advocate for Youth, Education and Leadership in the DFW area for the past 23 years. He uses his skills as a 16-year classroom educator, artist, mentor, curriculum designer, and program creator for all Big Thought projects. His diverse experiences include living and traveling the world as an Army brat, teaching for Dallas ISD and Arlington Classics Academy, mentoring at risk youth in afterschool programming, administrating afterschool academic, mentoring, and Arts programs, mentoring student teachers from area universities, teaching adult citizenship night classes, and creating district curriculum for writing initiatives. Armando utilizes his Master of Arts in Educational Innovation, from St. Edward's University, to work with partners to facilitate innovative ways to create experiential skills development that will help our Big Thought Youth advocate for their definition of "best life" and step into Self-Authorship.

254 AUTHOR BIOGRAPHIES

Evan Cleveland, Sr. Director Programs, Big Thought

Evan Cleveland has spent 20 years in the nonprofit sector, leading efforts to create and effect change. His work often resides within informal learning spaces and their intersections with school systems, universities, nonprofit organizations, and corporate diversity and inclusion. He has designed, assessed, and deployed programs for youth and adults, with a focus on equitable outcomes across diverse populations.

Currently, he serves as the Senior Director of Programs at Big Thought, a nonprofit in Dallas, TX, that seeks to close the opportunity gap for all youth in marginalized communities. At Big Thought, he oversees the teams leading the direct-to-youth programs, which engage youth from the ages of 4 to 24. These students come to Big Thought through programs in out-of-school and in-school spaces, community locations, and alternative education and juvenile justice settings. Taken together, Big Thought's programs touch thousands of students each year.

Evan comes at this work through the arts. He began his career leading creative writing programs with youth in schools, museums, hospitals, and detention centers. He has a Master of Fine Arts degree in Fiction, and his writing has appeared in national and international journals. He lives in Dallas with his wife, two teenage children, and a revolving cast of fish.

Nancy Deutsch, Associate Dean for Faculty Affairs, Linda K. Bunker Professor of Education, Director, Youth-Nex, University of Virginia

Nancy Deutsch is the associate dean for faculty affairs. In this role, Deutsch supports the professional growth and welfare of faculty through inclusive recruitment, retention, and professional development. This work includes—among many other things—meeting with faculty recruits, managing conversations about retirements, creating mentoring systems, and providing opportunities to celebrate our faculty. Deutsch is also the director of Youth-Nex, the UVA Center to Promote Effective Youth Development at the School of Education and Human Development. Deutsch is an editor of the *Journal of Adolescent Research*. She also sits on the editorial board for Qualitative Psychology and the Research Advisory Board for the National Mentoring Resource Center (NMRC).

Deutsch's research examines the socio-ecological contexts of adolescent development, particularly issues related to identity. She has focused on the role of afterschool programs and relationships with important adults and is especially interested in the process of adolescent learning and development as it unfolds within local environments for a better understanding of how to create settings that better support youth, especially those at risk due to economic or sociocultural factors.

Author Biographies   255

In addition to journal articles, she has published two books on youth in afterschool programs, *Pride in The Projects: Teens Building Identifies in Urban Contexts* (NYU Press, 2008) and *After-School Programs and Youth Development* (with Bart Hirsch & David DuBois, Cambridge University Press, 2011). Her works have been funded by agencies including the William T. Grant Foundation, the Department of Justice, the Office of Juvenile Justice and Delinquency Prevention, and the U.S. Department of Education.

Deutsch was a recipient of a University Teaching Award in 2017 and a Student Council Distinguished Teaching Award in 2016. In 2013, she received the School of Education and Human Development Outstanding Faculty award.

Teresa Drew, Deputy Director, STEM Next Opportunity Fund

Teresa Drew is the Deputy Director of STEM Next Opportunity Fund where she oversees and manages complex multi-stakeholder projects that build systems of support for STEM learning opportunities in all 50 states. She also manages STEM Next's grantmaking portfolio. Teresa also directs the Million Girls Moonshot, a transformative nationwide initiative from STEM Next that re-imagines who can engineer, who can build and who can invent. This project applies her expertise in and personal passion for gender equity and prosperity and aims to help close the gender gap in STEM.

Prior to joining STEM Next, Teresa was the co-founder of San Diego United Parents for Education, where she was active in education reform efforts—from local to federal, advocating and empowering the most under-engaged stakeholders in the education system. Teresa holds a California multiple-subject teaching credential and was the co-creator of a long-running early-childhood education program in San Diego. Teresa is a graduate of the University of San Diego's Master of Arts in Nonprofit Leadership and Management program.

Nicole Evans, Senior Director of Donor Communications at United Way Worldwide

An attorney, fundraiser, and nonprofit leader, Nicole has served in senior roles for national and global organizations advancing social causes, including the United Way, STEM Next Opportunity Fund, Boys & Girls Clubs of America, and the American Association of University Women. She is also a Lecturer at Johns Hopkins University, where she teaches graduate-level courses on nonprofit management.

Nicole holds a Juris Doctor from the American University Washington College of Law and a Master of Public Affairs degree in Nonprofit

256 AUTHOR BIOGRAPHIES

Management from the Truman School of Public Affairs at the University of Missouri. She is an active member of the District of Columbia Bar and involved with Reading Partners DC, serving on their Young Professionals Board.

Terri Ferinde, EdD, Partner, Collaborative Communications

Dr. Terri Ferinde is a connector, convenor, and communicator who believes that all young people should have opportunities and supports to explore their passions and achieve their dreams. As a partner with Collaborative Communications, she has created and led solutions and systems that build capacity in networks, foundations, nonprofits, and education organizations that address inequity and help children and youth learn and thrive. A champion for afterschool learning, in 2014, Terri was named one of the 25 most influential people in the afterschool sector by the National AfterSchool Association. Known for her work in afterschool systems building, she manages the 50 State Afterschool Network funded by the Charles Stewart Mott Foundation. Terri is the publisher of and a contributing author to the groundbreaking compendium focused on afterschool and summer learning, Expanding Minds and Opportunities, and the publisher of a companion collection, STEM Ready America. She has managed hundreds of convenings—from small task forces to large conventions—bringing to each a sharp focus on outcomes that lead to youth success. Terri earned a doctorate in education from Vanderbilt University's Peabody College focused on organizational leadership and learning. She holds a master's degree in public administration from George Mason University and a bachelor's degree in communications and government from American University.

Rebecca Goldberg, Rebecca Goldberg Consulting

Rebecca is a nonprofit and philanthropic advisor who is passionate about uplifting the youth development sector and creating equitable learning environments for all young people. She facilitates two funder groups and designs programming for Grantmakers for Education focused on out-of-school time and equitable grantmaking practice and works with other clients on leadership transition, partner engagement, research, and grant-making strategy.

She spent seven years in philanthropy leading a national youth development portfolio at the S.D. Bechtel, Jr. Foundation working with large, national youth organizations and intermediaries in California to bolster social-emotional learning, improve program quality, develop organizational capacity and sustainability, and infuse equitable policies and prac-

Author Biographies 257

tices within the organizations. Rebecca also previously led career pathway programs at a local community-based organization in Los Angeles and professional and workforce development initiatives at California School-Age Consortium supporting afterschool professionals in California.

Ania Hodges, Youth Advancement Coordinator, Big Thought

Ania graduated from the University of North Texas at Dallas and is on the advisory board for the National Institute to Unlock Potential. She is a dedicated member of the Community Action Team at Big Thought and works to make an impact in the Dallas community! In her role as Youth Advancement Coordinator, at Big Thought, Hodges is dedicated to empowering and equipping youth with the opportunities to create and imagine their best lives.

Gabrielle L. Kurlander, founding CEO (retired), All Stars Project, Inc.

Gabrielle Kurlander is an innovative nonprofit entrepreneur, award-winning theatre director, actor and philanthropist. She is a founder of the All Stars Project, Inc. (ASP). As its CEO (1989–2023), she led the organization's transformation from a small, New York City-based all-volunteer effort into a national nonprofit located in New York City, Newark, Chicago, Dallas and the San Francisco Bay Area. Using an innovative performance approach, ASP provides afterschool development opportunities for poor and underserved young people and builds bridges between diverse communities.

Ms. Kurlander has decades of experience in all aspects of performance and theatrical production. She began her career as a working actor, touring nationally with the Broadway tour of Biloxi Blues. Since then, she has been involved in over 40 theatrical productions. Productions she has directed have been recognized with six AUDELCO Awards for Excellence in Black Theatre.

Ms. Kurlander sits on the boards of the All Stars Project and TACA (The Arts Community Alliance) and is a member of the Women's Forum of New York. She has a Bachelor of Arts degree from SUNY Empire State College and resides in Dallas, Texas.

Melissa K. Levy, Associate Professor, Youth and Social Innovation Program Director, University of Virginia

As a faculty member, Melissa Levy's overarching goals are to foster community, nurture a sense of purpose, and cultivate spaces for growth and transformation. Levy's academic home is the youth and social innovation

258 AUTHOR BIOGRAPHIES

(YSI) degree, which prepares students to pursue work with or on behalf of youth, with an emphasis on the development and implementation of innovations that are informed by an understanding of both individual developmental and policy contexts. Her teaching frames the degree program (Introduction to YSI; YSI Capstone I & II) and prepares students to engage with youth and communities responsibly and effectively (Foundations of Community Engagement; Issues Facing Adolescent Girls, the course taken by mentors in the Young Women Leaders Program [YWLP]). As the YSI program area director and YWLP education coordinator, Levy advises and mentors undergraduate students considering the YSI major, students enrolled in her courses, students in YWLP, and students in the YSI major. Melissa Levy also mentors graduate students whose work and roles overlap with hers through teaching and research.

Bobbi R. Macdonald, Senior Partner for Ecosystem Growth and Advancement, Education Reimagined

Bobbi R. Macdonald, EDLD, is a social entrepreneur who believes in joyful work that illuminates the wisdom of communities, the importance of honoring the unique gifts of every child, and the significance of centering relationships and belonging. As Senior Partner for Ecosystem Growth and Advancement at Education Reimagined, she leads initiatives working with communities to catalyze the invention of transformational models of public education that bring to life equitable, community-based, learner-centered ecosystems. With a Doctorate of Education Leadership from Harvard Graduate School of Education, and a background in human development and family studies, Bobbi brings a wealth of knowledge and expertise to her work.

Prior to her current role, Bobbi spearheaded the creation of the City Neighbors Network of Schools (K–12) in Baltimore, MD. Her leadership was instrumental in bringing together the community to participate in a model of inquiry based design asking pivotal questions such as: "What would it take for every student to be Known, Loved, and Inspired?" These inquiries led to the successful growth of City Neighbors, including the establishment of the City Neighbors Foundation. For 15 years, Bobbi served as its Co-Founder and Executive Director, steering its mission to enhance public education, provide professional development for educators, and foster the ongoing advancement of City Neighbors schools.,

Bobbi's dedication to community empowerment has been recognized through prestigious fellowships such as the Annie E. Casey Foundation's Children and Family Fellowship, The Greater Baltimore Committee Leadership program, and her selection as a Finnegan Fellow at the Harvard Graduate School of Education.

Beyond her professional endeavors, Bobbi finds joy in expressing her creativity as a singer-songwriter, sharing her love for music with her husband, Rob, and their four wonderful children. Together, they explore New England, enjoy bike rides and hikes, and embrace a life filled with love and adventure.

Greg MacPherson, Chief Big Thought Institute Officer, Big Thought

As Chief Big Thought Institute Officer, Greg MacPherson oversees a talented team focused on building organizational and community capacity through a suite of services that include professional learning, program and curriculum design, research and evaluation, and consulting. Greg joined Big Thought in 2010 and has helped lead the organization's participation in both the National Summer Learning Initiative and the Partnerships for Social and Emotional Learning Initiative in conjunction with The Wallace Foundation. Prior to Big Thought, Greg worked with the City of Dallas Office of Arts and Culture and also the Classics Theater & Art for Children. Greg is an alumnus of Leadership Dallas, the National Guild for Community Arts Education Leadership Institute, and is a graduate of Baylor University.

Naomi McSwain, Executive Director (Retired) & Board Member, Al Wooten Jr. Youth Center

Naomi McSwain grew up in South Los Angeles, where an afterschool program helped her leave a life of gang activity in the 1970s. They helped her apply to college and go on to earn a BA degree in journalism from CSU Northridge. Naomi spent the next 15 years as a newspaper reporter and magazine editor before too many stories on gang violence led her to complete an MA degree in intercultural studies and children at risk from Fuller Theological Seminary where she wrote her thesis paper on gang prevention in Los Angeles. A year later, she returned to her previous work as executive director of the Al Wooten Jr. Youth Center, an agency Naomi helped found in 1990 in honor of her cousin, killed in a drive-by shooting.

Naomi retired from the Wooten Center in 2023 after a total of 17 years as executive director. She served seven years in the position at a sister site in Riverside County. Naomi received a certificate in nonprofit management from USC in 2020 and has completed several courses at the Center for Nonprofit Management, the Grantmanship Center, Bridgespan Group, and other capacity-building agencies. She is currently serving on the board of directors at the Wooten Center and the California School-Age Consortium, where she is also a certified trainer.

260 AUTHOR BIOGRAPHIES

Naomi is on the advisory board for ExpandLA, a Los Angeles mayor's office intermediary for expanded learning providers. Recognitions for her work in the field include the United Way of Greater Los Angeles' first Power of Her Award in 2018 and the Los Angeles Rams' pLAymaker Award in 2022.

Melea Meyer MFA EdD, Senior Specialist, ASAPconnect

Melea is the proud mom of two amazing humans (since 2008) and one of three Co-founders of Shanél Valley Academy (since 2021): a TK–6th grade charter school in rural Northern California, where she continues to serve on the Board of Directors. A passion for learning is the foundation upon which Melea has composed her personal and professional life. As Senior Specialist with ASAPconnect (since 2023), Melea supports the expanded learning workforce through building a statewide capacity for technical assistance that is grounded in equity, quality, and compassion.

Dr. Meyer's leadership expertise spans community schools, non-profit governance, systems design, curriculum planning, workforce development, and project management. Energized by California's statewide transformation of expanded learning programs and schools, Melea recently completed her Compassionate Systems Master Practitioner Certification and her Doctorate in Organizational Innovation, where she researched how to promote growth and transformation in times of complexity and renewal.

Prior to her role with the Foundation for Community Colleges as ASAP-connect-Senior Specialist, Melea worked as the Region 1 STEAM hub lead out of Mendocino County Office of Education, where she expanded access to high quality STEAM learning experiences for youth and expanded learning staff in Northern California. She also taught English, ESL and college readiness at Los Angeles Trade Technical Community College for seven years, where she discovered her passion for building trust with reluctant learners of all ages in nontraditional learning settings.

Monique Miles, Vice President, Aspen Institute; Director, OYF; Managing Director, FCS, Aspen Institute

Monique Miles is a Vice President of the Aspen Institute, the Director of the Opportunity Youth Forum, and Managing Director of the Aspen Institute Forum for Community Solutions.

Prior to joining the Forum for Community Solutions, Monique was the Director, Postsecondary Achievement at the National Youth Employment Coalition (NYEC). In her role at NYEC, Monique oversaw the Postsecondary Success Initiative, a national pilot that supported Community Based

Organizations (CBOs) across the country to design and implement post-secondary programming, in partnership with local institutions of higher learning, for students who were disconnected from education.

Monique began her career in education reform working as a Literacy Instructor at Youth Opportunity Boston. In this role Monique worked directly with students remanded to the Massachusetts Department of Youth Services (DYS) to design and deliver education and career development curriculum. Monique went on to serve the same population of students through political advocacy initiatives at the Commonwealth Corporation (CommCorp).

Monique earned a Bachelor of Science from Springfield College and a master's in education, policy, and management from the Harvard Graduate School of Education. Monique serves as the Vice-Chair of the Board of Trustees at the Pomfret School. She also serves on the Advisory Board of Tulane University Cowen Institute of Public Education Initiatives. She is on the board of Independent Trust and the Corps Network.

Angelica Portillo, Director of Advocacy and Workforce Initiatives, National Afterschool Association

Angelica Portillo's passion for education and public policy led her to advocate for the Out-of-School Time (OST) field. She has spent over a decade working in afterschool programs and providing quality assistance to OST programs, ultimately led her to serve as NAA's Director of Advocacy and Workforce Development.

Before her role at NAA, Portillo worked at as the Director of Advocacy at Dallas Afterschool, increasing access to afterschool programs for children across Dallas County. In 2018, the National Afterschool Association (NAA) honored her with the Next Generation of Afterschool Leaders award. Angelica holds a bachelor's degree in political science and public administration from the University of North Texas (UNT). She is a Board Member of Current Issues in Out-of-School Time Book Series. She also takes pride in being an alumnus of The Dallas Regional Chamber's Young Professionals Advisory Board, Leadership ISD Civic Voices, Mayor's Star Council, and the LBJ Women's Campaign School.

Fernande Raine, Founder and Co-Lead of The History Co:Lab

Fernande Raine is founder and Co-Lead of The History Co:Lab. The History Co:Lab is an intergenerational impact-driven collective that co-creates learning experiences and catalyzes communities with and for young people so they all can thrive in their roles as makers of our shared history.

Together with our partners, we work toward a world in which a model of youth-centered learning grounded in the complexity and possibility of human history has become the norm, preparing young people to renew and revitalize democracy for our collective wellbeing. With a strong belief in the power of youth voice and intergenerational dialogue to shape the future of education, the team incubated and produces the award-winning teen-led youth podcast UnTextbooked. Fernande has a PhD in history from Yale, started her career as a strategy consultant at McKinsey and Co. and spent 15 years with Ashoka launching programs in systems-change and growing the institution around the globe. She is the mom of four young women and loves hiking, cooking and celebrating community.

Carlos Santini, CEO, Mizzen Education

As CEO of Mizzen Education, Carlos Santini leads and helps grow the Mizzen platform as a key resource in elevating the quality of afterschool programs for young people across the United States.

Since 2002, Santini has worked closely with school districts, foundations, corporations, and local, state and national leaders to expand the scope and improve the quality of afterschool programming for young people. He previously served as executive vice president of programs for After-School All-Stars, a national nonprofit offering comprehensive afterschool programs for middle school youth in 19 cities across the country. Prior to that, Santini was the associate executive director for After-School All-Stars, Los Angeles, one of California's most influential expanded learning programs. He recently served on the National Afterschool Association board of directors and is currently serving on the advisory committee for the 21st Century National Technical Assistance Center (NTAC). Santini is also a featured speaker demonstrating best practices and leadership competencies in the expanded learning field.

Santini also has had a successful career in marketing and public relations placing high-tech corporate clients in top-tier media outlets, including *Time, Fortune,* and *The Wall Street Journal.*

Santini immigrated to the U.S. from Honduras at age seven and credits his experience as an English learner for paving his path towards a career in education. He attended the University of California, Los Angeles, where he first began his work in youth development with UCLA UniCamp. He is married and has two daughters. His wife, Alejandra, has been an elementary school teacher for more than 30 years and is a former nonprofit executive leader.

Author Biographies 263

Chris Street, President & CEO, All Stars Project, Inc.

Chris Street is a change maker with a talent for unifying diverse individuals around transformative causes. His involvement with the All Stars Project (ASP) began as a volunteer in 1992, and he has dedicated over 30 years to building it from a small, local, community-based nonprofit into a national organization operating in six cities and serving youth in over 20 states through in-person and virtual programs.

Chris assumed the role of CEO in November 2023 and continues to serve as president, just two of several leadership roles he has played over the last 23 years. A leading social entrepreneur who provides strategic direction to the organization's operations nationwide, he works closely with national and regional board members on advancing ASP's impact and oversees the planning and execution of all programming, operations, and community building activities. In addition to leading the design of strategic initiatives, Chris has engaged with elected officials and government leaders in New York City, Chicago, Dallas, and Newark to create public-private partnerships and launch new initiatives, such as Operation Conversation: Cops & Kids, with Mayor Ras Baraka's administration in New Jersey. More recently, he has led discussions with education institutions like Dallas College and ICA Cristo Rey Academy in San Francisco about creating new kinds of workforce development solutions for their student bodies, bringing the performatory developmental approach into engagements with institutions focused on learning.

After graduating from New Canaan High School in Connecticut and the London School of Economics in 1992, Chris dedicated his life to public service and community organizing initiatives that focus on advancing equality of opportunity, diverse civic leadership, and social entrepreneurship. In 2022, he graduated from the Integral Leadership Program of the Stagen Leadership Academy in Dallas. He currently resides in Dallas and travels regularly to each ASP market.

Emily Wegner, Network Lead and Co-Founder, Kansas City History Co:Lab

Emily Wegner serves as the Network Lead and co-founder of the Kansas City History Co:Lab where she is responsible for connecting teachers, students, and schools to local museums and community institutions. She thrives in an environment of collaboration and shared experience. Emily actively works to support Kauffman's Real-World Learning Initiative, student voice and engagement, Inquiry Design Model (IDM) development, and the development of quality and balanced assessments.

264 AUTHOR BIOGRAPHIES

Emily also serves as the Social Studies Curriculum Specialist for Lee's Summit School District. She actively supports curriculum grades K–12 by participating in the development of assessment and resource development for the State of Missouri. She has coordinated and developed professional learning for teachers representing over 25 school districts across the KC region and the state of Missouri and has presented at a variety of state and national conferences since 2013. She currently serves as a Board Member of the Missouri Council for History Education and is a member of the Missouri Council of Social Studies.

Sheronda Witter, Senior Advisor for Out-of-School Time Partnerships, STEM Next Opportunity Fund

Sheronda Witter, PhD, is a senior advisor for Out-of-School Time Partnerships with the STEM Next Opportunity Fund. Previously, Dr. Witter served as the Out-of-School Time Partnerships Fellow in the Office of the Secretary at the U.S. Department of Education. In this capacity, Dr. Witter helped to drive and coordinate the Department's Engage Every Student Initiative, which is a bold new call to action to provide high-quality out-of-school time learning opportunities for every child who wants to participate.

Dr. Witter served as the Director of the North Carolina Center for Afterschool Programs, where she provided visionary and strategic leadership of North Carolina's statewide afterschool network to make North Carolina a place where all youth have access to high-quality learning opportunities beyond the school day that prepare them for success in education, career and life. Dr. Witter earned a Bachelor of Arts degree in Intercultural Youth Development from Furman University, a Master of Science degree in Youth Development Leadership at Clemson University and a Doctor of Philosophy degree in Educational Research and Policy Analysis for K–12 Education at North Carolina State University.

Jill Young, Senior Researcher, American Institutes for Research

Jill Young is a senior researcher in the Youth, Family, and Community Development program at AIR. Her primary responsibilities include leading research, evaluation, and capacity-building projects. Dr. Young's work is focused on youth development, out-of-school time programming, and social and emotional learning at the national, state, and local levels. She specializes in both quantitative and qualitative data collection and analysis, with a focus on mixed methods. She currently serves on the research advisory committee for Youth Today, and on the publication board for the Information Age Publishing book series on Current Issues in Out-of-School Time.

Prior to joining AIR, Dr. Young supported Chicago's largest afterschool system, After School Matters, where she served as the Senior Director of Research and Evaluation, leading research and evaluation efforts for afterschool and summer programs. She also supported program design and led implementation studies for special initiative programs, including those focused on post-secondary services and opportunity youth. She also worked as a statistical analyst at the University of Chicago and as a research manager at Northwestern University.

Printed in the United States
by Baker & Taylor Publisher Services